FOR CLIVE OGDEN

What was said? What was done? was there prosing or rhyming?
  Was nothing noteworthy in deed or in word? –
Why, just as the hour of the supper was chiming,
  The only event of the evening occurred.
Up jumped, with his neck stretching out like a gander,
  Master Swinburne, and squealed, glaring out thro' his hair,
'All Virtue is bosh! Hallelujah for Landor!
  I disbelieve wholly in everything! – There!'

With language so awful he dared then to treat 'em, –
  Miss Ingelow fainted in Tennyson's arms,
Poor Arnold rushed out, crying '*Saecl' inficetum!*'
  And great bards and small bards were full of alarms.
Till Tennyson, flaming and red as a gipsy,
  Struck his fist on the table and utter'd a shout:
'To the door with the boy! Call a cab! He is tipsy!'
  And they carried the naughty young gentleman out.

Robert Buchanan, *The Session of the Poets* (1866)

Contents

Acknowledgements		xi
Introduction		1

1 Tennyson   19

W. J. Fox on *Poems, Chiefly Lyrical* (1830) in the *Westminster Review* (1831) — 22

John Wilson Croker on *Poems* (1833) in the *Quarterly Review* (1833) — 25

John Stuart Mill on *Poems, Chiefly Lyrical* (1831) and *Poems* (1833) in the *London Review* (1835) — 27

Leigh Hunt on *Poems* (1842) in the *Church of England Quarterly* (1842) — 30

Charles Kingsley on Tennyson in *Fraser's Magazine* (1850) — 32

In Memoriam (1850) from Hallam Tennyson, *Alfred, Lord Tennyson* (1897) — 37

Hippolyte Taine on *Maud* (1855) and *In Memoriam* (1850) from *A History of English Literature* (1856-9) — 41

R. J. Mann on *Maud* (1855) in *Tennyson's* Maud *Vindicated: An Explanatory Essay* (1856) — 45

Matthew Arnold on Tennyson in *On Translating Homer* (1861-2) and in *Letters* (1895) — 47

Walter Bagehot on *Idylls of the King* (1859) in the *National Review* (1859) — 50

R. H. Hutton on Tennyson in *Literary Essays* (1888) — 52

W. E. Henley on Tennyson in *Views and Reviews* (1890) — 56

Leslie Stephen on Tennyson in *Studies of a Biographer* (1899) — 57

Harold Nicolson on Tennyson in *Tennyson* (1923) — 59

F. R. Leavis on Tennyson in *New Bearings in English Poetry* (1932) — 61

T. S. Eliot on *In Memoriam* (1850) in *Essays Ancient and Modern* (1936) — 63

2   Browning 67

W. J. Fox on *Pauline* (1833) in the *Monthly Repository* (1833) 69

An anonymous reviewer on *Paracelsus* (1835) in the *Spectator* (1835) 70

John Forster on *Paracelsus* (1835) in the *Examiner* (1835) 72

Leigh Hunt on *Paracelsus* (1835) in the *London Journal* (1835) 73

An anonymous reviewer on *Sordello* (1840) in the *Dublin Review* (1840) 75

An anonymous reviewer on *Dramatic Lyrics and Romances* (1845) in the *Examiner* (1845) 77

An anonymous reviewer on Browning in the *English Review* (1845) 78

Anonymous reviewers on *Christmas-Eve and Easter-Day* (1850) in the *Leader* (1850) and *Chamber's Edinburgh Journal* (1853) 79

W. M. Rossetti on *Christmas-Eve and Easter-Day* (1850) in the *Germ* (1850) 82

An anonymous reviewer on *Men and Women* (1855) in the *Athenaeum* (1855) 83

An unsigned review of *Men and Women* (1855) in the *Saturday Review* (1855) 85

George Eliot on *Men and Women* (1855) in the *Westminster Review* (1856) 87

D. G. Rossetti on *Men and Women* (1855) in his letters to William Allingham (1855–6) 89

William Morris on *Men and Women* (1855) in the *Oxford and Cambridge Magazine* (1856) 91

John Ruskin on Browning in *Modern Painters*, Volume IV (1856) 92

An anonymous reviewer on 'A poet without a public' in *Chamber's Journal* (1863) 95

E. P. Hood on Browning in the *Eclectic and Congregational Review* (1863) 97

Walter Bagehot on *Dramatis Personae* (1864) in the *National Review* (1864) 99

R. W. Buchanan on *The Ring and the Book* (1868–9) in the *Athenaeum* (1869) 101

H. B. Forman on 'Browning's poetry' in the *London Quarterly Review* (1869) 104

An anonymous reviewer on *Red Cotton Night-Cap Country*
(1873) in the *Spectator* (1873) — 105

G. K. Chesterton on 'Browning in later life' and 'The
philosophy of Browning' in *Robert Browning* (1903) — 107

Donald Thomas on 'The madhouse and the shrine' in *Robert
Browning: A Life within Life* (1982) — 109

3 Arnold — 114

Charles Kingsley on *The Strayed Reveller and Other Poems*
(1849) in *Fraser's Magazine* (1849) — 115

W. E. Aytoun on *The Strayed Reveller and Other Poems*
(1849) in *Blackwood's Magazine* (1849) — 118

G. D. Boyle on *Empedocles on Etna* (1852) in the *North
British Review* (1853) — 119

Matthew Arnold in his Preface to *Poems* (1853) — 121

G. H. Lewes on *Poems* (1853) in the *Leader* (1853) — 124

J. A. Froude on *Poems* (1853) in the *Westminster Review*
(1854) — 125

Coventry Patmore on *Poems* (1853) in the *North British
Review* (1854) — 127

Leslie Stephen on *New Poems* (1867) in the *Saturday Review*
(1867) — 128

Isidore G. Ascher on *New Poems* (1867) in the *St James's
Magazine* (1868) — 130

R. H. Hutton on 'The poetry of Matthew Arnold' in the
British Quarterly Review (1872) — 131

Lionel Johnson on Matthew Arnold in *Post Liminium* (1912) — 134

4 Clough — 137

Charles Kingsley on *The Bothie* (1848) in *Fraser's Magazine*
(1849) — 138

Ralph Waldo Emerson on *The Bothie* (1848) in the
Massachusetts Quarterly Review (1849) — 141

An anonymous reviewer on *Ambarvalia* (1849) in the
Guardian (1849) — 142

Matthew Arnold on Clough in *Last Words on Translating
Homer* (1862) — 145

An anonymous critic on *Poems by Arthur Hugh Clough* (1862)
in the *Saturday Review* (1862) — 146

Henry Fothergill Chorley on *Poems by Arthur Hugh Clough*
(1862) in the *Athenaeum* (1862) — 149

CONTENTS

William Allingham on 'Arthur Hugh Clough, 1819–1861' in
Fraser's Magazine (1866)   150

John Addington Symonds on 'Arthur Hugh Clough' in the
Fortnightly Review (1868)   154

Arthur T. Lyttelton on 'The poetry of doubt' in the *Church
Quarterly Review* (1878)   156

Lytton Strachey on Dr Arnold in *Eminent Victorians* (1918)   157

5 **Swinburne**   160

Edmund Gosse on 'Swinburne' in *Portraits and Sketches* (1912) 162

Donald Thomas on *'Poems and Ballads'* in *Swinburne: The
Poet in his World* (1979)   163

John Morley on *Poems and Ballads* (1866) in the *Saturday
Review* (1866)   166

A. C. Swinburne in *Notes on Poems and Reviews* (1866)   171

W. M. Rossetti in *Swinburne's Poems and Ballads: A Criticism*
(1866)   174

George Saintsbury on 'Mr Swinburne' in *A History of
Nineteenth Century Literature* (1896)   177

6 **Later critical texts**   184

Additional bibliography   193

Acknowledgements

We are grateful for permission given to reproduce extracts from the following:

T. S. Eliot, *Collected Poems 1909-1962*, Faber and Faber Ltd and Harcourt Brace Jovanovich, Inc., 1936, copyright 1963, 1964 T. S. Eliot.

T. S. Eliot, on *In Memoriam*, in *Selected Essays*, Faber and Faber Ltd, 1932 and Harcourt Brace Jovanovich, Inc., 1950, copyright renewed by Esme Valerie Eliot 1978.

F. R. Leavis, *New Bearings in English Poetry*, Chatto and Windus and University of Michigan Press, 1932, reprinted by permission of the Executors of the F. R. Leavis Estate.

Harold Nicolson, *Tennyson*, Constable, 1923, and Hutchinson Grey Arrow paperback, 1960.

Donald Thomas, *Robert Browning: A Life Within Life*, Weidenfeld and Nicolson, 1982.

Donald Thomas, *Swinburne: The Poet in his World*, Weidenfeld and Nicolson, 1979.

Introduction

THE LEGACY OF THE FIRST ROMANTICS

To define romanticism is like trying to catch the bubble in a spirit-level. No one doubts that it exists, for everyone can see it. Yet at the first attempt to imprison it in a formula, it changes shape and dances away. But what cannot be defined may be described. Romanticism and its legacy are, in this sense, a matter of history rather than of theory or definition.

The flowering of the first English romantic movement, like some of its most famous names, had been short-lived. Its contemporary fame lasted from the publication of *Lyrical Ballads* in 1798 until the death of Byron in 1824. By then, Keats and Shelley too were dead. Wordsworth and Coleridge were burnt-out stars: Coleridge was in thrall to opium and Wordsworth, the revolutionary sympathizer of the 1790s, had long since accepted a pension from the reactionary government of Lord Liverpool. 'Just for a handful of silver he left us', wrote the young Robert Browning sardonically in 'The Lost Leader', after meeting Wordsworth in 1836, 'Just for a riband to stick in his coat'.

In the last decade of the romantic movement itself, Byron and Shelley had been the poetic idols of the rebellious young and of radical dissent. Indeed, Byron had died on his way to fight for Greece in her war of liberation against Turkey. The poetry of these two patrician Englishmen had been a revolutionary call to arms and a red rag to the authorities. Their publishers were convicted of blasphemy for issuing Byron's *Cain* and Shelley's *Queen Mab* and for a libel on George III in the case of Byron's *Vision of Judgment*. Shelley's description of European monarchy as 'privileged gangs of murderers and swindlers' was suppressed for seventy years after that.

With the sudden death of these two heroes, it was not hard to understand why the aspiring adolescent poets of the day felt like orphans. Robert Browning nourished an adulation of Shelley, even

1

imitating the older poet's atheism and vegetarianism for a while, and writing poems in the manner of Shelley that had the effect of destroying his own early prospects of success. Revolutionary romanticism even persuaded the young Tennyson to play a small part in an abortive *coup d'état* in Spain. He escaped the fate of other sympathizers who were executed by a firing-squad on the esplanade at Malaga.

A brief but revolutionary movement in English culture was at a sudden end in 1824. But the great names of Victorian poetry were not the immediate successors of these first romantics. When Byron died, Tennyson was fifteen years old and Browning twelve. Clough was five, Matthew Arnold two, and Swinburne was not born for another thirteen years.

There was to be an interregnum until new forces gave momentum to English poetry again. Few of the poets belonging to this period of the 1820s and 1830s yet had the ability to capitalize on the romantic legacy. The literary annuals of the period promoted poetry whose aim was to avoid bringing a blush to a maiden's cheek. An essential quality was to be its suitability for family reading. Thomas Bowdler had begun *The Family Shakespeare* in 1818, cutting from the plays anything that had the least air of vulgarity or indecency. This was followed by *The Family Classical Library*, which pruned away erotic and bloodthirsty passages from the authors of Greece and Rome until they were suited to babes and sucklings. Evangelical poets like Robert Montgomery wrote pious verses on such subjects as 'The Effects of Indiscriminate Novel-Reading'. New popular poetry was too often represented by the type of Mrs Felicia Hemans and her famous recitation-pieces like 'Casabianca' ('The boy stood on the burning deck, whence all but he had fled').

The great romantics themselves suffered eclipse. Byron was taboo, in part for his treatment of his wife and for fathering a daughter on his half-sister; in part for his creation of the amoral dandy in *Don Juan*. Shelley was only to be read in carefully chosen poems about skylarks or the west wind. His collected poems were the subject of a successful prosecution for blasphemous libel in 1840-1. Keats was not truly popular until he had been rescued by Richard Monckton Milnes' *Life and Letters of John Keats* in 1848. Wordsworth, at least, was safe. He had repented of his early enthusiasms and was to be made Poet Laureate in 1843.

But even under such conditions as this, characteristic elements of romanticism survived. The movement had always nourished a Gothick theme, sometimes sentimental but often macabre. Thomas Hood took this and wrote superb narrative poems of which the murder and detection described in 'Eugene Aram' remains graphic and compellingly readable. His taste for the bizarre found expression in the epic-length *Miss Kilmansegg and her Precious Leg*, the story of a rich young lady who lost a leg and had a gold one fitted. Courted by men for the wealth of this artificial limb, Miss Kilmansegg married a foreign nobleman who at last beat her to death with it. The verdict was suicide because her own leg had killed her. More popular still was *Hood's Annual* and its family verses on the comic and the macabre, including 'Mary's Ghost', in which the apparition of the girl whose corpse has been dug up by body-snatchers for an anatomy class appears to her lover.

> You thought that I was buried deep,
> Quite decent like and chary,
> But from her grave in Mary-bone
> They've come and bon'd your Mary.

Hood was but one example of the energy of English writing in the raffish and turbulent period of the 1830s and early 1840s. Indeed, the young Charles Dickens was demonstrating a parallel energy in prose, a similar blend of the grotesque and the sentimental in *Oliver Twist* and *Nicholas Nickleby*. Hood, in his most outlandish whimsy, kept alive one important strain of romanticism. It also appeared in Thomas Lovell Beddoes who worked on *Death's Jest-Book* for many years until his suicide in 1840. These macabre preoccupations in poetry became more important to the post-romantics than to most of their forebears.

Though the great stream of romanticism might seem to be dribbling away in the sand, the vitality of writing during the 1830s was not in question. The last years of Byron, Keats, and Shelley were also the period of the Regency, whose splendid animal spirits characterized a section of English society that was sporting, patrician, gallant, and military. From this came the mocking and wistful *vers de société* of Winthrop Mackworth Praed and Richard Barham's *Ingoldsby Legends*. The poetry captured the tone and rhythm of speech in a manner common to both Praed and Browning's later monologues, to Barham and to Clough.

Akin to the macabre was romantic fascination with a medieval past, evident in the Gothick Novel after Horace Walpole's *Castle of Otranto* (1764) and in a new curiosity over ballad poetry and 'reliques'. Upon this, in the 1820s and the 1830s, Sir Walter Scott built a reputation in poetry and fiction as the best-selling author of all time. When he was overtaken, it was by another great popularizer of the past, Lord Macaulay, whose *History of England* appeared volume by volume between 1849 and 1861 with immediate commercial success.

In a different sphere of English poetry, the 'peasant-poet' John Clare wrote poems of rural life and personal reflection so limpid and easy that they made Wordsworth seem burdened by bourgeois self-consciousness. *Graves of Infants* is a subject booby-trapped for the unwary by sentimentality and sermonizing. Not so for John Clare. He never appears lugubrious or sententious:

> Infants have naught to weep for ere they die;
> All prayers are needless, beads they need not tell,
> White flowers their mourners are, nature their passing-bell.

Before 1840 the first volumes of Tennyson and Browning had been published. In Browning's case, they made little impact and were indifferently received by most of the critics who bothered to notice them. There was rarely such a case of a major poet who began with so little promise. Not until he was in his fifties did he make any money at all from the poetry he had been writing assiduously since his teens. Indeed, most of it would never have appeared in print at all had there not been family money to pay for publishing the earlier volumes.

If the English hesitated over what the romantic legacy represented, the French and Germans had a clearer view. They had given a more precise account of the European romantic revival. It was not enough for Wordsworth to assure his readers that poetry was the spontaneous overflow of powerful feeling. Pope or Dryden might have thought that as they set about their enemies in satire. But while England treated literature in a robustly pragmatic way, Europe saw more clearly the direction that a new post-romanticism might take.

A NEW ROMANTICISM:
BEAUTY AND THE BEAST

In 1798, the year of Wordsworth's and Coleridge's *Lyrical Ballads* in England, the German romantic August Wilhelm von Schlegel founded a magazine, the *Athenaeum*. In its pages, and in his own lectures, he described what modern romanticism should be. Since the Renaissance, European culture and science had been governed by the rediscovered classicism of Greece and Rome. Dante was seen as a new Virgil. Raphael and Michelangelo were regarded as the descendants of Grecian or Roman art.

This adulation of classical antiquity, Schlegel thought, had been carried to an absurd degree. The world needed a change, taking as its model not classical antiquity but the medieval world of romance. But the new romantic age would not be mere medievalism. It was to be the basis of modern art. The characteristic of Grecian culture had been harmony and perfection. The new romanticism, Schlegel wrote, was to be characterized by struggle and opposition. Perfection was dead or sterile. Imperfection, or even discord, was the stimulus to progress.

Madame de Staël, a French exile living in Germany and an acquaintance of Schlegel, became the first writer to use the specific term 'romanticism' for this new development. She took the argument a stage further in her book *De l'Allemagne*, published in 1810:

> We sometimes use the word classic as synonymous with perfection. I use it here in a different manner, considering classic poetry as that of the ancients, and romantic, as that which is generally connected with the traditions of chivalry. . . . Romantic literature is the only kind capable of further improvement. Rooted in our own soil, it alone can continue to grow and acquire fresh life. It expresses our religion. It recalls our history. Its origin is ancient, although not of classical antiquity.

That, in a paragraph, was the argument for romanticism as modern art. It could hardly be expected that a profoundly rooted modern movement would wither after twenty or thirty years because its first leaders had died young or withdrawn from it.

In any case, a new generation of European post-romantics wanted more than those leaders had offered. It was not enough to say that the romantic was modern. In what way was it modern? By 1827, the young Victor Hugo had no doubt. The middle ages were over. The Renaissance and its classicism were outmoded. Modern Europe had embarked on its 'third civilization'. 'Another era is about to begin for the world and for poetry,' Hugo wrote in the preface to his play *Cromwell*. It was not merely to be a world where romantic imperfection took precedence over classical perfection. The great subject of the moderns was to be the grotesque, as a rival to the sublime. Indeed, the grotesque was a necessary complement to the beautiful in modern art. It was what made it modern. 'Everything tends to show its close creative alliance with the beautiful in the so-called "romantic" age,' Hugo wrote, 'Even among the simplest popular legends there are none which do not somewhere, with an admirable instinct, solve this mystery of modern art. Antiquity could not have produced *Beauty and the Beast*.'

This was to be the new world of the post-romantics, the home of

Tennyson, Browning, and Swinburne in England, as well as of Gautier, Baudelaire, and Hugo himself in France. It would never do for the romantic century to be a mere revival of the middle ages. The German romantic poet Heinrich Heine, writing in exile in Paris in 1834, explained why. An infatuation with medievalism led all too soon to a suppression of intellectual freedom. The grotesque might be acceptable but pure medievalism was reactionary. 'A propaganda of priests and gentlemen who had conspired against the religion and political freedom of Europe had a hand in the game. It was really Jesuitism which was enticing German youth to ruin with the soft melodies of romance.'

Even in such a traditional aspect of beauty as feminine appearance and conduct, European post-romanticism took a turn towards the bizarre. Feminine beauty by the standards of classicism had, of course, been mathematically definable; twenty-two inches from the foot to knee, twenty-two inches from the knee to hip were the dimensions of perfection. But romantic eroticism saw a greater fascination in the imperfections of sexuality. Théophile Gautier's novel *Mademoiselle de Maupin*, later hailed by the young Swinburne as 'the holy writ of beauty', was an erotic *tour de force* of its age. Yet its subject was a lesbian and androgynous infatuation. A similar theme led to the prosecution of Baudelaire's publisher in 1859 and the removal of several poems from the author's *Les Fleurs du Mal*, in itself perhaps the most famous work of European poetry in the last two centuries.

In a less sensational way, Walter Pater was to cast a strange light on the feminine beauty of the past in *The Renaissance* (1873). Leonardo da Vinci's *Mona Lisa* was to many the best-known painting in the world but Pater's view of it reflected the bizarre rather than the beautiful, the grotesque rather than the sublime. He saw in the *Mona Lisa* 'strange thoughts and fantastic reveries and exquisite passions'. A portrait of beauty became an enigma of moral and sexual alienation. 'Set it for a moment beside one of those white Greek goddesses or beautiful women of antiquity, and how would they be troubled by this beauty, into which the soul with all its maladies has passed!' The triumph of the Renaissance humanist is made a subject of the macabre and the Gothick. 'She is older than the rocks among which she sits; like the vampire, she has been dead many times, and learned the secrets of the grave.'

By the time that Pater wrote, post-romanticism was rapidly running its course towards the 'decadence' of the 1890s. Long before that, there were hints of unacknowledged influences from the past working under its surface. The French critic Sainte-Beuve, writing in the *Revue des Deux Mondes* in 1843, suggested two names that bourgeois culture might have preferred to forget. 'I dare to affirm, without any fear of being contradicted, that Byron and Sade (forgive me for putting them together) have perhaps been the two great inspirations of the moderns. One of them is well-advertised and visible, the other is hidden — but not too hidden.'

That the flamboyant hedonism of Lord Byron and the dark spirit of the Marquis de Sade should be thought of as the major sources of inspiration for modern literature showed how far the romantics and the post-romantics had come since the publication of *Lyrical Ballads* forty-five years earlier. Yet, even in England, Swinburne was soon to profess himself a disciple of Sade, while the darkest human preoccupations characterized Browning's 'morbid anatomy', as it was called.

The period of post-romanticism was not, after all, to be a mere continuation of the romantic revival of 1798-1824. It was a development in some ways profoundly different and often disturbingly so. A monster like Guido Franceschini in Browning's *The Ring and the Book* - regretting that he had not cut off his wife's fingers joint by joint each time she misbehaved, because then he might not have had to put her to death - is further removed from Wordsworth than ever Wordsworth was from Pope or Dryden. It was not a matter of style. The post-romantics were children of a modern world. Neither Wordsworth nor Pope had been that.

Charles Baudelaire, writing in his *Salon de 1846*, called romanticism merely 'a mode of feeling'. In a sentence he summed up the moral self-discovery that was modern post-romanticism, as opposed to the first romantics a generation before. 'They looked for it outside themselves', he remarks of his predecessors, 'but it was only to be found within.'

THE DANGEROUS EDGE OF THINGS

'Our interest's on the dangerous edge of things,' says Browning's speaker in 'Bishop Blougram's Apology'. It was this element of the romantic which could most easily be seen as modern. Whether the subject was Franceschini, the self-righteous killer, or the poet torn on the rack of religious doubts, the age inspired a style of writing in which the imperfect, the inconclusive, the grotesque, and the morally uneasy played an increasing part. The progress of the Victorian romantic soul was no longer a steep and rocky ascent with a reward waiting at the top for the persistent and the virtuous. It seemed often a mad caper on a tightrope stretched above a Niagara of doubt and destruction.

Of the facets of Victorian poetry that owed most to romantic innovation, the confessional or autobiographical mode of writing appeared almost universally. There were romantic precedents in the *Confessions* of Jean-Jacques Rousseau, published in 1782, and Wordsworth's long poem *The Prelude, or Growth of a Poet's Mind*, completed in 1805 though not published until 1850. Poetry as mood or state of mind was important equally to the interpretation of landscape in Tennyson or the personal debate on faith and doubt in Arnold or Clough. It was crucial to the mental analysis of moral character, which Browning practised upon his subjects.

As a modern development, this belonged to the age as a whole and not just to its poetry. John Henry Newman's *Apologia Pro Vita Sua* (1864) was as vivid a portrayal of the soul's progress as the poems of Clough and Arnold, though mingled with autobiography and polemic. Indeed, the whole science of mental analysis had changed under the impact of cultural and political revolution. The revolutionary regime in France after 1789 thought it intolerable that patients in asylums should be visited and mocked like exhibits at a freak show. Moral therapy was pioneered. Philippe Pinel's *Treatise on Insanity* appeared in England in 1806 and advocated the importance of understanding the minds and thoughts of the mentally sick. As so often, poetry represented one aspect of an intellectual development that was common to contemporary culture as a whole. By no means all mental states portrayed in post-romantic poetry were of madness, uncertainty, delusion, or alienation. Yet these seemed to be characteristic of the new style, as its critics pointed out in the case of Tennyson's *Maud*, Browning's dramatic monologues, or even the interior debates of Clough's poetry.

The use of the Gothick, the medieval, or the Arthurian offered, in the Victorian period, a world of unreality as well as the mechanism for the sinister and the evil. The same had been true, indeed, of Coleridge or Keats. In Tennyson's *Idylls of the King*, no less than in the vividly enamelled images of Dante Gabriel Rossetti or William Morris, it unveiled a land of finely coloured make-believe. That the same Gothick decoration might be used to enhance what Hugo had called the grotesque was a truism of popular fiction and art.

Added to this, the new poetry inherited a shift in moral perceptions. More specifically, the good and the pious by the standards of evangelical morality were not the most interesting subject for poetry. 'I want a hero,' Byron had written at the beginning of Canto I of *Don*

Juan. But what he wanted in fact was known long afterwards by the type of the anti-hero. Don Juan the seducer and Cain the biblical murderer were evidence of it. That Byron himself and the Marquis de Sade should have seemed at one time like the guiding spirits of the age suggested that he was not alone in his preference.

It was not merely that the post-romantics preferred bad people to good. The interesting flaw of character was what stamped Browning's subjects, Tennyson's narrator in *Maud*, or even the tyrannical father and the doomed lovers in *Aylmer's Field*. A spiritual ambivalence was evident in Clough's religious poems or in a more languid social piece like his *Amours de Voyage*. Psychological paradox was at the heart of it. Browning, talking of this interest on the 'dangerous edge' of sanity, lists the honest thief, the tender murderer, the superstitious atheist, and the woman who hungers equally for sex and salvation as being truly interesting. How, then, could Napoleon, the grandiose dreamer who almost conquered Europe from Moscow to Lisbon, from Copenhagen to the Nile – and yet who brought death and devastation as well – fail to be the great Byronic hero of his day? He was a fit partner for the doomed warrior Satan of Milton's *Paradise Lost*, whom both Blake and Shelley saw as the hero of the poem.

At the very least, the romantic succession had proved Schlegel right in one thing. Classicism might be about perfection, but romanticism was the creed of imperfection, uncertainty, debate, turmoil, and revolution. A murderer or a devil was interesting for being odd and aberrant – grotesque, as Hugo said. But the same was no less true of a saint. Tranquillity, prudence, safety, normality, certainty, agreement, and peace, were the seven deadly virtues in the eyes of the new generation.

THE POST-ROMANTICS: BROWNING

Of the major poets after 1824, Robert Browning was most self-consciously the heir of the first romantics. Yet it was also Browning who showed the most uncompromising modernism. Shelley was his idol, to whom Browning paid tribute by such youthful poems as *Pauline* and *Paracelsus*. They were not bad poems, being strange and suggestive in their labyrinthine felicities. To many common-sense critics of the 1830s, however, they often seemed obscure and pretentious. Nor was his modernity much more welcome. In *Pippa Passes* (1843), Browning saw the world of northern Italy with the technique of a camera's eye that suggests the naturalism of European

9

cinema more than a hundred years later. Naturalistically, he picks up the ordinary objects and decoration in the lovers' bedroom as the morning light comes through the shutter's chink. Ottima, from the bed, nags Sebald in play as he gets up:

> Mind how you grope your way, though! How these tall
> Naked geraniums straggle! Push the lattice –
> Behind that frame! – Nay, do I bid you? – Sebald,
> It shakes the dust down on me! Why, of course
> The slide-bolt catches. – Well, are you content,
> Or must I find you something else to spoil?

The couple have murdered Ottima's elderly husband. Sebald recalls the peasants laughing at the shutters of the bedroom still closed suggestively at noon, imagining how 'The old man sleeps with the young wife!' Ottima draws to Sebald, her back naked against him, just inside the window to point out the black streak on the morning horizon that is the campanile of St Mark's at Venice. 'Look o'er my shoulder – follow my finger.'

Such writing was more revolutionary than anything in *Lyrical Ballads*. In reading the new poetry, it was easy to see why Baudelaire and others regarded the romanticism of the day as synonymous with modernity. Browning's scene has an air of Visconti and films like *Ossessione* (1942) even before the world had heard of *Wuthering Heights* or *Jane Eyre*. Compared with such fiction, the poetry of the day seemed to have leap-frogged into another century. Browning's fame was long delayed, however. His poetry was thought obscure and his plays were failures. At last he combined dramatic dialogue and poetic realism in poems whose speakers seemed to step from the pages into life and to evoke the worlds they lived in, their persecution, holiness, sadism, cheating, and above all sexual love.

Browning, more systematically than his contemporaries, anatomized those who dwelt on this 'dangerous edge of things': lovers at the moment of falling in love or parting for ever; troubled saints and self-righteous tricksters. His first two widely published poems were *Madhouse Cells*. In one of these, the psychopathic 'Porphyria's Lover' explains how he had to strangle the girl during the night because otherwise she would have left him in the morning. It was the logical thing do to. And now she will never be able to leave him again. But he does not talk like a criminal. 'No pain felt she,' he says reassuringly, 'I am quite sure she felt no pain.' And so that makes it all right. He broke no divine law, for God 'has not said a word'. Like many of

Browning's people, Porphyria's lover speaks with the patient and inflexible logic of the morally insane.

Browning's preoccupation was, as he said, 'Original Sin, the Corruption of Man's Heart'. But in modern terms his preoccupation was also with the morally and mentally alienated, the misfits and the psychopaths, the abnormally infatuated and the dangerously holy. Guido Franceschini in *The Ring and the Book* never doubts that he was right to kill Pompilia, whom he bought at twelve years of age when she was still playing with her toys. She betrayed him with another man. To put such a wife to death was as much his right as to dispose of anything else he had purchased and found defective. It was Browning's way to let his monsters – and his saints – speak for themselves. The author would not intervene to reassure or comfort the reader.

Not surprisingly, even some of Browning's friends found his interest in 'morbid anatomy' repellent. He had taken Hugo's belief in the grotesque to its limit. But he also exemplified perfectly the post-romantic as the modern. He would anticipate the cinema in *Pippa Passes*, or he might rival Zola and Maupassant in a bizarre tale of sexual infatuation and religious guilt, *Red Cotton Night-Cap Country*, in 1873. That scandal was so topical that most of those involved were still alive when Browning published his verse novel.

TENNYSON

If Browning began as a self-proclaimed disciple of Shelley, then Tennyson seemed to owe a good deal to Keats. Among the early poems, 'Mariana' has the air of a Keatsean ode, though evoking the flat fenland of Tennyson's boyhood at Somersby, the little channels draining down to the windy shore and the cold line of the verge of the North Sea. The homely vividness seems in a line of descent from the 'Ode to Autumn':

> With blackest moss the flower-pots
>   Were thickly crusted, one and all,
> The rusted nails fell from the knots
>   That held the peach to the garden wall.

Tennyson was, from the first, what John Betjeman called the 'lord of landscape'. But landscape was the means rather than the fulfilment of his poetic sensibility. He was primarily an example of Baudelaire's latter-day romantic who knew that what he sought was in himself and not in the world around him. Tennyson's art lay in the subtlety and flexibility with which he made landscape an extension of the poetic mind. Indeed, much of the medieval scene in 'The Lady of Shalott' or the Odyssean idyll of 'The Lotos-Eaters' was entirely of the mind. The lazy warmth and beauty of the eastern Mediterranean, or the southern seas in the latter poem, were actually the result of a day-trip to Torquay.

Like Keats in 'The Eve of St Agnes' and 'Ode on a Grecian Urn', Tennyson exploited the myths of chivalry and of the ancient world. But, as in Browning, there was modernity and sometimes it was thrust upon the reader. When he wrote his fantasy of 'Godiva', Tennyson began in the thick of the industrial revolution with steam engines and 'the flying wheel'. His readers were not to forget that he anchored such fantasy in Victorian reality. The tone, as well as the imagery, might have been John Betjeman's a century later:

> I waited for the train at Coventry:
> I hung with grooms and porters on the bridge,
> To watch the three tall spires; and there I shaped
> The city's ancient legend into this . . .

Ironically, the image of Tennyson on the railway bridge was more enduring than that of Godiva naked on her horse, the blind walls full of chinks and holes, the crowding gables staring overhead.

By 1850 he was Poet Laureate and in the following year established his fame with *In Memoriam*. The poem revealed a soul torn by the agony of religious doubt after the death of his greatest friend. He seemed to care more for the death of Arthur Hallam than the possible death of God. Neither Wordsworth nor Baudelaire, let alone Shelley in *Adonais*, ever revealed the morbid intensity of fear and longing which Tennyson displayed to the world in the fiftieth section of the great poem:

> Be near me when my light is low.
>   When the blood creeps, and the nerves prick
> And tingle; and the heart is sick,
>   And all the wheels of Being slow.

Fear and loneliness, faith overcome by doubt, assume dramatic power in one man, isolated in the face of death and extinction. In all the laments and elegies of a hundred years past, no one had written with such intensity. Here, if anywhere, was the precipice of the mind's endurance. Gerard Manley Hopkins experienced something of the same in his sonnets of 1885:

O the mind, mind has mountains; cliffs of fall
Frightful, sheer, no-man-fathomed. Hold them cheap
May who n'er hung there.

But Tennyson also had a taste for the macabre, as if to bring melancholy under the control of reason and wit. He shows it early in the irony of his *Song* of 1830, when a sick man in the 'damp and hush'd' air of his bedroom takes a nap, not knowing that he will die in an hour's time and get all the sleep he needs. We see it in poems like 'A Vision of Sin' where evolution goes dizzily into reverse and life is 'slowly quickening into lower forms' as the worms eat men and horses alike. We see it on a larger scale in his verse novel *Maud*. A good many well-fleshed Victorian tenors had sung 'Come into the garden, Maud', with its lines, 'My heart would hear her and beat/ Were it earth in an earthy bed,' knowing that it was just a figure of speech. But those who read the entire poem knew that the hero would be buried alive in his madness. 'Why have they not buried me deep enough?' He can still see and hear, all too vividly, as the living burial of the madhouse engulfs him.

After 1851, Tennyson was a great public poet of the Victorian age and the creator of Arthurian fantasy in *Idylls of the King*. Some of his poetry for public occasions was not good. It showed 'Schoolmiss Alfred' at his worst. But 'The Charge of the Light Brigade' captured the mood of England when the news of folly and glory at Balaclava reached the press. His 'Ode on the Death of the Duke of Wellington' is a superb evocation of that chill and silent day when the hero of Waterloo and the Peninsula was borne through the packed streets of London to his resting place in St Paul's. Tennyson catches the mood as well as the sights and sounds, in a manner that any radio or television commentator might envy. From the booming of the minute-guns to the wintry light on the golden cross of the cathedral dome, the picture is complete.

Tennyson and Browning chose different paths through the post-romantic world of the Victorian period. Yet they had a good deal in common. Both were enthralled by legends of the past and yet both were modern in thought and expression, far more so than many novelists until the 1860s. Indeed, the novel usually tailored its material to what was suitable for children as well as adults. Poetry was freer from this restraint. Browning and Tennyson also shared a central interest in the uneasy and the aberrant, the curious and the unbalanced. So did Hood and Beddoes. The difference between Browning or Tennyson and a poet like Hood was in their greater range of subject-matter and tone, subtler representation of conduct, and profounder analysis of human mentality. By contrast, Hood played well, but he played like a virtuoso on one string.

MATTHEW ARNOLD

Arnold lacked the range and intensity of his two great predecessors. He had an elegiac gift and could evoke the pastoral beauty of Victorian Oxford or the sublime austerity of Rugby chapel with a skill that also owed something to the example of Keats. In 'The Scholar-Gipsy' the sound of Oxford river water running against the boat's movement is conveyed with the immediacy of Keats:

> Crossing the stripling Thames at Bab-lock-hithe,
>   Trailing in the cool stream thy fingers wet,
>   As the punt's rope chops round.

Yet Arnold was a meditative philosopher in verse and, of all the major Victorians, perhaps the most obvious descendant of Wordsworth. Like Wordsworth, he was a poet of proclaimed human sympathies, which appeared as much in his 'Shakespeare' sonnet as in 'A Gipsy-Child by the Seashore'.

To his detractors, he was apt to seem academic or dilettante. For them, a poem like 'Sohrab and Rustum' was a little like a mere exercise in the Homeric style. Arnold owed too much to the models of classicism. He was the contrary of Browning who thrived by being energetic, objective, and analytical. Arnold was thoughtful, speculative, and too spiritually self-indulgent for those like F. R. Leavis who saw in 'The Scholar-Gipsy' merely a flight from 'this strange disease of modern life'. His detractors sensed a fatal charm in Arnold's poetic 'scenery' that would reduce Wordsworthian romanticism to the level of a tourist vignette. To his admirers, however, he combined scene and mood with a suppleness of philosophic purpose. In 'Dover Beach' he had produced a limpid and elegiac manifesto of the age of doubt.

Alone among the five poets, Arnold abandoned poetry in favour of prose. It was hard to think of his verse as having been in anything but a minor key. At his best, he evoked the agreeable sweeetness of melancholy in landscape, sometimes the sublimity of Rugby chapel or the Grande Chartreuse. It would be hard to find a consistent 'philosophy' in Tennyson or Browning. Arnold, writing of Wordsworth, thought it a mistake to look for such a thing in poetry.

Yet perhaps of all his contemporaries he came closest to embodying the philosopher-poet in his pursuit of poetry as 'a criticism of life'.

In him, the personal debate is decorous and subdued. He is the voice of honest doubt but not of desperation. There are no fervent outbursts as there had been during *In Memoriam*. Arnold is agreeable and intelligent. His nerves do not prick and tingle, nor is his heart sick at the thought of death and extinction, as Tennyson claimed to be. Arnold's spiritual struggle is civilized and urbane. His poems are a beautiful place to be. The dreaming spires and the Oxford countryside are a heaven in the mind, without God or angels, as if to compensate for the Christian heaven that Arnold cannot allow himself.

He does not seem to suffer as much as a Christian believer like Gerard Manley Hopkins in the so-called 'Sonnets of Desolation'. But he shows a humanity and an ability to capture character and nature as a painter might. He combines the influences of romanticism with an anticipation of modernity. In a poem like 'A Summer Night' there are lines and phrases that look forward to the urban scenes of English poetry in the 1920s.

CLOUGH

Friendship and intellectual preoccupation linked Arnold and Clough. Both were the products of Rugby school as reformed by Thomas Arnold, the earnest and questioning Christian father of the poet. Both were at Balliol in the first years of Benjamin Jowett's influence as Fellow. Both were doubters in the religious debate of mid-century. But Arnold's 'high seriousness' gave way in Clough to apparent moments of cynicism, amusement, and downright flippancy.

Clough died at forty-two, in 1861, commemorated by Arnold in 'Thyrsis'. At one extreme, he was a poet of spiritual drama in 'Easter Day', his realization, while walking 'the great sinful streets of Naples', that 'Christ is not risen'. But in the second part of the poem 'Hope conquers cowardice'; Christ is risen, after all, in 'the true creed', which Clough does not precisely define.

Clough represented what his biographer Lady Chorley called 'the uncommitted mind'. But a life of open-minded doubt might have proved more destructive to poetry than either Browning's firm Christian belief or Shelley's doctrinaire atheism. Clough seemed to practise the romanticism of disengagement, as Byron sometimes appeared to do. Like Byron, he became the gifted and amused observer of fashionable society. His long poems are almost novels in verse. *The*

Bothie of Tober-na-Vuolich is a laconic account of an Oxford reading-party in the Highlands during the long vacation. *Amours de Voyage* is an exchange of letters describing an English family in Rome. He wrote these in the metre of Latin hexametres, a rhythm that rarely suggests solemnity in English verse:

> Dear Eustacio, I write that you may write me an answer,
> Or at the least to put us again *en rapport* with each other.
> Rome disappoints me much, — St Peter's, perhaps, in especial;
> Only the Arch of Titus and the view from the Lateran please me.

The poem has a decorous romantic interest, and the voice of Claude to Eustace is matched by that of Georgina Trevellyn writing to her friend Louisa:

> At last, dearest Louisa, I take up my pen to address you.
> Here we are, you see, with the seven-and-seventy boxes,
> Courier, Papa and Mamma, the children, and Mary and Susan:
> Here we all are at Rome, and delighted of course with St Peter's.

Clough at his best was urbane and sophisticated, an acute and witty observer of humanity. In his major poems, like 'Dipsychus', he allowed moral and religious arguments their separate voices. He might almost have believed either voice, though he was assumed to be Faust fighting off Mephistopheles. He gave the impression of himself as a man who had been to the 'dangerous edge of things' and had no intention of taking the plunge.

SWINBURNE

To a third generation of Victorians, who were young men in the 1860s, the philosophizing of Clough and the earnestness of Matthew Arnold were profoundly unappealing:

> Literary history will hardly care to remember or to register the fact that there was a bad poet named Clough, whom his friends found it useless to puff: for the public, if dull, has not quite such a skull as belongs to believers in Clough.

In these words, Swinburne gave the public *coup de grâce* to Clough's reputation. Clough, of course, hardly lived to see the 1860s, a decade of the revolutionary young as much as the 1960s were to be. Swinburne, said Gosse, seemed not only a flag of rebellion but 'the red flag incarnate'. The European revolutions of 1848 were his childhood memories. The new Italian uprisings of Garibaldi and Mazzini against

Austrian oppression claimed his adulation. After Eton and Balliol, the young revolutionary burst upon a world where the Marquis de Sade was to be the new messiah and Algernon Charles Swinburne would be his prophet.

Poems and Ballads in 1866 took subjects thinly veiled by classical or historical allusions. Murder and rape, lesbians and sado-masochism were thrust upon startled readers in drawing-rooms and deaneries. Their outrage was the stuff of life to the shrill-voiced poet with the bright red hair that gave him the air of a cockatoo. In private, he circulated his novelettes in which Queen Victoria proved to be the twin sister of a Haymarket prostitute and in which Victoria herself confessed to having been seduced by William Wordsworth. Her sexual passion had been inflamed by his reading of *The Excursion*, safely short-listed among the most tedious poems in the English language.

In his pornographic writing, Swinburne sought to turn the schoolroom into a brothel and nearly killed himself by chronic brandy-drinking. But the *enfant terrible* became a tame middle-aged poet. He had a lyric gift and a pure brilliance that he squandered as if in a nursery tantrum. But it was not all wasted. There were passages in *Atalanta in Calydon* and pieces in *Poems and Ballads* that deserved all the praise of his followers. Like Wordsworth and Coleridge, he was burnt out long before his death in 1909 but he burnt with a flame in which many contemporaries saw the brightest falling star of the age.

THE CRITICS

These five poets collectively inspired some of the best criticism of poetry in the nineteenth century as well as in our own. They were not the only poets of importance in the sixty years between 1830 and 1890, yet they represented the mainstream of the romantic tradition. Rossetti, Morris, and the Pre-Raphaelites, as well as imperial Kipling, the genius of Hopkins, and the romantic decadence of the Nineties were culturally their successors even if they were not always so chronologically.

The Victorians had a deep intellectual scepticism about English literature as a subject to be taught in universities or elsewhere. It was proper that every intelligent man and woman should be familiar with it. It was part of culture and the nation's heritage. But the notion of awarding degrees for knowing about it seemed as unsuitable as awarding them for hairdressing or embalming.

In consequence, comparatively few critics were professional 'English' specialists. John Wilson Croker, the man who 'killed John Keats', by his scathing criticism of 'Endymion' in the *Quarterly Review* in 1818, was Secretary to the Admiralty; Gladstone was Prime Minister; Walter Bagehot was a political economist; Charles Kingsley was a clergyman, politician, and scientific thinker as well as a novelist and poet; John Morley was a barrister and minister in the Liberal government in 1886, his *Life of Gladstone* a classic of political biography; W. M. Rossetti was an officer of the Inland Revenue; Frederic Harrison was an international lawyer. Later still, T. S. Eliot was a banker and Harold Nicolson a Foreign Office diplomat.

Such men were quite as capable of reading poetry and commenting upon it as any professor of English. But perhaps they wrote a little differently. They had had a good deal of experience in public life and this encouraged a tendency towards forthright common-sense. And because most criticism appeared in commercially run publications there was more open debate. A good fight sold the magazine. Writers of literature used these columns on occasion to settle old scores with enemies, to promote their own interests, to defend their friends. They were not much activated by media publicity or 'hype', but by healthy old-fashioned likes and hates, prejudice and rancour, even by critical honesty or enthusiasm for what was beautiful and fine.

Nor was it a bad thing that this should be so. It served as another reminder that literature, in the first place, was not an academic discipline but an arena for the display of human conduct at its best and its worst.

1

Tennyson

Tennyson's reputation is difficult to appreciate without some sense of what it meant to be the first popular poet in an age of mass publishing. Popularity almost destroyed him. But first it made him what he was. Even Byron had never enjoyed such a reputation as his. Tennyson could not take a summer walk in the gardens of his home at Farringford on the Isle of Wight without the heads of trippers appearing here and there to gawp at the object of their pilgrimage. His verse was set to music and sung round thousands of drawing-room pianos in suburbs or country towns. 'Crossing the Bar' was carved on tombstones and memorials. His specially written verses were read out at such occasions as the 1886 opening of the Indian and Colonial Exhibition. The *Tennyson Birthday Book* had an inspiration-al verse for each day of the year. He was chosen by Thomas Edison as one of three famous English voices to be recorded on wax. The other two were Queen Victoria and Gladstone. Victoria refused, Gladstone and Tennyson agreed. He died as the first Lord Tennyson.

Tickets were issued for his funeral. Arthur Munby saw a vast crowd converging on Westminster Abbey, people jostling to buy penny photographs of the poet and copies of 'Crossing the Bar'. Eight years later, a biography by Robert F. Horton appeared in J. M. Dent's 'Saintly Lives Series', excluding such incidents as Tennyson's advice to young Maisie Ward to move away a little because 'I'm going to tell your father a dirty story.'

Despite some hostile reviews, Tennyson had not truly been out of favour since 1830. It was not the critics who bore his reputation highest but a procession of public figures, led by Queen Victoria. In 1845 her Prime Minister, Sir Robert Peel, recommended Tennyson for a Civil List pension as 'a poet of whose powers of imagination and expression many competent judges think highly'. In 1850, Lord John Russell, the new Prime Minister, told Prince Albert that 'Mr Tennyson is a fit person to be Poet Laureate.' After Albert's death, Victoria recorded in her journal on 14 April 1862 a meeting on the Isle of Wight:

I went down to see Tennyson, who is very peculiar-looking, tall, dark, with a fine head, long black flowing hair and a beard; oddly dressed but there is no affectation about him. I told him how much I admired his glorious lines to my precious Albert, and how much comfort I found in his *In Memoriam*. He was full of unbounded appreciation of beloved Albert. When he spoke of my own loss, of that to the nation, his eyes quite filled with tears.

The consolation found by the Queen in the lines of *In Memoriam* was mirrored in thousands of her subjects. The average age of death during her reign was forty, and in some areas it had been seventeen. Tennyson's great poem spoke comfort to the bereaved. Twenty-one years later he visited Victoria again, at Osborne, on 7 August 1883. Again she noted their conversation:

He spoke of the many friends he had lost, and what it would be if he did not feel and know that there was another world where there would be no partings, of his horror of unbelievers and philosophers, who would try to make one believe that there was no other world, no immortality, who tried to explain everything away in a miserable manner. . . . I told him what a comfort *In Memoriam* had always been to me, which seemed to please him; but he said I could not believe the numbers of shameful letters of abuse he had received about it. Incredible!

It did not need literary critics to promote or explain Tennyson's fame. *In Memoriam* promised no narrow religious certainty but vague reunion with loved ones whom the reader mourned. At that level, its success seemed inevitable.

Tennyson thought he had also been unjustly abused for the darkness and madness in *Maud*. The future Margot Asquith, as a young woman, once asked him to read it to her before dinner. 'That was the poem I was cursed for writing!' the old man said. 'When it came out no word was bad enough for me! I was a blackguard, a ruffian and an atheist! You will live to have as great a contempt for literary critics and the public as I have, my child!' He finished, 'Come into the garden, Maud', pulled her on to his knee and said, 'Many have written as well as that, but nothing that ever *sounded* so well.'

In October 1892 Benjamin Jowett heard that Tennyson was dying. He urged Lady Tennyson to comfort herself by reading her husband's poems, 'beginning with *In Memoriam*'. A few days later Queen Victoria had the final word:

Heard that dear old Lord Tennyson had breathed his last, a great national loss. He was a great poet, and his ideas were ever grand, noble and elevating. He was very loyal, and always very kind and sympathizing to me, quite remarkably so. What beautiful lines he wrote for my darling Albert and for my children and Eddy! He died with his hand on his Shakespeare and the moon shining full into the window and over him. A worthy end to such a remarkable man.

Sentiment, nostalgia, veneration were swept away by the new and impatient century. 'In literature her tastes were more restricted,' wrote Lytton Strachey of Victoria in 1921. 'She was devoted to Lord Tennyson.' When Harold Nicolson's biography was published in 1923, Strachey refused to review it. 'I can't face Lord Tennyson', he told Maynard Keynes, dismissing the idea of Nicolson's book as 'so stupid and disgusting'. Bloomsbury and Chelsea wondered if Tennyson and the Victorians were, on the whole, more contemptible or absurd. Roger Fry, writing about drawing-room furniture in the *Athenaeum* in 1919 (reprinted in Roger Fry, *Vision and Design*, 1920), suggested that whatever sexual passion was roused by intimacy on the cushioned ottoman would soon be rebuked and assuaged by the sight of volumes of Lord Tennyson on the shelves of the whatnot.

In 1932, F. R. Leavis swept aside Tennyson and his age in a few pages of *New Bearings in English Poetry*. John Collier, in the same year, wrote of Tennyson, 'No failure has been so absurd and tragic as his.' W. J. Turner, also in 1932, remarked that 'Victorian poetry is, to the present generation, more contemptible than any other literary product in the history of England.'

But the pendulum swung again. Nicolson in 1923 and T. S. Eliot in 1936 saw in Tennyson not the self-confident public bard but a great poet of the post-romantic age, one who had known the precipice of the soul, in both the differing perspectives of Browning and Hopkins. The rediscovery of Tennyson once more gave his work a promise first seen in the early reviews, when William IV was still king and the future laureate of *In Memoriam* and *Maud* was known only as a clever young man from Trinity, who had lately won the Chancellor's Medal for a poem on 'Timbuctoo'.

W. J. Fox on *Poems, Chiefly Lyrical* (1830) in the *Westminster Review* (1831)

In 1827, Tennyson was part-author with his brother Charles of Poems
by Two Brothers. *In 1830, while still an undergraduate at Trinity
College, Cambridge, he published his own* Poems, Chiefly Lyrical. *W.
J. Fox reviewed it in the* Westminster Review *in January 1831. The*
Westminster *had been founded in 1824 by Jeremy Bentham and James
Mill as the voice of philosophical radicals and, specifically, of
utilitarianism. It was not, on the whole, well disposed towards poetry
as mere beauty or ornament. 'Literature is a seducer', it warned in
1825, 'we had almost said a harlot. She may do to trifle with; but woe
be to the state whose statesmen write verses, and whose lawyers read
more in Tom Moore than in Bracton.'*[1]

Fox was a Nonconformist minister who edited his own Monthly
Repository, *in which the two* Madhouse Cells *of the young Robert
Browning were published in 1834. He was a perceptive and precise
critic who seized on the two significant characteristics of Tennyson as
a natural successor to the first romantics. Tennyson's poetry was
graceful and impassioned but that alone was not enough. More
important, Fox saw him as one who explored and opened up the
landscape of the mind rather than merely reflecting external nature.
'He climbs the pineal gland as if it were a hill.' In that respect,
Tennyson at twenty-one already anticipated Baudelaire's comment of
1846 on the error of the earlier romantics and their romanticism.
'They looked for it outside themselves, but it was only to be found
within.'*

Why is Shakspeare the greatest of poets? Because he was one of the
greatest of philosophers. We reason on the conduct of his characters
with as little hesitation as if they were real living human beings.
Extent of observation, accuracy of thought, and depth of reflection,
were the qualities which won the prize of sovereignty for his
imagination, and the effect of these qualities was practically to
anticipate, so far as was needful for his purposes, the mental
philosophy of a future age. Metaphysics must be the stem of poetry
for the plant to thrive; but if the stem flourishes we are not likely to
be at a loss for leaves, flowers, and fruit. Now whatever theories may
have come into fashion, and gone out of fashion, the real science of

mind advances with the progress of society like all other sciences. The poetry of the last forty years already shews symptoms of life in exact proportion as it is imbued with this science. There is least of it in the exotic legends of Southey, and the feudal romances of Scott. More of it, though in different ways, in Byron and Campbell. In Shelley there would have been more still, had he not devoted himself to unsound and mystical theories. Most of all in Coleridge and Wordsworth. They are all going or gone; but here is a little book as thoroughly and unitedly metaphysical and poetical in its spirit as any of them; and sorely shall we be disappointed in its author if it be not the precursor of a series of productions which shall beautifully illustrate our speculations, and convincingly prove their soundness.

Do not let our readers be alarmed. These poems are anything but heavy; anything but stiff and pedantic; anything but cold and logical. They are graceful, very graceful; they are animated, touching, and impassioned. And they are so, precisely because they are philosophical; because they are not made up of metrical cant and conventional phraseology; because there is sincerity where the author writes from experience, and accuracy whether he writes from experience or observation; and he only writes from experience or observation, because he has felt and thought, and learned to analyze thought and feeling; because his own mind is rich in poetical associations, and he has wisely been content with its riches; and because, in his composition, he has not sought to construct an elaborate and artificial harmony, but only to pour forth his thoughts in those expressive and simple melodies whose meaning, truth, and power, are the soonest recognized and the longest felt.

The most important department in which metaphysical science has been a pioneer for poetry is in the analysis of particular states of mind; a work which is now performed with ease, power, and utility as much increased, as in the grosser dissections of the anatomical lecturer. Hence the poet, more fortunate than the physician, has provision made for an inexhaustible supply of subjects. A new world is discovered for him to conquer. The poets of antiquity rarely did more than incidentally touch this class of topics; the external world had not yet lost its freshness; situations, and the outward expression of the thoughts, feelings and passions generated by those situations, were a province so much nearer at hand, and presented so much to be done and enjoyed, that they rested there content, like the two tribes and a half of Israel, who sought not to cross the narrow boundary that separated them from a better and richer country. Nor let them be blamed; it was for the philosophers to be the first discoverers and settlers, and for poetry afterwards to reap the advantage of their labours. This has only been done recently, or rather is only beginning to be done at all.

Mr. Tennyson has some excellent specimens of this class. He seems to obtain entrance into a mind as he would make his way into a landscape; he climbs the pineal gland as if it were a hill in the centre of the scene; looks around on all objects with their varieties of form, their movements, their shades of colour, and their mutual relations and influences; and forthwith produces as graphic a delineation in the one case as Wilson[2] or Gainsborough could have done in the other, to the great enrichment of our gallery of intellectual scenery. In the 'Supposed Confessions of a second-rate sensitive mind not in unity with itself', there is an extraordinary combination of deep reflection, metaphysical analysis, picturesque description, dramatic transition, and strong emotion. The author personates (he can personate anything he pleases from an angel to a grasshopper) a timid sceptic, but who must evidently always remain such, and yet be miserable in his scepticism; whose early associations, and whose sympathies, make religion a necessity to his heart; yet who has not lost his pride in the prowess of his youthful infidelity; who is tossed hither and thither on the conflicting currents of feeling and doubt, without that vigorous intellectual decision which alone could 'ride in the whirlwind and direct the storm', until at last he disappears with an exclamation which remains on the ear like

> the bubbling cry
> Of some strong swimmer in his agony.

Now without intruding any irreverent comparison or critical profanity we do honestly think this state of mind as good a subject for poetical description as even the shield of Achilles itself. Such topics are more in accordance with the spirit and intellect of the age than those about which poetry has been accustomed to be conversant; their adoption will effectually redeem it from the reproach of being frivolous and enervating; and of their affinity with the best pictorial qualities of poetry we have conclusive evidence in this very composition. The delineations of the trustful infant, the praying mother, the dying lamb, are as good as anything of the kind can be; while those of the supposed author's emotions as he gazes on 'Christians with happy countenances', or stands by the Christian grave, or realizes again, with a mixture of self-admiration and self-reproach, 'the unsunned fresh-ness of his strength', when he 'went forth in quest of truth', are of a higher order, and are more powerfully, though not less gracefully finished.

John Wilson Croker on *Poems* (1833) in the *Quarterly Review* (1833)

Tennyson's friends and well-wishers had overdone the praise in 1831. He had been favourably compared with Milton and Aeschylus. Leigh Hunt wrote in the Tatler *that there had been 'no such poetical writing since the last volume of Mr Keats'. Tennyson's closest friend, Arthur Hallam, reviewed the poems in the* Englishman's Magazine, *quoting from 'Adeline' and asking, 'Is this not beautiful? When this Poet dies, will not the Graces and the Loves mourn over him?' Admiration toppled into absurdity.*

In 1833, Tennyson's second volume was reviewed in the Quarterly *by John Wilson Croker, the man who was said in the limerick to have 'killed John Keats' by the savagery of his criticism. Croker was a former Secretary to the Admiralty and a prominent Tory politician. He set about young Alfred Tennyson in a brisk, no-nonsense manner. Croker, whatever his more obvious failings, had a nose for the pretentious. He seemed to scent a pungent whiff of it in this young man for whom the 'Loves' and 'Graces' were so concerned. Croker began with a sardonic comment on the 'popularity' of the earlier volume and the controversy over his 'killing' of Keats. Then he went on to have a little savage fun at the expense of Tennyson's own poems.*

This is, as some of his marginal notes intimate, Mr. Tennyson's second appearance. By some strange chance we have never seen his first publication, which, if it at all resembles its younger brother, must be by this time so popular that any notice of it on our part would seem idle and presumptuous; but we gladly seize this opportunity of repairing an unintentional neglect, and of introducing to the admi-ration of our more sequestered readers a new prodigy of genius—another and a brighter star of the galaxy or *milky way* of poetry of which the lamented Keats was the harbinger; and let us take this occasion to sing our palinode on the subject of 'Endymion'. We certainly did not discover in that poem the same degree of merit that its more clear-sighted and prophetic admirers did. We did not foresee the unbounded popularity which has carried it through we know not how many editions; which has placed it on every table; and, what is still more unequivocal, familiarized it in every mouth. All this splendour of fame, however, though we had not the sagacity to anticipate, we have the candour to acknowledge; and we request that the publisher of the new and beautiful edition of Keats's works now in the press, with graphic illustrations by Callcott[3] and Turner, will do us the favour and the justice to notice our conversion in his pro-legomena.

Warned by our former mishap, wiser by experience, and improved, as we hope, in taste, we have to offer Mr. Tennyson our tribute of unmingled approbation, and it is very agreeable to us, as well as to our readers, that our present task will be little more than the selection, for their delight, of a few specimens of Mr. Tennyson's singular genius, and the venturing to point out, now and then, the peculiar brilliancy of some of the gems that irradiate his poetical crown.

A prefatory sonnet opens to the reader the aspirations of the young author, in which, after the manner of sundry poets, ancient and modern, he expresses his own peculiar character, by wishing himself to be something that he is not. The amorous Catullus aspired to be a sparrow; the tuneful and convivial Anacreon (for we totally reject the supposition that attributes the Ἔιθε λύρη καλὴ γενοίμην[4] to Alcæus)[5] wished to be a lyre and a great drinking cup; a crowd of more modern sentimentalists have desired to approach their mistresses as flowers, tunicks, sandals, birds, breezes, and butterflies;—all poor conceits of narrow-minded poetasters! Mr. Tennyson (though he, too, would, as far as his true-love is concerned, not unwillingly be 'an earring', 'a girdle', and 'a necklace') in the more serious and solemn exordium of his works ambitions a bolder metamorphosis—he wishes to be—*a river*!

SONNET.

Mine be the strength of spirit fierce and free,
Like some broad river rushing down *alone*—

rivers that travel in company are too common for his taste—

With the self-same impulse wherewith he was thrown—

a beautiful and harmonious line—

From his loud fount upon the echoing lea:—
Which, with *increasing* might, doth *forward flee*—

Every word of this line is valuable—the natural progress of human ambition is here strongly characterized—two lines ago he would have been satisfied with the *self-same* impulse—but now he must have *increasing* might; and indeed he would require all his might to accomplish his object of *fleeing forward*, that is, going backwards and forwards at the same time.

The next piece is a kind of testamentary paper, addressed 'To ——', a friend, we presume, containing his wishes as to what his friend should do for him when he (the poet) shall be dead—not, as we shall see, that he quite thinks that such a poet can die outright.

> Shake hands, my friend, across the brink
>   Of that deep grave to which I go.
> Shake hands once more; I cannot sink
>   So far—far down, but I shall know
>   Thy voice, and answer from below!

Horace said 'non omnis moriar',[6] meaning that his fame should survive—Mr. Tennyson is still more vivacious, 'non *omnino* moriar'—'I will not die at all; my body shall be as immortal as my verse, and however *low I may go*, I warrant you I shall keep all my wits about me,—therefore'

> When, in the darkness over me,
>   The four-handed mole shall scrape,
> Plant thou no dusky cypress tree,
>   Nor wreath thy cap with doleful crape,
>   But pledge me in the flowing grape.

Observe how all ages become present to the mind of a great poet; and admire how naturally he combines the funeral cypress of classical antiquity with the crape hatband of the modern undertaker.

John Stuart Mill on *Poems, Chiefly Lyrical* (1831) and *Poems* (1833) in the *London Review* (1835)

Two years after Croker had done his best to make young Tennyson look a fool, John Stuart Mill came to the rescue. Though better known

as a political economist and author of the essay On Liberty *(1859),*
Mill was an important literary critic of the 1830s. He began but never
finished a review of Browning's first poem, Pauline, *in 1832.*

Here he responds sharply to the literal-minded philistinism of men
like Croker and recommends Tennyson as a poet of colour and
imagination. In the following extracts, he discusses 'The Lady of
Shalott', 'Isabel', and 'The Lotos-Eaters'. He begins with 'The Lady of
Shalott'.

The next poem which we shall quote is one of higher pretensions. Its
length exceeds the usual dimensions of an extract. But the idea which
would be given of the more perfect of Mr. Tennyson's poems, by
detached passages, would be not merely an incomplete but a false idea.
There is not a stanza in the following poem which can be felt or even
understood as the poet intended, unless the reader's imagination and
feelings are already in the state which results from the passage next
preceding, or rather from all which precedes. The very breaks, which
divide the story into parts, all tell.

If every one approached poetry in the spirit in which it ought to be
approached, willing to feel it first and examine it afterwards, we
should not premise another word. But there is a class of readers, (a
class, too, on whose verdict the early success of a young poet mainly
depends,) who dare not enjoy until they have first satisfied
themselves that they have a warrant for enjoying; who read a poem
with the critical understanding first, and only when they are convinced that it is right to be delighted, are willing to give their
spontaneous feelings fair play. The consequence is, that they lose the
general effect, while they higgle about the details, and never place
themselves in the position in which, even with their mere under-
standings, they can estimate the poem as a whole. For the benefit of
such readers, we tell them beforehand, that this is a tale of enchantment; and that they will never enter into the spirit of it unless they
surrender their imagination to the guidance of the poet, with the same
easy credulity with which they would read the *Arabian Nights*, or,
what this story more resembles, the tales of magic of the middle ages.

Though the agency is supernatural, the scenery, as will be
perceived, belongs to the actual world. No reader of any imagination
will complain, that the precise nature of the enchantment is left in
mystery.

In powers of narrative and scene-painting combined, this poem
must be ranked among the very first of its class. The delineation of

outward objects, as in the greater number of Mr. Tennyson's poems, is, not picturesque, but (if we may use the term) statuesque; with brilliancy of colour superadded. The forms are not, as in painting, or unequal degrees of definiteness; the tints do not melt gradually into each other, but each individual object stands out in bold relief, with a clear decided outline. This statue-like precision and distinctness, few artists have been able to give to so essentially vague a language as that of words: but if once this difficulty be got over, scene-painting by words has a wider range than either painting or sculpture; for it can represent (as the reader must have seen in the foregoing poem), not only with the vividness and strength of the one, but with the clearness and definiteness of the other, objects in motion. Along with all this, there is in the poem all that power of making a few touches do the whole work, which excites our admiration in Coleridge. Every line suggests so much more than it says, that much may be left unsaid: the concentration, which is the soul of narrative, is obtained, without the sacrifice of reality and life. Where the march of the story requires that the mind should pause, details are specified; where rapidity is necessary, they are all brought before us at a flash. Except that the versification is less exquisite, the 'Lady of Shalott' is entitled to a place by the side of the 'Ancient Mariner' and 'Christabel'.

Mr. Tennyson's two volumes contain a whole picture-gallery of lovely women: but we are drawing near to the limits of allowable quotation. The imagery of the following passage from the poem of 'Isabel', in the first volume, is beautifully typical of the nobler and gentler of two beings, upholding, purifying, and, as far as possible, assimilating to itself the grosser and ruder:—

> A clear stream flowing with a muddy one,
>   Till in its onward current it absorbs
>   With swifter movement and in purer light
>   The vexed eddies of its wayward brother—
>   A leaning and upbearing parasite,
>   Clothing the steam, which else had fallen quite,
>   With clustered flowerbells and ambrosial orbs
>   Of rich fruitbunches leaning on each other.

The length to which our quotations have extended, and the unsatisfactoriness of short extracts, prevent us from giving any specimen of one of the finest of Mr. Tennyson's poems, the 'Lotos-Eaters'. The subject is familiar to every reader of the *Odyssey*. The poem is not of such sustained merit in the execution as some of the others; but the general impression resembles an effect of climate in a landscape: we see the objects through a drowsy, relaxing, but dreamy atmosphere, and the inhabitants seem to have inhaled the like. Two lines near the commencement touch the key-note of the poem:

> In the afternoon they came unto a land
> Wherein it seemèd always afternoon.

The above extracts by no means afford an idea of all the variety of beauty to be found in these volumes. But the specimens we have given may, we hope, satisfy the reader, that if he explore further for himself, his search will be rewarded.

Leigh Hunt on *Poems* (1842) in the *Church of England Quarterly* (1842)

The publication of his Poems *in two volumes in 1842 represented a collection of the best that Tennyson had so far written. This edition established him as the great poetic talent of his day in the estimation of most contemporaries. Leigh Hunt, poet and essayist, was a survivor of the romantic revival, a friend of Shelley and Keats, a political journalist imprisoned for two years in 1813 after denouncing the Prince Regent, the nation's ruler, as 'a corpulent gentleman of fifty . . . a violator of his word, a libertine over head and ears in debt and disgrace, a despiser of domestic ties, the companion of gamblers and demireps, a man who has just closed half a century without one single claim on the gratitude of his country, or the respect of posterity'. Leigh Hunt was later to be lampooned himself by Dickens as Harold Skimpole in* Bleak House *(1853).*

In the following extracts from the review of Tennyson, he balances praise and reservation more judiciously than he had done in 1831. He begins by rebuking Tennyson gently for talking too much about the revisions he has made or how the poems came to be written.

We are compelled to say, then, in justice to the very respect which we entertain, and the more which we desire to entertain, for the genius of Mr. Tennyson, that the above 'lettings out of the bag' of his dates and alterations, are a little too characteristic of a certain mixture of timidity and misgiving with his otherwise somewhat defying demands upon our assent to his figments and his *hyphens*, and that we have greater objections to a certain air of literary dandyism, or fine-gentlemanism, or fastidiousness, or whatever he may *not* be pleased to call it, which leads him to usher in his compositions with such exordiums as those to 'Morte d'Arthur', and 'Godiva'; in the former of which he gives us to understand that he should have burnt his poem but for the 'request of friends'; and, in the latter, that he 'shaped' it while he was waiting 'for the train at Coventry', and hanging on the bridge 'with grooms and porters'. Really this is little better than the rhyming fine-ladyism of Miss Seward,[7] who said that she used to translate an ode of Horace 'while her hair was curling'. And, if the 'grooms and porters' have any meaning beyond a superfluous bit of the graphic, not in keeping with his subject, it is a little worse, for why should not Mr. Tennyson, in the universality of his poetry, be as content to be waiting on a bridge, among 'grooms and porters', as with any other assortment of his fellow-men? Doubtless he would disclaim any such want of philosophy; but this kind of mixed tone of contempt and nonchalance, or, at best, of fine-life phrases with better fellowship, looks a little instructive, and is, at all events, a little perilous. There is a drawl of Bond-street in it. We suspect that these poems of 'Morte d'Arthur' and 'Godiva' are among those which Mr. Tennyson thinks his best, and is most anxious that others should regard as he does; and therefore it is that he would affect to make trifles of them. The reader's opinion is at once to be of great importance to him, and yet none at all. There is a boyishness in this, which we shall be happy to see Mr. Tennyson, who is no longer a boy, outgrow.

He has fancy, imagination, expression, thought, knowledge, and music, too—in short, all the materials of an admirable contemplative poet, and in some instances his success has been already great, and his name, we trust, will be lasting. But at present he still shows a little too much of the spoiled child. He is indolent, over-refining, is in danger of neutralizing his earnestness altogether by the scepticism of thought not too strong, but not strong enough to lead or combine, and he runs, or rather reposes, altogether upon feelings (not to speak it offensively) too sensual. His mind lives in an atmosphere heavy with perfumes. He grows lazy by the side of his Lincolnshire water-lilies; and, with a genius of his own sufficient for original and enduring purposes (at least we hope so), subjects himself to the charge of helping it too much with the poets gone before him, from Homer to Wordsworth, and to Shelley and Keats. But we will touch upon most of the poems in their order, and thus best show what we mean. The beautiful passages that we shall have to quote in eulogy will luckily far more than repay the reader and ourselves for any unpleasant necessity of finding fault.

'Claribel', who 'low-lieth' where the 'beetle *boometh*' (not a good word), and the 'wild bee hummeth', and the 'lintwhite smelleth', and the 'mavis dwelleth', *et cetera, et cetera*, is rather a series of descriptive items in obsolete language than a dirge in earnest.

'Lilian' is as light and pretty as its subject; but

> Till the lightning laughters dimple
> The baby roses in her cheeks,

is an instance of that injudicious crowding of images which sometimes results from Mr. Tennyson's desire to impress upon us the abundance of his thoughts.

The style of 'Isabel' reminds us both of Wordsworth's solemnity and Shelley's Grecisms and penultimate accents. It is a panegyric of chastity in that ultra-super-exalting spirit of Beaumont and Fletcher, which renders the sincerity of it suspicious; and the conclusion unluckily corroborates the impression by informing us that 'the world hath not such another', for a 'finished, chastened purity', as this lady! This is awkward for the sex in general, and for their gratitude to the poet. The expression '*blanched* tablets of the heart', will not do at all after its beautiful original in the old poet, 'the *red-leaved* tablets of the heart'. There is a charming verisimilitude and warmth of feeling in the latter image, full of grace and cordiality.

'Mariana', in the 'Moated Grange', brings us at once into the thick of the real beauties of the author; and, as we have not noticed him in this publication before, and wish our article to give as thorough an idea of his genius as it can, we will quote the whole of it, though at the hazard of the reader's having seen it years ago. The loose, rusty nails on the garden wall, the 'glooming flats', the low of the oxen coming from the dark fens, the blue fly singing in the pane, and the mouse shrieking behind the mouldering wainscot, are part of a heap of images all painted from nature, and true to the feeling of the subject.

Charles Kingsley on Tennyson in
Fraser's Magazine (1850)

Charles Kingsley, famous by 1850 as a Christian Socialist, as well as for his novels of political debate, Yeast (1848) *and* Alton Locke

(1850), looked back on Tennyson's work before In Memoriam *and his appointment as Poet Laureate. Like many contemporary assessments, this measures Tennyson against the first romantics and considers the extent to which the landscape of the mind combined a naturalistic and mystical account of the outer world. It also reflects Kingsley's preoccupations and begins a systematic perception of Tennyson as preacher or teacher.*

Kingsley then discusses Tennyson as the poet of modern man, of Christian man with strength and faith for the future. He contrasts this with the moral lassitude of earlier romanticism, 'Werterism' as he calls it. Goethe's *romance,* Sorrows of Young Werther *(1774) described the despair and suicide of its hero when his beloved Charlotte married another man. Morbid and unhealthy to the more muscular Victorians, it was mocked by Thackeray in a satirical poem with Goethe's title:*

> *Charlotte, having seen his body*
> *Borne before her on a shutter,*
> *Like a well-conducted person,*
> *Went on cutting bread and butter.*

Some of our readers, we would fain hope, remember as an era in their lives the first day on which they read those earlier poems; how, fifteen years ago, 'Mariana in the Moated Grange', 'The Dying Swan', 'The Lady of Shalott', came to them as revelations. They seemed to themselves to have found at last a poet who promised not only to combine the cunning melody of Moore, the rich fulness of Keats, and the simplicity of Wordsworth, but one who was introducing a method of observing Nature different from that of all three, and yet succeeding in everything which they had attempted, often in vain.

This deep, simple faith in the divineness of Nature as she appears, which, in our eyes, is Mr. Tennyson's *differentia*,[8] is really the natural accompaniment of a quality at first sight its very opposite, and for which he is often blamed by a prosaic world; namely, his subjective and transcendental mysticism. It is the mystic, after all, who will describe Nature most simply, because he sees most in her; because he is most ready to believe that she will reveal to others the same message which she has revealed to him. Men like Boehme,[9] Novalis,[10] and Fourier,[11] who can soar into the inner cloud-world of man's spirit, even though they lose their way there, dazzled by excess of wonder— men who, like Wordsworth, can give utterance to such subtle anthropologic wisdom as the ode on the 'Intimations of Immortality', will for that very reason most humbly and patiently 'consider the lilies of the field, how they grow'. And even so it is just because Mr. Tennyson is, far more than Wordsworth, mystical, and what an ignorant and money-getting generation, idolatrous of mere sensuous activity, calls 'dreamy', that he has become the greatest naturalistic poet which England has seen for several centuries: the same faculty which enabled him to draw such subtle subjective pictures of womanhood as 'Adeline', 'Isabel', and 'Eleänore' enabled him to see, and, therefore simply to describe in one of the most distinctive and successful of his earlier poems, how

> The creeping mosses and clambering weeds,
>   And the willow branches hoar and dank,
> And the wavy swell of the soughing reeds,
>   And the wave-worn horns of the echoing bank,
> And the silvery marish-flowers that throng
> The desolate creeks and pools among,
> Were flooded over with eddying song.

No doubt there are in the earlier poems exceptions to this style,— attempts to adorn Nature, and dazzle with a barbaric splendour akin to that of Keats,—as, for instance, in the 'Recollections of the Arabian Nights'. But how cold and gaudy, in spite of individual beauties, is that poem by the side of either of the 'Marianas', and especially of that one in which the scenery is drawn, simply and faithfully, from those counties which the world considers the quintessence of the prosaic— the English fens.

> Upon the middle of the night
>   Waking she heard the night-fowl crow;
> The cock sung out an hour ere light:
>   From the dark fen the oxen's low
> Came to her: without hope of change,
>   In sleep she seem'd to walk forlorn,
>   Till cold winds woke the grey-eyed morn
> About the lonely moated grange.
>
> About a stone-cast from the wall
>   A sluice with blacken'd waters slept,
> And o'er it many, round and small,
>   The cluster'd marish-mosses crept.
> Hard by a poplar shook alway,

> All silver-green with gnarled bark,
> For leagues no other tree did dark
> The level waste, the rounding gray.

Throughout all these exquisite lines occurs but one instance of what the vulgar call 'poetic diction'. All is simple description, in short and Saxon words, and yet who can deny the effect to be perfect—superior to almost any similar passage in Wordsworth? And why? Because the passage quoted, and indeed the whole poem, is perfect in what artists call *tone*—tone in the metre and in the sound of the words, as well as in the images and the feelings expressed. The weariness, the dreariness, the dark mysterious waste, exist alike within and without, in the slow monotonous pace of the metre and the words, as well as in the boundless fen, and the heart of her who, 'without hope of change, in sleep did seem to walk forlorn'. The same faith in Nature, the same instinctive correctness in melody, springing from the correct insight into Nature, ran through the poems inspired by mediæval legends. The very spirit of the old ballad writers, with their combinations of mysticism and objectivity, their freedom from any self-conscious attempt at reflective epithets or figures, runs through them all. We are never jarred in them, as we are in all the attempts at ballad-writing and ballad-restoring before Mr. Tennyson's time, by discordant touches of the reflective in thought, the picturesque in Nature, or the theatric in action.

In Mr. Tennyson alone, as we think, the spirit of the middle age is perfectly reflected.—Its delight, not in the 'sublime and picturesque', but in the green leaves and spring flowers for their own sake,—the spirit of Chaucer and of the *Robin Hood Garland*,—the naturalism which revels as much in the hedgerow and garden as in alps, and cataracts, and Italian skies, and the other strong stimulants to the faculty of admiration which the palled taste of an unhealthy age, from Keats and Byron down to Browning, has rushed abroad to seek. It is enough for Mr. Tennyson's truly English spirit to see how

> On either side the river lie
> Long fields of barley and of rye,
> That clothe the wold and meet the sky;
> And through the field the road runs by
> To many-tower'd Camelot.

Or how,

> In the stormy east-wind straining,
> The pale yellow woods were waning,
> The broad stream in his banks complaining,
> Heavily the low sky raining
>   Over tower'd Camelot.

Give him but such scenery as that, which he can see in every parish in England, and he will find it a fit scene for an ideal myth, subtler than a casuist's questionings, deep as the deepest heart of woman.

But in this earlier volume we have only the *disjecta membra poetæ*.[12] The poet has not yet arrived at the art of combining his new speculations on man with his new mode of viewing Nature. His objective pieces are too exclusively objective, his subjective too exclusively subjective; and where he deals with natural imagery in these latter, he is too apt, as in 'Eleänore', to fall back upon the old and received method of poetic diction, though he never indulges in a commonplace or a stock epithet. But in the interval between 1830 and 1842 the needful interfusion of the two elements took place. And in 'Locksley Hall' and the 'Two Voices' we find the new doubts and questions of the time embodied naturally and organically, in his own method of simple natural expression. For instance, from the 'Search for Truth' in the 'Two Voices',—

> Cry, faint not, climb: the summits slope
> Beyond the furthest flights of hope,
> Wrapt in dense cloud from base to cope.

> Sometimes a little corner shines,
> As over rainy mist inclines
> A gleaming crag with belts of pines.

> 'I will go forward,' sayest thou;
> 'I shall not fail to find her now.
> Look up, the fold is on her brow.'

Or, again, in 'Locksley Hall', the poem which, as we think deservedly, has had most influence on the minds of the young men of our day—

> Eager-hearted as a boy when first he leaves his father's field,
> And at night along the dusky highway near and nearer drawn,
> Sees in heaven the light of London flaring like a dreary dawn;
> And his spirit leaps within him to be gone before him then,
> Underneath the light he looks at, in among the throngs of men;
> Men, my brothers, men the workers, ever reaping something
>   new:

That which they have done but earnest of the things which they
   shall do:

and all the grand prophetic passage following, which is said, we know
not how truly, to have won for the poet the respect of that great
statesman whose loss all good men this day deplore.

In saying that 'Locksley Hall' has deservedly had so great an
influence over the minds of the young, we shall, we are afraid, have
offended some who are accustomed to consider that poem as Werterian
and unhealthy. But, in reality, the spirit of the poem is simply anti-
Werterian. It is man rising out of sickness into health,—not conquered
by Werterism, but conquering his selfish sorrow, and the moral and
intellectual paralysis which it produces, by faith and hope,—faith in the
progress of science and civilization, hope in the final triumph of good.
Doubtless, that is not the highest deliverance,—not a permanent
deliverance at all. Faith in God and hope in Christ alone can deliver a
man once and for all, from Werterism, or any other moral disease; that
truth was reserved for *In Memoriam*: but as far as 'Locksley Hall' goes,
it is a step forward—a whole moral æon beyond Byron and Shelley; and
a step, too, in the right direction, just because it *is* a step forward,—
because the path of deliverance is, as 'Locksley Hall' sets forth, not
backwards towards a fancied paradise of childhood—not backward to
grope after an unconsciousness which is now impossible, an implicit
faith which would be unworthy of the man, but forward on the road on
which God has been leading him, carrying upward with him the
aspirations of childhood, and the bitter experience of youth, to help the
organized and trustful labour of manhood. There are, in fact, only two
deliverances from Werterism possible in the nineteenth century; one is
into Popery, and the other is—

   Forward, forward, let us range;
Let the peoples spin for ever down the ringing grooves of
   change;
Through the shadow of the world we sweep into the younger
   day:
Better fifty years of Europe than a cycle of Cathay.

In Memoriam (1850) from Hallam Tennyson, *Alfred, Lord Tennyson* (1897)

Publication of In Memoriam *turned Tennyson from an admired poet
into a figure of English public life. The poem had been written over a*

period of seventeen years, in short sections, a monument to his grief at the sudden death of his closest friend, Arthur Hallam. But it was published anonymously and not generally recognized as Tennyson's work. Indeed, because Tennyson speaks of himself as 'widowed' and because the intensity of loss was expressed so openly, it was thought by some readers and reviewers to be written by a woman for her dead husband. After the poet's death his son, Hallam Tennyson, christened in tribute to Arthur Hallam, published Tennyson's account of the poem's composition and the reactions of individual readers to it.

"It must be remembered," writes my father, "that this is a poem, *not* an actual biography. It is founded on our friendship, on the engagement of Arthur Hallam to my sister, on his sudden death at Vienna, just before the time fixed for their marriage, and on his burial at Clevedon Church. The poem concludes with the marriage of my youngest sister Cecilia. It was meant to be a kind of *Divina Commedia*, ending with happiness. The sections were written at many different places, and as the phases of our intercourse came to my memory and suggested them. I did not write them with any view of weaving them into a whole, or for publication, until I found that I had written so many. The different moods of sorrow as in a drama are dramatically given, and my conviction that fear, doubts, and suffering will find answer and relief only through Faith in a God of Love. 'I' is not always the author speaking of himself, but the voice of the human race speaking thro' him."

Hallam Tennyson went on to summarize critical reaction to the poem, on the part of controversial theologians like Frederick Robertson and F. D. Maurice, one of the founders of Christian Socialism, as well as eminent scientists.

At first the reviews of the volume were not on the whole sympathetic. One critic in a leading journal, for instance, considered that "a great deal of poetic feeling had been wasted," and "much shallow art spent on the tenderness shown to an Amaryllis[13] of the Chancery Bar." Another referred to the poem as follows: "These touching lines evidently come from the full heart of the widow of a military man." However, men like Maurice and Robertson thought that the author had made a definite step towards the unification of the highest religion and philosophy with the progressive science of the day; and that he was the one poet who "through almost the agonies of a death-struggle" had made an effective stand against his own doubts and difficulties and those of the time, "on behalf of those first principles which underlie all creeds, which belong to our earliest childhood, and on which the wisest and best have rested through all ages; that all is right; that darkness shall be clear; that God and Time are the only interpreters; that Love is King; that the Immortal is in us; that, which is the keynote of the whole, 'All is well, tho' Faith and Form be sundered in the night of Fear.' " Scientific leaders like Herschel, Owen, Sedgwick and Tyndall[14] regarded him as a champion of Science, and cheered him with words of genuine admiration for his love of Nature, for the eagerness with which he welcomed all the latest scientific discoveries, and for his trust in truth. Science indeed in his opinion was one of the main forces tending to disperse the superstition that still darkens the world.

A future Prime Minister, W. E. Gladstone, added a double homage to Tennyson and to his dead friend. 'What can be a nobler tribute than this, that for seventeen years after his death, a poet fast rising towards the lofty summits of his art, found that young fading image the richest source of his inspiration, and of thoughts that gave him buoyancy for a flight such as he had not hitherto attained?'

From two other men, a bishop and a philosopher, came impressions of the poem. Hallam Tennyson quotes them as representative of the great intellectual debate of mid-century, in which In Memoriam *had played its part. Brooke Foss Westcott, Bishop of Durham, was a leading thinker and theologian, a conciliator in the Durham coal strike of 1892, close to Maurice's Christian Socialism. Henry Sidgwick was Professor of Moral Philosophy at Cambridge and a member of the Society for Psychical Research.*

Bishop Westcott and Professor Henry Sidgwick have written me interesting letters which respectively give the impressions the poem made on Cambridge men in 1850, and in 1860, and I quote them *in extenso*.

The Bishop writes:

When "In Memoriam" appeared, I felt (as I feel if possible more strongly now) that the hope of man lies in the historic realization of the Gospel. I rejoiced in the Introduction, which appeared to me to be the mature summing up after an interval of the many strains of thought in the "Elegies." Now the stress of controversy is over, I think so still. As I look at my original copy of "In Memoriam," I recognise that what impressed me most was your father's splendid faith (in the face of the frankest acknowledgement of every difficulty) in the growing purpose of the sum of life, and in the noble destiny of the individual man as he offers himself for the fulfilment of his little part (LIV., LXXXI., LXXXII. and the closing stanzas). This faith has now largely entered into our common life, and it seems to me to express a lesson of the Gospel which the circumstances of all time encourage us to master.

Professor Sidgwick writes:

Well, the years pass, the struggle with what Carlyle used to call "Hebrew old clothes" is over, Freedom is won, and what does Freedom bring us to? It brings us face to face with atheistic science: the faith in God and Immortality, which we had been struggling to clear from superstition, suddenly seems to be *in the air*: and in seeking for a firm basis for this faith we find ourselves in the midst of the "fight with death" which "In Memoriam" so powerfully presents.

What "In Memoriam" did for us, for me at least, in this struggle was to impress on us the ineffaceable and ineradicable conviction that *humanity* will not and cannot acquiesce in a godless world: the "man in men" will not do this, whatever individual men may do, whatever they may temporarily feel themselves driven to do, by following methods which they cannot abandon to the conclusions to which these methods at present seem to lead.

The force with which it impressed this conviction was not due to the *mere intensity* of its expression of the feelings which Atheism outrages and Agnosticism ignores: but rather to its expression of them along with a reverent docility to the lessons of science which also belongs to the essence of the thought of our age.

I remember being struck with a note in *Nature*, at the time of your father's death, which dwelt on this last-mentioned aspect of his work, and regarded him as preeminently the Poet of Science. I have always felt this characteristic important in estimating his effect on his generation. Wordsworth's attitude towards Nature was one that, so to say, left Science unregarded: the Nature for which Wordsworth stirred our feelings was Nature as known by simple observation and interpreted by religious and sympathetic intuition. But for your father the physical world is always the world as known to us through physical science: the scientific view of it dominates his thoughts about it; and his general acceptance of this view is real and sincere, even when he utters the intensest feeling of its inadequacy to satisfy our deepest needs. Had it been otherwise, had he met the atheistic tendencies of modern Science with more confident defiance, more confident assertion of an Intuitive Faculty of theological knowledge, overriding the results laboriously reached by empirical science, I think his antagonism to these tendencies would have been far less impressive.

Hippolyte Taine on *Maud* (1855) and *In Memoriam* (1850) from *A History of English Literature* (1856-9)

The French historian and positivist Hippolyte Taine took a contrary view of Tennyson's poetry from that of most English critics. In England, the great elegy to Arthur Hallam had made Tennyson's name. Maud, *which followed in 1855, was widely known for its famous lyric, 'Come into the garden, Maud', but not much appreciated otherwise. It is certainly possible to read* Maud *as poetic drama, which is Taine's suggestion. Tennyson described it as 'A Monodrama'. Its narrator is the son of an ill-fated family, ruined by the old lord of the hall. He falls in love with Maud, daughter of the old lord, and wins her love in return, only to be ousted by a 'new-made lord' who is to be her husband. In the quarrels which ensue, he kills the girl's brother in a duel, goes abroad, and is overtaken by madness. He recovers from this, spurred on by enthusiasm for serving his country on the field of battle.*

The poem was not particularly well received. Tennyson called it his 'little Hamlet', *but that was not how it was regarded. However, both the Brownings praised it and Jowett wrote that it was the best thing of its kind since Shakespeare. All the same, it was not what the public or the reviewers had expected after* In Memoriam. *The subject was unpalatable. It was not uplifting. Moreover the poem, with its celebration of the cleansing effect of war, appeared just as the expedition to the Crimea proved to be the military miscalculation that its critics had feared. The British army lost some 20,000 dead to little political purpose.*

Taine, standing back from such preoccupations, saw the strange attraction of the poem more clearly. It was In Memoriam *that seemed to him a failure, an attempt to yoke the spirit of poetry and beauty to the paraphernalia of the undertaker and the cold ceremony of a Victorian funeral. Poetry, in Taine's view, belonged to the world of beauty and imagination, drama, and even fantasy. It had no business with social or philosophic realities of the kind that Tennyson's elegy for Arthur Hallam embraced. Taine begins by praising* Maud *as frank and strong, and continues with his account of it.*

In it the rapture broke forth with all its inequalities, familiarities, freedom, violence. The correct, measured poet betrayed himself, for he seemed to think and weep aloud. This book is the diary of a gloomy young man, soured by great family misfortunes, by long solitary meditations, who gradually became enamoured, dared to speak, found himself loved. He does not sing, but speaks; they are the hazarded, reckless words of ordinary conversation; details of everyday life; the description of a toilet, a political dinner, a service and sermon in a village church. The prose of Dickens and Thackeray did not more firmly grasp real and actual manners. And by its side, most splendid poetry abounded and blossomed, as in fact it blossoms and abounds in the midst of our commonplaces. The smile of a richly dressed girl, a sunbeam on a stormy sea, or on a spray of roses, throws all at once these sudden illuminations into impassioned souls. What verses are these, in which he represents himself in his dark little garden:

> "A million emeralds break from the ruby-budded lime
> In the little grove where I sit—ah, wherefore cannot I be
> Like things of the season gay, like the bountiful season bland,
> When the far-off sail is blown by the breeze of a softer clime,
> Half lost in the liquid azure bloom of a crescent of sea,
> The silent sapphire-spangled marriage ring of the land"?

What a holiday in his heart when he is loved! What madness in these cries, that intoxication, that tenderness which would pour itself on all, and summon all to the spectacle and the participation of his happiness! How all is transfigured in his eyes; and how constantly he is himself transfigured! Gaiety, then ecstasy, then archness, then satire, then disclosures, all ready movements, all sudden changes, like a crackling and flaming fire, renewing every moment its shape and colour: how rich is the soul, and how it can live a hundred years in a day! The hero of the poem, surprised and insulted by the brother of

Maud, kills him in a duel, and loses her whom he loved. He flees; he is seen wandering in London. What a gloomy contrast is that of the great busy careless town, and a solitary man haunted by true grief! We follow him down the noisy thoroughfares, through the yellow fog, under the wan sun which rises above the river like a "dull red ball," and we hear the heart full of anguish, deep sobs, insensate agitation of a soul which would but cannot tear itself from its memories. Despair grows, and in the end the reverie becomes a vision:

> "Dead, long dead,
>   Long dead!
> And my heart is a handful of dust,
> And the wheels go over my head,
> And my bones are shaken with pain,
> For into a shallow grave they are thrust,
> Only a yard beneath the street,
> And the hoofs of the horses beat, beat,
> The hoofs of the horses beat,
> Beat into my scalp and my brain,
> With never an end to the stream of passing feet,
> Driving, hurrying, marrying, burying,
> Clamour and rumble, and ringing and clatter. . . .
> O me! why have they not buried me deep enough?
> Is it kind to have made me a grave so rough,
> Me, that was never a quiet sleeper?
> Maybe still I am but half-dead;
> Then I cannot be wholly dumb;
> I will cry to the steps above my head,
> And somebody, surely, some kind heart will come
> To bury me, bury me
> Deeper, ever so little deeper."

However, he revives, and gradually rises again. War breaks out, a liberal and generous war, the war against Russia; and the big, manly heart, wounded by deep love, is healed by action and courage.

> "And I stood on a giant deck and mix'd my breath
> With a loyal people shouting a battle cry. . . .
> Yet God's just wrath shall be wreak'd on a giant liar;
> And many a darkness into the light shall leap,
> And shine in the sudden making of splendid names,
> And noble thought be freer under the sun,
> And the heart of a people beat with one desire;

> For the peace, that I deem'd no peace, is over and done,
> And now by the side of the Black and the Baltic deep,
> And deathful-grinning mouths of the fortress, flames
> The blood-red blossom of war with a heart of fire."

This explosion of feeling was the only one; Tennyson has not again encountered it. In spite of the moral close, men said of *Maud* that he was imitating Byron; they cried out against these bitter declamations; they thought that they perceived the rebellious accent of the Satanic school; they blamed this uneven, obscure, excessive style; they were shocked at these crudities and incongruities; they called on the poet to return to his first well-proportioned style. He was discouraged, left the storm-clouds, and returned to the azure sky. He was right; he is better there than anywhere else. A fine soul may be transported, attain at times to the fire of the most violent and the strongest beings: personal memories, they say, had furnished the matter of *Maud* and of *Locksley Hall*; with a woman's delicacy, he had the nerves of a woman. The fit over, he fell again into his "golden languors," into his calm reverie. After *Locksley Hall* he wrote the *Princess*; after *Maud* the *Idylls of the King*.

The great task of an artist is to find subjects which suit his talent. Tennyson has not always succeeded in this. His long poem, *In Memoriam*, written in praise and memory of a friend who died young, is cold, monotonous, and too prettily arranged. He goes into mourning; but, like a correct gentleman, with bran new gloves, wipes away his tears with a cambric handkerchief, and displays throughout the religious service, which ends the ceremony, all the compunction of a respectful and well-trained layman. He was to find his subjects elsewhere. To be poetically happy is the object of a dilettante-artist. For this many things are necessary. First of all, that the place, the events, and the characters shall not exist. Realities are coarse, and always, in some sense, ugly; at least they are heavy; we do not treat them as we should like, they oppress the fancy; at bottom there is nothing truly sweet and beautiful in our life but our dreams. We are ill at ease whilst we remain glued to earth, hobbling along on our two feet, which drag us wretchedly here and there in the place which impounds us. We need to live in another world, to hover in the wide-air kingdom, to build palaces in the clouds, to see them rise and crumble, to follow in a hazy distance the whims of their moving architecture, and the turns of their golden volutes. In this fantastic world, again, all must be pleasant and beautiful, the heart and senses must enjoy it, objects must be smiling or picturesque, sentiments delicate or lofty; no crudity, incongruity, brutality, savageness, must come to sully with its excess the modulated harmony of this ideal perfection. This leads the poet to the legends of chivalry. Here is the fantastic world, splendid to the sight, noble and specially pure, in which love, war, adventures, generosity, courtesy, all spectacles and all virtues which suit the instincts of our European races, are assembled, to furnish them with the epic which they love, and the model which suits them.

R. J. Mann on *Maud* (1855) in *Tennyson's* Maud *Vindicated: An Explanatory Essay* (1856)

Tennyson was, indeed, moving towards that dream world of chivalry and Arthurian legend, the newly contrived romanticism of the middle ages which Taine recommended. In 1859 the first Idylls of the King *were to appear. But* Maud *remained his own favourite, at least for public reading. The contempt that he expressed to young Margot Asquith for the critics and for public taste was the consequence of* Maud's *rejection. When he read the poem aloud, according to his son Hallam, he often prefaced it with part of R. J. Mann's essay,* Tennyson's Maud Vindicated. *Here, at least, was one critic prepared to stand against the tide of condemnation and to criticize the reviewers themselves. Mann was a doctor turned literary critic who was also the author of several successful scientific textbooks. Though the circumstances of the two poems were quite different, as surely as throughout* In Memoriam, *Dr Mann saw in Tennyson's* Maud *an analysis of human mind near the end of its tether.*

The world, if it had been left to its own inclinations and tendencies, would no doubt have received this production of his fancy and intellect reverentially, and with some measure of gratitude—taking occasion, perchance, in its own slow-paced way to master the full purport of the work, but, in the meantime, giving credit both for sense and excellence, until its perceptions had been matured in the legitimate way, through reflection and study. The guild of critics, however, true to its traditions, and to its own idea of its craft, acted upon the assumption that it held the vested right of seeing at a glance what high genius had only perfected through the expenditure of prolonged and patient labour, and proceeded forthwith to deliver its Protean judgments. One member of the fraternity immediately pronounced the poem to be *a spasm*; another acutely discovered that it was a careless, visionary, and unreal *allegory of the Russian war*; a third could not quite make up his mind whether the adjective *mud* or *mad* would best apply to the work, but thought, as there was only one small vowel redundant in the title in either case, both might do. A fourth found that the mud concealed *irony*; and a fifth, leaning rather to the mad hypothesis, nevertheless held that the madness was only assumed as *an excuse for* pitching the tone of the poetry in *a key of extravagant sensibility*. Others of the multifold judgments were that it was *an ægis covering startling propositions* from too close philosophic scrutiny;—a *political fever*;—an *epidemic* caught from the prevalent carelessness of thought and rambling contemplativeness of the time;—*obscurity mistaken for profundity;*—the *dead level of prose run mad*;—*circumstance proclaimed dominant* over free-will; *matrimony exhibited* as the soother of troubled dreams;—*absurdity, such as even partial friendship must blush to tolerate*, (and, therefore, it is to be presumed, exceeding even the seemingly unapproachable accomplishments of criticism in this line;)—rampant and rabid *bloodthirstiness of soul*. These are but a few of the pleasant suggestions which critical acumen brought forward as its explanations of the inspiration of numbers that most nevertheless admitted to be musical. When time shall have accomplished its appointed task of beneficence,—the crumbling of dry and unvital substance into indistinguishable vapour and harmless dust, the statement will never be believed that such were the views professed critics offered as interpretations of the object and meaning of Mr. Tennyson's *Maud*, at the period of its first appearance. That they were so is, however, strictly, soberly, and sadly a literary fact.

Maud is a drama;—that is, an action;—in which an exquisite tale of love and sorrow is revealed in a form that bears upon itself the impress at once of consummate art, and of simple nature. The *dramatis persona* of the action,—for there is but one individual who is ever brought forward in it *in person*,—exhibits his story through the mental influences its several incidents work in himself, and this exhibition is made, not directly and connectedly, but, as it were, inferentially and interruptedly, through a series of distinct scenes, which are as varied as the circumstances involved. It is in this peculiarity of the poem,—the one person revealing to the reader his own sad and momentous history, by fits and starts, which are themselves but so many impulsive utterances naturally called forth from a mind strung to the pitch of keen poetic sensibility,—that its absolute originality and the surpassing skill of the Laureate are displayed. Nothing can be more exquisitely consonant to the proceedings of nature than that such utterances should be made in fitful and broken strains, rather than that they should march steadily on to the measure of equal lines, and regularly recurring rhymes. It is one of the necessities of the poet-temperament that it must feel, what it does feel, to its inmost core, and that it must speak, when it does speak, in words that are actually articulate casts of what it feels. Every utterance, whether it be of sentiment, passion, or reflection, is an impulsive outburst; but it is an outburst that involuntarily clothes itself in language of the most appropriate character and vivid power. Such, both in the matter of sense and of music, is the language of *Maud.* The syllables and lines of the several stanzas actually trip and halt with abrupt fervour, tremble with passion, swell with emotion, and dance with joy, as each separate phase of mental experience comes on the scene. The power of language to symbolize in sound mental states and perceptions, has never before been so magically proved. In the successful employment of this kind of word-music, the author of *Maud* stands entirely unrivalled, as, in its general form of severe dramatic unipersonality, the poem itself is absolutely unique.

But *Maud* is moral, as well as passionate and musical. The drama has a purpose towards which its successive scenes steadily conduct. This purpose is so finely conceived, and so subtly enunciated, that it grows insensibly on the reader, until in the final movement of the action, he finds himself thoroughly possessed with it, although quite unable to determine when and how its perception was first caught. In this again consummate skill is shown.

Matthew Arnold on Tennyson in *On Translating Homer* (1861–2) and in *Letters* (1895)

There were moments in private when Matthew Arnold appeared to regard Tennyson as an unavoidable ill of Victorian literary life. 'One has him so much in one's head,' he wrote to John Duke Coleridge in 1853, 'one cannot help imitating him sometimes; but except in the last two lines I thought I had kept him out of "Sohrab and Rustum". Mark any other places you notice, for I would wish to alter such.'

Arnold had already told Clough in 1847 that 'To solve the Universe as you try to do is as irritating as Tennyson's dawdling with its painted shell is fatiguing to me to witness.'

In private, at least, it seemed that Arnold grew to dislike Tennyson on principle. He thought that Maud *was rather similar to Clough's* Bothie of Tober-na-Vuolich *and* Amours de Voyage, *a style of poetry that, 'as you know, I do not like'. But, as a way of writing, he told Clough in 1855, 'You use it with far more freedom, vigour and abundance than he does.' Six years later, he wrote to Clough, 'I care for his productions less and less and am convinced both Alfred de Musset and Henri [Heinrich] Heine are more profitable studies, if we are to study contemporaries at all.'*

Nor did Arnold care for Tennyson's later work in the Idylls of the King. *Oddly enough, he believed that Tennyson's characteristic weakness was lack of intellectual power, one of the strengths which others had found in poems like* In Memoriam.

> The fault I find with Tennyson in his *Idylls of the King* is that the peculiar charm and aroma of the Middle Age he does not give in them. There is something magical about it, and I will do something with it before I have done. The real truth is that Tennyson, with all his temperament and artistic skill, is deficient in intellectual power; and no modern poet can make very much of his business unless he is pre-eminently strong in this. Goethe owes his grandeur to his strength in this, although it even hurt his poetical operations by its immense predominance.

It was in 1860-2, as Professor of Poetry at Oxford, that Arnold gave his public verdict on Tennyson. The opinion he offered was more generous than his private mutterings. The subject of his lectures was On Translating Homer. *He tried to show that a simple English style was the only tolerable one for the task. In his first comment he suggests, by three lines of Tennyson's* Ulysses, *that the subtlety of the modern poet's thought in those three lines takes longer to unravel than a whole book of Homer. The style for Homeric translation must not, therefore, be Tennyson's.*

It must not be Mr. Tennyson's blank verse.

> For all experience is an arch, wherethro'
> Gleams that untravell'd world, whose distance fades[15]
> For ever and for ever, as we gaze—

it is no blame to the thought of those lines, which belongs to another order of ideas than Homer's, but it is true, that Homer would certainly have said of them, 'It is to consider too curiously to consider so.' It is no blame to their rhythm, which belongs to another order of movement than Homer's, but it is true, that these three lines by themselves take up nearly as much time as a whole book of the *Iliad*.

Mr. Tennyson is a most distinguished and charming poet; but the very essential characteristic of his poetry is, it seems to me, an extreme subtlety and curious elaborateness of thought, an extreme subtlety and curious elaborateness of expression. In the best and most characteristic productions of his genius, these characteristics are most prominent. They are marked characteristics, as we have seen, of the Elizabethan poets; they are marked, though not the essential, characteristics of Shakespeare himself. Under the influences of the nineteenth century, under wholly new conditions of thought and culture, they manifest themselves in Mr. Tennyson's poetry in a wholly new way. But they are still there. The essential bent of his poetry is towards such expressions as

> Now lies the Earth all Danaë to the stars . . .

or

> O'er the sun's bright eye
> Drew the vast eyelid of an inky cloud . . .

or

> When the cairn'd mountain was a shadow, sunn'd
> The world to peace again . . .

or

> The fresh young captains flash'd their glittering teeth,
> The huge bush-bearded barons heaved and blew . . .

or

> He bared the knotted column of his throat,
> The massive square of his heroic breast,
> And arms on which the standing muscle sloped
> As slopes a wild brook o'er a little stone,
> Running too vehemently to break upon it. . . .

And this way of speaking is the least *plain*, the most *unHomeric*, which can possibly be conceived. Homer presents his thought to you just as it wells from the source of his mind: Mr. Tennyson carefully distils his thought before he will part with it. Hence comes, in the expression of the thought, a heightened and elaborate air. In Homer's poetry it is all natural thoughts in natural words; in Mr. Tennyson's poetry it is all distilled thoughts in distilled words. Exactly this heightening and elaboration may be observed in Mr. Spedding's[16]

> While the steeds *mouth'd their corn aloof* . . .

(an expression which might have been Mr. Tennyson's), on which I have already commented; and to one who is penetrated with a sense of the real simplicity of Homer, this subtle sophistication of the thought is, I think, very perceptible even in such lines as these,

> And drunk delight of battle with my peers,
> Far on the ringing plains of windy Troy . . .

which I have seen quoted as perfectly Homeric. Perfect simplicity can be obtained only by a genius of which perfect simplicity is an essential characteristic.

Walter Bagehot on *Idylls of the King* (1859) in the *National Review* (1859)

Walter Bagehot, banker and shipowner, editor of the National Review *and* The Economist, *was also an eminent literary critic. He was the author of* The English Constitution *(1867) and* Physics and Politics *(1876) but also of* Literary Studies *(1879). In this review of the recently published* Idylls of the King, *including 'Enid', 'Vivien', 'Elaine', and 'Guinevere', Bagehot assesses Tennyson's reputation. He describes the two audiences for poetry. Those with more youthful enthusiasm are the poet's immediate admirers. But beyond these young men is a wider public, easily alienated by poetry that seems in some way disagreeable. The same 'narrowing influence' of the immediate admirers had been evident in Wordsworth and even in Keats and Shelley.*

His audience formerly consisted entirely of young men of cultivated tastes and susceptible imaginations; and it was so because his poetry contained most of the elements which are suitable to such persons in a country like England, and an age such as this is. But whatever be the cause,—whether or not our analysis of the ingredients in Mr. Tennyson's poetry which attracted young men of this kind be correct or otherwise,—the fact that it did so attract them, and that it attracted but few others with great force, is very certain. His public was limited and peculiar; it was almost as much so as Wordsworth's was at an earlier time.

When Mr. Tennyson published *Maud*, we feared that the influence of this class of admirers was deteriorating his powers. The subject was calculated to call out the unhealthier sort of youthful imaginations; and his treatment of it, so far from lessening the danger, seemed studiously selected to increase it. The hero of *Maud* is a young man who lives very much out of the world, who has no definite duties or intelligible occupations, who hates society because he is bound by no social ties and is conscious of no social courage. This young gentleman sees a young lady who is rich, and whose father has an unpleasant association with his own father, who was a bankrupt. He has all manner of feelings about the young lady, and she is partial to him; but there is a difficulty about their interviews. As he is poor and she is wealthy, they do not meet in common society; and a stolen visit in her garden ends, if we understand the matter, in his killing her brother. After this he leads a wandering life, and expresses his sentiments. Such a story is evidently very likely to bring into prominence the exaggerated feelings and distorted notions which we call unhealthy. The feelings of a young man who has nothing to do, and tries to do nothing; who is very poor, and regrets that he is not very rich; who is in love, and cannot speak to the lady he loves; who knows he cannot marry her, but notwithstanding wanders vaguely about her,—are sure to be unhealthy. Solitude, social mortification, wounded feeling, are the strongest sources of mental malaria; and all of these are here crowded together, and are conceived to act at once. Such a representation, therefore, if it was to be true, must be partially tinctured with unhealthiness. This was inevitable; and it was inevitable, too, that this taint should be rather agreeable than otherwise to many of the poet's warmest admirers. The Tennysonians, as we have said, were young men; and youth is the season of semi-diseased feeling. Keats, who knew much about such matters, remarked this. 'The imagination,' he said, 'of a man is healthy, and the imagination of a boy is healthy'; but between there is an uncertain time, when the fancy is restless, the principles are unfixed, the sentiments waver, and the highest feelings have not acquired consistency. Upon young men in such a frame of mind a delineation like that of the hero of *Maud*, adorned, as it was, with rare fragments of beautiful imagery, and abiding snatches of the sweetest music, could not but be attractive, and could not but be dangerous. It seemed to be the realised ideal of their hopes, of their hearts, of themselves; it half consecrated their characteristic defects, it confirmed their hope that their eccentricities were excellencies. Such a danger could not be avoided; but Mr. Tennyson, so far from trying to shun it, seemed intentionally to choose to aggravate it. He seemed to sympathize with the feverish railings, the moody nonsense, the very entangled philosophy, which he put into the mouth of his hero. There were some odd invectives against peace, against industry, against making your livelihood, which seemed by no means to be dramatic exhibitions of represented character, but on the contrary, confidential expositions of the poet's own belief. He not only depicted the natural sentiments of an inactive, inexperienced, and neglected young man, but seemed to agree with them. He sympathized with moody longings; he was not severe on melancholy vanity; he rather encouraged a general disaffection to the universe. He appeared not only to have written, but to have accepted the 'Gospel according to the Unappreciated'. The most charitable reader could scarcely help fancying, that in describing an irritable confusion of fancy and a diseased moodiness of feeling, the poet for the time imbibed a certain taint of those defects.

The *Idylls of the King* suggest to us a peculiar doubt. Was not Mr. Tennyson, after all, laughing at his admirers? *Did* he believe in *Maud*, though he seemed to say he did? We do not know; but at all events we have now a poem not only of a different, but of the very opposite kind. Every line of it is defined with the delicate grace of a very composed genius; shows the trace of a very mature judgment; will bear the scrutiny of the most choice and detective taste. The feelings are natural, the thoughts such as people in life have or might have. The situations, though in a certain sense unnatural, have, we believe, a peculiar artistic propriety. There is a completeness in the whole.

R. H. Hutton on Tennyson in *Literary Essays* (1888)

Four years before the poet's death the summaries of his life had begun to appear. Richard Holt Hutton was a Unitarian theologian, a writer on 'modern thought', and a Professor of Mathematics at Bedford

College, London, who became an editor of the Spectator. *In the first of the passages quoted below, he opposes the view that Tennyson was a gifted poet of image and lyricism who lost his power with age. To Hutton, it was the maturity of thought in the later poems that was most to be admired. In the second extract, discussing the presentation of women in Tennyson's poetry, Hutton sees the effectiveness of creating characters of legend who have the realism of modern womanhood.*

The Roman Catholics have, I believe, a doctrine that at a certain stage in the growth of the embryo body the soul is 'infused' into it, and from that stage it shapes and moulds all the structures of the body with a view to their subserviency to a moral and spiritual growth. Apply that analogy to Tennyson's poems, and the period before 1832 is the period before his vivid pictures had a soul in them, and consequently before they had a music of their own. He himself has told us very finely in one of his newer poems, when describing the building of Arthur's great capital,—which, like Ilium, was rumoured to have been built to a divine music,—how the highest works of the human spirit are created:—

> For an ye heard a music, like enow
> They are building still, seeing the city is built
> To music, therefore never built at all,
> And therefore built for ever.

There was no such music in Tennyson's earliest verses, but he himself has all but told us when the period in which his productiveness was due more to the 'lust of the eye' than to any true poetic gift, ceased. Curiously enough, the first poem where there is any trace of those musings on the legends of the Round Table to which he has directed so much of his maturest genius, is also a confession that the poet was sick of the magic mirror of fancy and its picture-shadows, and was turning away from them to the poetry of human life. 'The Lady of Shalott', the first poem of those published in the autumn of 1832—the same sad year which laid the foundation of Tennyson's most perfect, if not his greatest poem, *In Memoriam*—has for its real subject the emptiness of the life of fancy, however rich and brilliant, the utter satiety which compels any true imaginative nature to break through the spell which entrances it in an unreal world of visionary joys. The Lady of Shalott—a variation on Elaine—gazing in her magic mirror, sees a faithful picture of all that passes by her solitary isle, and copies it in the web she weaves:—

> There she weaves by night and day
> A magic web with colours gay.
> She has heard a whisper say,
> A curse is on her if she stay
> To look down to Camelot.
> She knows not what the curse may be,
> And so she weaveth steadily,
> And little other care hath she,
> The Lady of Shalott.

The curse, of course, is that she shall be involved in mortal passions, and suffer the fate of mortals, if she looks away from the shadow to the reality. Nevertheless, the time comes when she braves the curse:—

> But in her web she still delights
> To weave the mirror's magic sights,
> For often through the silent nights
> A funeral, with plumes and lights,
> And music, went to Camelot:
> Or when the moon was overhead,
> Came two young lovers lately wed:
> 'I am half sick of shadows,' said
> The Lady of Shalott.

And probably it was the vision of a 'funeral', at least as much as that other vision which made the fair Lady of Shalott more than half sick of shadows, that first led the author of this beautiful little poem into his true poetic work.

But even after the embryo period is past, even when Tennyson's poems are uniformly moulded by an 'infused' soul, one not unfrequently notices the excess of the faculty of vision over the governing conception which moulds the vision, so that I think he is almost always most successful when his poem begins in a thought or a feeling rather than from a picture or a narrative, for then the thought or feeling dominates and controls his otherwise too lavish fancy. 'Ulysses' and 'Tithonus' are far superior to 'Œnone', exquisite as the pictorial workmanship of 'Œnone' is; 'The Palace of Art' is finer than 'The Dream of Fair Women'; 'The Death of Lucretius', painful as the subject is, than 'Enoch Arden' or 'Aylmer's Field'; and, for the same reason, *In Memoriam* is perhaps an even more perfect whole than the poem of greatest scope, and in some respects the noblest of his imaginative efforts, the great Arthurian epic which he completed so much later. Whenever Tennyson's pictorial fancy has had it in any degree in its power to run away with the guiding and controlling mind, the richness of the workmanship has to some extent overgrown the spiritual principle of his poems.

Never was any cry more absurd than the cry made against *Maud* for the sympathy it was supposed to show with hysterical passion. What it *was* meant to be, and what it was, though inadequately,—the failure being due, not to sympathy with hysterics, but to the zeal with which Tennyson strove to caricature hysterics,—was an exposure of hysterics. The love of measure and order is as visible in Tennyson's pictures of character as in every other aspect of his poetry. His 'St. Simeon Stylites' is his hostile picture of the fanatic, just as his 'Ulysses' is his friendly picture of the insatiable craving for new experience, enterprise, and adventure, when under the control of a luminous reason and a self-controlled will.

And this love of measure and order in complexity shows itself even more remarkably in Lord Tennyson's leaning to the domestic, modern type of women. All his favourite women are women of a certain fixed class of social life, usually not the lowest; sometimes homely, like Alice the miller's daughter, and Rose the gardener's daughter, or Dora, or the wife of the Lord of Burleigh; sometimes women of the Drawing-room or the Palace, like Maud, Lady Flora in 'The Day-Dream', or the princess in the poem about women, or Lynette, and Enid, and Elaine, and Guinevere in *The Idylls of the King*; but always women of the quiet and domestic type (except indeed the heroine of 'The Sisters'), women whom you might meet every day in a modern home, women of the garden-flower kind rather than of the wild-flower kind. He has set even his exquisite poem on 'The Sleeping Beauty' in a drawing-room framework, *i.e.* made the 'Lady Flora' to whom it is related 'take her broidery frame and add a crimson to the quaint macaw'. In the beautiful little idyll called 'The Miller's Daughter', Mr. Tennyson even injures the rustic effect of the piece by introducing an artificial element, a song about Alice's earring and necklace, a touch which, however true it may be to life—(earrings and necklaces are just what millers' daughters would most value)—is idyllically false as destroying the simplicity of the picture, just as it might have been true to life, but would have been idyllically false, to call the heroine Juliana or Matilda, instead of Alice. The simplest and most lyrical heroines, heroines like Gretchen in *Faust* or Mignon in

Wilhelm Meister,[17] are hardly in Tennyson's way. He loves something of the air and manner which a fixed social status gives. His 'May Queen' has always seemed to me one of his few falsetto poems. There is art, in the sense of complex harmony, in all his greatest poems.

W. E. Henley on Tennyson in
Views and Reviews (1890)

W. E. Henley was himself a poet of the nineties, known for 'England, My England', and his account of Life as a whore and Death as her pimp in 'Madam Life's a Piece in Bloom':

> With his kneebones at your chest,
> And his knuckles in your throat,
> You would reason – plead – protest!
> Clutching at her petticoat . . .

And all, of course, to no avail. Life reminds you that 'you've had your fun', as Death does his work.

   Henley, in a brief comparison, looks at Tennyson as one technician admiring another. And then, in the face of a good deal of contrary opinion, suggests that the innovation and experiment of the Poet Laureate's old age is his most striking achievement.

In Keats' 'St. Agnes' Eve' nothing is white but the heroine. It is winter, and 'bitter chill'; the hare 'limps trembling through the frozen grass'; the owl is a-cold for all his feathers; the beadsman's fingers are numb, his breath is frosted; and at an instant of special and peculiar romance

> The frost-wind blows
> Like Love's alarum, pattering the sharp sleet
> Against the window-panes.

But there is no snow. The picture is pure colour: it blushes with blood of queens and kings; it glows with 'splendid dyes', like the tiger-moth's 'deep-damasked wings'—with 'rose bloom', and 'warm gules', and 'soft amethyst'; it is loud with music and luxurious with 'spiced dainties', with 'lucent syrops tinct wth cinnamon', with 'manna and dates', the fruitage of Fez and 'cedared Lebanon' and 'silken

Samarcand'. Now, the Laureate's 'St. Agnes' Eve' is an ecstasy of colourless perfection. The snows sparkle on the convent roof; the 'first snowdrop' vies with St. Agnes' virgin bosom; the moon shines an 'argent round' in the 'frosty skies'; and in a transport of purity the lady prays:

> Break up thy heavens, O Lord! and far,
>   Through all the starlight keen,
> Draw me thy bride, a glittering star,
>   In raiment white and clean.

It is all coldly, miraculously stainless: as somebody has said, 'la vraie *Symphonie en Blanc Majeur*'.

And at four-score the poet of 'St. Agnes' Eve' is still our greatest since the Wordsworth of certain sonnets and the two immortal odes: is still the one Englishman of whom it can be stated and believed that Elisha is not less than Elijah.[18] His verse is far less smooth and less lustrous than in the well-filed times of *In Memoriam* and the Arthurian idylls. But it is also far more plangent and affecting; it shows a larger and more liberal mastery of form and therewith a finer, stronger, saner sentiment of material; in its display of breadth and freedom in union with particularity, of suggestiveness with precision, of swiftness of handling with completeness of effect, it reminds you of the later magic of Rembrandt and the looser and richer, the less artful-seeming but more ample and sumptuous, of the styles of Shakespeare. And the matter is worthy of the manner. Everywhere are greatness and a high imagination moving at ease in the gold armour of an heroic style.

Leslie Stephen on Tennyson in *Studies of a Biographer* (1899)

At the end of his remarks on Tennyson, Henley had quoted Dickens. The novelist read the Idylls of the King *or* Maud *and said, 'Lord, what a pleasure it is to come across a man that can* write!' *As the century drew to its close, it began to seem that this ability might be Tennyson's weakness. His facility was so great that he had written too many poems with too little thought. He knocked out poems as other men knocked out cake-stands or coffins.*

The first and most obvious target as the reaction against him began was the work of his later years. There was a contemporary point to In Memoriam *or* Maud, *whether or not one liked the poetry. But what was the point of so much energy expended on medieval or Arthurian daydream in the* Idylls of the King *or even in the* Morte d'Arthur *and its companions of the 1842 volumes? Swinburne mocked the later* Idylls *as the apotheosis of the dead Prince Albert, done to curry favour with Victoria. He referred scornfully to the* Morte d'Albert *and the* Idylls of the Prince Consort. *Leslie Stephen, a clergyman turned agnostic and critic, father of Virginia Woolf and Vanessa Bell, put similar misgivings into print more soberly, seven years after Tennyson's death.*

To me, I humbly confess, 'allegory,' rightly or wrongly, means nuisance. The 'meaning' which it sticks on to a poem is precisely what the poem cannot properly 'mean.' The old *Morte d'Arthur*, as it appeared with the charming old setting, was one of the poems which we all knew by heart. One of the charms was surely that the behaviour of the persons was delightfully illogical and absurd. Rather, perhaps, it took one to the world in which true logic demands illogical behaviour. Things take place there according to a law of their own, which is the more attractive just because it is preposterous and apparently arbitrary. When Sir Bedivere throws Excalibur into the lake, the whole proceeding is, as indeed Sir Bedivere very properly perceives and points out, contrary to all commonsense. His reluctance gives us warning that we have got into the world governed by phantastic laws. Throwing a sword into a lake does not, within ordinary experience, produce a barge occupied by three queens with crowns of gold; just as shooting an albatross does not, as a rule, produce a dead calm and death of a ship's crew by thirst. But though things of dreamland follow laws of their own, even dreamland has laws, and they ought to be observed when once you get there. The 'Ancient Mariner' was ridden by a nightmare, and all things happened to him according to the genuine laws of the nightmare world. Arthur's Round Table was a dream of the mediaeval imagination, and the historian of its adventures should frankly put himself in the corresponding attitude of mind. It lends itself admirably to represent the ideals which were in the mind of the dreamer, and therefore unconsciously determined the constitution of the imaginary world. But when the personages, instead of obeying the laws of their own world, are converted into allegory, they lose their dream reality without gaining the reality of ordinary life. The arbitrariness especially ceases to be delightful when we suspect that the real creatures of the fancy have become the puppets of a judicious moralist. The question, What is the meaning? throws one's mind out of gear. When Sir Bedivere made his second appearance somebody asked Tennyson whether the three queens were not Faith, Hope, and Charity. The poet replied that they were, and that they were not. They might be the Virtues or they might be the Three Graces. There was, he said, an 'allegorical, or perhaps rather a parabolic, drift,' in the poem; but he added there was not a single fact or incident in the *Idylls* which might not be explained without any mystery or allegory whatever. This explanation may be very satisfactory to some readers, and if they are satisfied, their state is the more gracious; but I humbly confess that so soon as genuine inhabitants of Fairyland can be interpreted as three virtues or three graces, they cease to fascinate me. In the *Holy Grail* the mystical purpose is most distinctly avowed. We are told to learn what it means by studying the visions of Sir Percival, and his 'subsequent fall and nineteenth-century temptations.' The result of my study is that the visions are turned into waking shams, and leave a residuum of edifying sermon. The intrusion of the nineteenth century is simply disenchantment. If I want to be moral, I should get much more instruction out of *Mme. Bovary* or some other 'masterful transcript of actuality' than out of Tristram and Iseult, and if I want to be romantic, the likeness of King Arthur to the Prince Consort takes all the vigour out of the prehistoric personage. The Prince Consort, no doubt, deserved Tennyson's profound respect; but when we find him masquerading among the knights of the Round Table, his admirable propriety of behaviour looks painfully like insipidity and incapacity for his position.

Harold Nicolson on Tennyson in *Tennyson* (1923)

From the years of Tennyson's eclipse came the most readable account of him and the best introduction to his work that the twentieth century has produced. Harold Nicolson was a young but distinguished diplomat who had served in Madrid, Berlin, Tehran, and Istanbul. He was soon to turn to politics, journalism, and biography.

His life of Tennyson, which so irritated Bloomsbury as represented by Lytton Strachey, was not a rehabilitation of the Victorian period. It saw Tennyson by the light of the new century, the influence of Freud, and the experience of a great war. Penetrating the disguise of the gruff self-confident Poet Laureate, Nicolson found within a man plagued by phobias and uncertainty, a child crying in the night, as Tennyson described himself in his great elegy for Hallam.

Nicolson's success was in sweeeping away the reputation that had been conferred on Tennyson by his admirers. In place of that he put the poet, as the poet described himself in his own work. The comforting assurances vanished. Tennyson appeared a victim of that doomed world which another great post-romantic, Cardinal Newman, described in his own autobiography as the scene of man's 'terrible aboriginal calamity'. The self-righteous Tennyson vanished. Nicolson's readers watched the anatomizing of a poet who might almost have belonged to the age of The Waste Land *and a later* Ulysses. *At the end of his book, Nicolson returned to the great centrepiece of* In Memoriam *and Tennyson's boyhood by the remote fenland of the Lincolnshire coast.*

This haunting wail of fear and loneliness piercing at moments through the undertones of *In Memoriam*, echoes a note which runs through all the poetry of Tennyson, and which, when once apprehended, beats with pitiful persistence on the heart. It proceeds from that grey region between the conscious and the unconscious; from the dim glimmering land where mingle the 'Voices of the Dark' and the 'Voices of the Day'; from the uncertain shadow-edges of consciousness in which stir the evanescent memories of childhood or the flitting shapelessness of half-forgotten dreams. It is a cry that mingles with the mystery of wide spaces, of sullen sunsets or of sodden dawns; the cry of a child lost at night time; the cry of some stricken creature in the dark; 'the low moan of an unknown sea':—

> The first gray streak of earliest summer-dawn,
> The last long stripe of waning crimson gloom,
> As if the late and early were but one—
> A height, a broken grange, a grove, a flower
> Had murmurs 'Lost and gone and lost and gone!'
> A breath, a whisper—some divine farewell—
> Desolate sweetness—far and far away.

And thus, in that 'ever-moaning battle in the mist' which was the spiritual life of Tennyson, there were sudden penetrating moments when he would obtain:—

A glimpse of that dark world where I was born;

when, once again, the 'old mysterious glimmer' would steal into his soul, and when in a sombre flash of vision, he would see his life:—

> all dark and red—a tract of sand,
> And someone pacing there alone,
> Who paced for ever in a glimmering land,
> Lit with a low large moon.

To the vibration of so sad a cadence I should wish to leave him, trusting that the ultimate impression, thus attuned, will prove more poignant and more durable than any hollow reverence for what was once admired. The age of Tennyson is past; the ideals which he voiced so earnestly have fallen from esteem. The day may come, perhaps, when the conventions of that century will once again inspire the thoughtful or animate the weak. But, for the moment, it is not through these that any interest can be evoked. And thus, if we consider it reasonable and right that Tennyson should also stand among the poets, let us, for the present, forget the delicate Laureate of a cautious age; the shallow thought, the vacant compromise; the honeyed idyll, the complacent ode; let us forget the dulled monochrome of his middle years, forget the magnolia and the roses, the indolent Augusts of his island-home; forget the laurels and the rhododendrons.

Let us recall only the low booming of the North Sea upon the dunes; the grey clouds lowering above the wold; the moan of the night wind on the fen; the far glimmer of marsh-pools through the reeds; the cold, the half-light, and the gloom.

F. R. Leavis on Tennyson in
New Bearings in English Poetry (1932)

As literary criticism became institutionalized in the new English departments of universities, so academic critics appeared who were often to become the figureheads of cults or movements. I. A. Richards was identified as the originator of 'practical criticism' in the Cambridge of the 1920s. But, as an influence, Richards was overtaken by F. R. Leavis in the following decade. In many respects Leavis had the air of an evangelist rather than a critic. He preached literary criticism – and literature itself – as a moral and intellectual training. In this he

represented one of the best legacies of the English Puritan tradition.
He did much for the reputation of those authors whom he adopted,
Joseph Conrad, Ezra Pound, and T. S. Eliot among them.

But Leavis had little time for dalliance or mere amusement.
Victorian poetry, as he described it in 1932, was largely escapism and
not worthy of detailed consideration. It was a weakness in his own
style that he would assert rather than argue, on such occasions, and
then behave as though he had argued none the less. It made him seem
petulant and merely irascible, rather than usefully provocative which
he was at his best. He dismissed Browning and all his works with a
single swipe. Browning was not escapist but 'There are kinds of
strength a poet is best without. And it is too plain that Browning
would have been less robust if he had been more sensitive and
intelligent.' Writing of this kind probably won more friends for
Browning than for Leavis. Tennyson leaves little more scope for
argument. Leavis sees him as seduced from public debate, in the end,
by an artificial notion of the poetical and a flight from reality.

The mischievousness of the nineteenth-century conventions of 'the
poetical' should by now be plain. They had behind them the prestige
of the Romantic achievement and found their sanction in undoubted
poetic successes. But as the situation changed and the incidence of
stress for the adult sensitive mind shifted, more and more did they
tend to get between such a mind and its main concerns. It clearly could
not take the day-dream habit seriously, though to cut free from the
accompanying conventions and techniques would not be so easy as
one might think. The other habits and conventions that have been
indicated would be still harder to escape. But they would be equally
disabling. For a sensitive adult in the nineteenth century could not fail
to be preoccupied with the changed intellectual background, and to
find his main interests inseparable from the modern world. Tennyson
did his best. But, in spite of a great deal of allusion to scientific ideas
('If that hypothesis of theirs be sound'), and in spite of the approval of
contemporary savants, his intellectual interests (of which, therefore,
we need not discuss the quality) have little to do with his successful
poetry, which answers to the account of 'the poetical' given above.
Indeed, there could be no better illustration. To justify his ambition
would have taken a much finer intelligence and a much more robust
original genius than Tennyson's—much greater strength and courage.
He might wrestle solemnly with the 'problems of the age,' but the

habits, conventions and techniques that he found congenial are not those of a poet who could have exposed himself freely to the rigours of the contemporary climate. And in this he is representative. It was possible for the poets of the Romantic period to believe that the interests animating their poetry were the forces moving the world, or that might move it. But Victorian poetry admits implicitly that the actual world is alien, recalcitrant and unpoetical, and that no protest is worth making except the protest of withdrawal.

T. S. Eliot on *In Memoriam* (1850) in *Essays Ancient and Modern* (1936)

By far the most powerful influence in restoring the reputation of a major nineteenth-century poet was the praise of the most acclaimed poet of the twentieth century. It was as if the amateurs had been put in their place by a professional. But it was more than that. As time passed, the so-called division between the two literary cultures seemed increasingly artificial. There was poetry that might almost have belonged to either:

> The noise of life begins again,
> And ghastly thro' the drizzling rain
> On the bald street breaks the blank day.

The lines might open one of Eliot's Preludes. *As it happens, they come from* In Memoriam.

> And at the corner of the street
> A lonely cab-horse steams and stamps.

It might be In Memoriam *but this time it is the* Preludes. *The literary journals' hunger for novelty and the treatment of poetry as 'fashion' were shown as the stupidity they always are.*

Tennyson, in Eliot's view, was a minor Virgil, but a Virgil of the shades as seen by Dante, 'the saddest of all English poets . . . the most instinctive rebel against the society in which he was the most perfect conformist'. That he was also one of the greatest English poets seemed now to be beyond question.

Tennyson is a great poet, for reasons that are perfectly clear. He has three qualities which are seldom found together except in the greatest poets: abundance, variety, and complete competence. We therefore cannot appreciate his work unless we read a good deal of it. We may not admire his aims: but whatever he sets out to do, he succeeds in doing, with a mastery which gives us the sense of confidence that is one of the major pleasures of poetry. His variety of metrical accomplishment is astonishing. Without making the mistake of trying to write Latin verse in English, he knew everything about Latin versification that an English poet could use; and he said of himself that he thought he knew the quantity of the sounds of every English word except perhaps *scissors*. He had the finest ear of any English poet since Milton.

> Dark house, by which once more I stand
> Here in the long unlovely street,
> Doors, where my heart was used to beat
> So quickly, waiting for a hand,
>
> A hand that can be clasp'd no more —
> Behold me, for I cannot sleep,
> And like a guilty thing I creep
> At earliest morning to the door.
>
> He is not here; but far away
> The noise of life begins again,
> And ghastly thro' the drizzling rain,
> On the bald street breaks the blank day.

This is great poetry, economical of words, a universal emotion related to a particular place; and it gives me the shudder that I fail to get from anything in *Maud*. But such a passage, by itself, is not *In Memoriam*: *In Memoriam* is the whole poem. It is unique: it is a long poem made by putting together lyrics, which have only the unity and continuity of a diary, the concentrated diary of a man confessing himself. It is a diary of which we have to read every word.

Apparently Tennyson's contemporaries, once they had accepted *In Memoriam*, regarded it as a message of hope and reassurance to their rather fading Christian faith. It happens now and then that a poet by some strange accident expresses the mood of his generation, at the same time that he is expressing a mood of his own which is quite remote from that of his generation. This is not a question of insincerity; there is an amalgam of yielding and opposition below the level of consciousness. Tennyson himself, on the conscious level of the man who talks to reporters and poses for photographers, to judge from remarks made in conversation and recorded in his son's Memoir, consistently asserted a convinced, if somewhat sketchy, Christian belief. And he was a friend of Frederick Denison Maurice – nothing seems odder about that age than the respect which its eminent people felt for each other. Nevertheless, I get a very different impression from *In Memoriam* from that which Tennyson's contemporaries seem to have got. It is of a very much more interesting and tragic Tennyson. His biographers have not failed to remark that he had a good deal of the temperament of the mystic – certainly not at all the mind of the theologian. He was desperately anxious to hold the faith of the believer, without being very clear about what he wanted to believe: he was capable of illumination which he was incapable of understanding. The 'Strong Son of God, Immortal Love', with an invocation of whom the poem opens, has only a hazy connexion with the Logos, or the Incarnate God. Tennyson is distressed by the idea of a mechanical universe; he is naturally, in lamenting his friend, teased by the hope of immortality and reunion beyond death. Yet the renewal craved for seems at best but a continuance, or a substitute for the joys of friendship upon earth. His desire for immortality never is quite the desire for Eternal Life; his concern is for the loss of man rather than for the gain of God.

NOTES

1 Henry de Bracton, died 1268, ecclesiastic and judge; *De Legibus et Consuetudinibus Angliae* written between 1235 and 1259.
2 Sir Richard Wilson, RA (1714–82), Welsh landscape-painter.
3 Sir Augustus Wall Callcott, ARA (1779–1844), known for his English and Dutch landscapes, and such subjects as 'Raphael and the Fornarina' (1837) and 'Milton dictating to his Daughters' (1838).
4 'Ειθε λύρη καλή γενοίμην – 'Oh, that I might become a beautiful lyre!'
5 Anacreon and Alcaeus were lyric poets of the sixth century BC.
6 '*Non omnis moriar*' – 'I shall not die altogether'.
7 Anna Seward, 'The Swan of Litchfield' (1747–1809), acquainted with Johnson and Boswell; *Poetical Works* published posthumously in 1810.
8 *differentia* – a species, as opposed to a genus.
9 Jakob Boehme (1575–1624), German theosophist and mystic, author of *Aurora* (*c.* 1612), widely influential in Germany, Holland, and England.
10 Novalis, the pen-name of Friedrich von Hardenberg (1772–1801), a German poet regarded as a prophet of romanticism.
11 François Marie Charles Fourier (1772–1837), French social theorist who advocated the division of society into *phalanges* or self-sufficient social units of 1,500 people, reconciling individual and communal interest. A practical experiment in 1832 was not a success.

12 *disjecta membra poetae* – Horace. Otherwise adapted by Dryden in *MacFlecknoe* (1682), lines 98-9:

> No *Persian* Carpets spread th' Imperial way,
> But scatter'd Limbs of mangled Poets lay.

13 Amaryllis, a pastoral sweetheart, a name taken from Theocritos and Virgil; cf. Milton, *Lycidas*, line 68: 'To sport with Amaryllis in the shade.'

14 Sir William Herschel (1738–1822), astronomer; Sir Richard Owen (1804–92), naturalist; Adam Sedgwick (1785–1873), geologist; John Tyndall (1820–93), physicist.

15 Arnold misquotes Tennyson's *Ulysses*, which reads, 'that untravell'd world whose margin fades/For ever and for ever when I move'.

16 James Spedding (1808–81), Fellow of Trinity College, Cambridge, and a member of the Civil Service Commission, also the editor of Francis Bacon.

17 *Faust*, a dramatic poem, and *Wilhelm Meister*, a biographical romance, were both written by Johann Wolfgang Goethe (1749-1832), the former occupying him from 1770 until 1832, the latter from 1786 until 1830.

18 Elisha succeeded the prophet Elijah. His miracles are described in 2 Kings iii *et seq.*

2

Browning

Robert Browning's career and his literary personality might almost have made a novel, as his courtship of Elizabeth Barrett made a play in *The Barretts of Wimpole Street*. Indeed, Henry James used them as the subject of his short story, 'The Private Life', published in 1893, four years after Browning's death.

Browning's first book, the long poem *Pauline*, appeared in 1833 when he was twenty. It might not have seen the light of day had not his aunt, Mrs Silverthorne, paid for publication. 'A strange, wild (in parts singularly magnificent) poet biography,' Joseph Arnould called it fifteen years later. This long confessional poem in tribute to Shelley received a few reviews, which treated it gently as a promise of things to come. John Stuart Mill was to have reviewed it in the liberal Sunday paper, the *Examiner*. He made some notes but never wrote the review. 'With considerable poetic powers, the writer seems to me possessed with a more intense and morbid self-consciousness than I ever knew in any sane human being.' Browning's analysis of human psychology and its aberrations had begun early.

Not a single copy of the poem was sold. It was followed by another tribute to Shelley, *Paracelsus*, in 1835. This time the book was better received, though the critics liked the poem despite its Shelleyan qualities and not because of them. Then, in 1840, Browning published what was intended to be his masterwork, the long poem *Sordello*. The press regarded it with dismay and exasperation. Most could not begin to understand the poem. It was a public disaster which sank Browning's uncertain reputation and tagged him with 'obscurity' for the rest of his life. Five hundred copies were printed. Fifteen years later only 157 had been sold.

He still contrived to get his poetry into print. The publisher Edward Moxon agreed to issue his books so long as Browning's father paid the costs. But, throughout the 1840s, most critics were unimpressed by the successive volumes of *Bells and Pomegranates* which contained such titles as *Pippa Passes* and poems like 'Porphyria's

Lover', 'My Last Duchess', and 'The Bishop Orders his Tomb in St Praxed's Church'. It was also the decade of his courtship of Elizabeth Barrett, their elopement and early life together in Florence. But she was then far better known and established than he. By the time that Browning published *Men and Women*, one of the most splendid collections in the whole of English poetry, he was forty-three. He had still earned nothing from poetry and the critical reception of the book was tepid. Even nine years later, in 1864 when he was fifty-two, his royalty payment amounted to only £15.

Family money and a bequest from a friend kept him going. Recognition was so long delayed that when it came, in the 1860s, he seemed like a new poet and a successor to the fame of Tennyson. He appeared as a truly 'modern' writer. The great drama of his 'Roman murder case' in *The Ring and the Book* (1868) made his reputation at last. Based on a trial of 1698, when Guido Franceschini defended his right to kill his supposedly adulterous wife, it was a dark-coloured story of wickedness and nobility in which the participants themselves were the voices. Even his old critical enemy, the *Athenaeum*, conceded that this tale of murder and virtue, brutality and humanity, was 'the most precious and profound spiritual treasure that England has produced since the days of Shakespeare'. Contrary to the notion that all true art is non-commercial, Browning began to make some money from his work.

There was soon more disapproval. 'Original Sin, the Corruption of Man's Heart' was Browning's description of his interest. He came under attack – or criticism – for an obsession with 'morbid anatomy'. *Red Cotton Night-Cap Country* (1873) was a true and recent story of Antoine Mellerio, an international jeweller in Paris. A devout Catholic, he was infatuated with a young married woman in Normandy. Stricken by sudden remorse, he held in the fire a casket of her letters until even his own hands had been reduced to 'crackling stumps' of bone. Changing his mind again, he went back to his mistress with artificial hands fitted. He began to believe that he might obtain pardon by the grace of a statue of the Virgin on a nearby church, to which he prayed. He would throw himself from the tower of his country house on the Normandy coast. Our Lady would not let him fall but would bear him up. He would be seen flying above the landscape in a public miracle that would restore the age of faith. He threw himself from the tower and fell dead below.

All this was true. Browning used the story, in a poem that sometimes reads like a novel of Maupassant or Zola. Even friends had doubts about his later style. Julia Wedgwood had written to him after *The Ring and the Book*: 'I wish I could apprehend the attraction of this subject to you. I thought I shared your interest in morbid anatomy.' Browning was unperturbed. 'My wife would have subscribed to every one of your bad opinions of the book,' he replied cheerfully, 'she never took the least interest in the story, so much as to wish to inspect the papers.' Miss Wedgwood accused him of being ruled by the theme that 'human beings are devilish'; Browning agreed, except that he thought of their devilishness as the stuff of literature.

His interest in the grotesque matched Hugo's prophecy in 1827. Browning shrugged off criticism and pursued a long-felt curiosity over articles 'that have helped great murderers to their purposes'. The 'devilishness' of the human race fascinated him. He lavished his imaginative skills on the subtle Genoese daggers, whose little teeth ripped the wound wider as they were drawn out of the victim. He was intrigued by the custom of embellishing knives and whips as if to add art to pain and murder. Yet he was one of the first and most vociferous opponents of the use of animals for medical experiments. He was a convinced Liberal in politics and a Christian in religion. When he was buried in Westminster Abbey, Henry James wrote of him, 'A good many oddities and a good many great writers have been entombed in the Abbey, but none of the odd ones have been so great and none of the great ones so odd.'

He never received adulation to match Tennyson. He was not disliked as much as Tennyson by his successors. The clever young men and women of Bloomsbury could be sharp and sardonic but they were mere amateurs at it compared with Browning himself. Still, for many years he remained in eclipse, emerging at last as perhaps the great modernist of the Victorian period and certainly the great postromantic. It was not his Victorianism that made him so but his affinity with Europeanism, past and present. To read him was to be reminded of Florence and the Medici, but also of Byron and Sade, Hugo and Baudelaire.

W. J. Fox on *Pauline* (1833) in the *Monthly Repository* (1833)

Browning was twenty when his aunt paid for Pauline *to be published. Unlike Tennyson, he was not at the centre of culture and privilege but a rather solitary figure living at home in Camberwell. He was privately and self-educated, apart from a short spell at the new*

University of London. The poem was anonymous and made little impact. An early review in the Literary Gazette *on 23 March 1833 called it, 'Somewhat mystical, somewhat poetical, somewhat sensual, and not a little unintelligible . . . a dreamy volume, without an object, and unfit for publication.'*

William Manginn, in the December 1833 number of Fraser's Magazine, *dismissed the author as 'The Mad Poet of the Batch'. He was 'as mad as Cassandra, without any of the power to prophesy like her, or to construct a connected sentence like anybody else'. Manginn suggested that the poem was written by the members of the government, because it showed 'the same folly, incoherence, and reckless assertion' as their remarks on parliamentary reform.*

But Allan Cunningham, in the Athenaeum *on 6 April, found 'not a little true poetry'. Opening* Pauline *at random, 'fine things abound'. Only W. J. Fox ranked Browning with Tennyson in the April number of his* Monthly Repository.

These thoughts have been suggested by the work before us, which, though evidently a hasty and imperfect sketch, has truth and life in it, which gave us the thrill, and laid hold of us with the power, the sensation of which has never yet failed us as a test of genius. Whoever the anonymous author may be, he is a poet. A pretender to science cannot always be safely judged of by a brief publication, for the knowledge of some facts does not imply the knowledge of other facts; but the claimant of poetic honours may generally be appreciated by a few pages, often by a few lines, for if they be poetry, he is a poet. We cannot judge of the house by the brick, but we can judge of the statue of Hercules by its foot. We felt certain of Tennyson, before we saw the book, by a few verses which had straggled into a newspaper; we are not less certain of the author of *Pauline* . . .

An anonymous reviewer on *Paracelsus* (1835) in the *Spectator* (1835)

Two years after Pauline, *Tennyson had won recognition while Browning was still struggling.* Paracelsus *was a dramatic poem showing the crises in the life of the historical sixteenth-century figure, driven by a hunger for learning and fame. His tragedy lies in forfeiting love by intellectual and spiritual arrogance. The poem owed much to Shelley's philosophy and to the example of* Alastor. *Yet it showed a subtle power of description in its evocation of the sunlit garden at Würzburg or the gorgeous evening panorama of Constantinople:*

> Over the waters in the vaporous west
> The sun goes down as in a sphere of gold
> Behind the outstretched city, which between,
> With all that length of domes and minarets
> Athwart the splendour, black and crooked runs
> Like a Turk verse along a scimitar.

The first anonymous reviewer, in the Athenaeum *on 2 August 1835, was unimpressed. 'There is talent in this dramatic poem . . . but it is dreamy and obscure.' As for Browning's literary idol, 'Writers would do well to remember . . . that though it is not difficult to imitate the mysticism and vagueness of Shelley, we love him and have taken him to our hearts as a poet, not* because *of these characteristics – but* in spite *of them.' On 15 August, an unsigned review in the* Spectator *supplemented this adverse criticism.*

The defect in the structure of this poem is palpable: there is neither action nor incident, scarcely even a story to excite the attention of the reader. Of this the author seems to be in some sort conscious; stating that he has endeavoured to write a poem, not a drama, and to reverse the method usually adopted by writers whose aim it is to set forth any phœnomenon of the mind or of the passions by the operations of persons and events; and that instead of having recourse to an external machinery of incidents to create and evolve the crisis he desired to produce, he has ventured to display somewhat minutely the mood itself in its rise and progress, and has suffered the agency by which it is influenced and determined to be generally discernible in its effects alone. But admitting all this to have been designed, the design may still be very injudicious: for the form of dialogue precludes those descriptions and digressions by which the author in a narrative poem can vary his subjects and 'interchange delights'; whilst the fundamental plan renders the whole piece a virtual soliloquy, each person of the drama *speaking up* to Paracelsus, in order to elicit his feelings, thoughts, or opinions. For these reasons we conceive that such a poem contains in its structure the elements of tediousness, which no execution could obviate; and, unfortunately, the execution of *Paracelsus* is not of a nature to overcome difficulties. Evidences of mental power, perhaps of poetical talent, are visible throughout; but there is no nice conception and development of character, nothing peculiar or striking in the thoughts, whilst the language in which they are clothed gives them an air of mystical or dreamy vagueness.

John Forster on *Paracelsus* (1835) in the *Examiner* (1835)

John Forster, editor and biographer, is probably best known for his life of Dickens (1872–4) and his editorship of the radical Daily News *in 1846. He was Browning's contemporary and in this unsigned* Examiner *review on 6 September he stemmed the almost universal critical hostility to* Paracelsus. *In December, Browning met Forster through the actor William Macready and the two men became friends. Through Forster, Browning also met Charles Lamb and Leigh Hunt. Forster was to review* Paracelsus *again, after meeting Browning, in the* New Monthly Magazine and Literary Journal *for March 1836. In that later review he summarized in a sentence the skill of Browning's dramatic monologues. 'We never think of Mr Browning while we read his poem; we are not identified with him, but with the persons into whom he has flung his genius.'*

Even before knowing Browning, Forster had no doubts of his ability. He put his opinion forcefully in the 1835 Examiner *review. 'It is some time since we read a work of more unequivocal power than this. We conclude that its author is a young man, as we do not recollect his having published before. If so, we may safely predict for him a brilliant career, if he continues true to the present promise of his genius. He possesses all the elements of a fine poet.' Forster begins by ranking Browning with Henry Taylor, whose dramatic romance,* Philip von Artevelde, *had been published in the previous year.*

Since the publication of *Philip Von Artevelde*, we have met with no such evidences of poetical genius, and of general intellectual power, as are contained in this volume. It is a philosophical view of incident, to create and evolve the crisis he desires to produce, prefers to display somewhat minutely the mood itself in its rise and progress, and to suffer the agency by which it is influenced and determined, to be generally discernible in its effects alone, and subordinate, if not altogether excluded. The effect of this mode of treatment is necessarily severe, and the reader who takes up the volume must be prepared accordingly. He will find enough of beauty to compensate him for the tedious passages, were they ten times as obscure and tedious. A rich vein of internal sentiment, a deep knowledge of humanity, an intellect subtle and inquisitive, will soon fix his interest, and call forth his warmest admiration. He will probably read the book twice—as we have done.

Leigh Hunt on *Paracelsus* (1835) in the *London Journal* (1835)

Between Forster's two reviews, Leigh Hunt delivered judgment on Browning's poetry. It was not so much Paracelsus *itself as the latent talents of the young poet that preoccupied him. The dangers and the potential of his style came under notice more intensely than in the case of* Pauline. *By this time, it was clear that* Paracelsus *had become a critical success. If Browning took advice and heeded certain warnings about obscurity of thought or convoluted syntax, his future as a poet seemed assured.*

In its chief constituent qualities Mr Browning's style and manner of writing is, like that of every man of cultivated powers, a sufficiently true representative of his manner of thinking; even its peculiarities, whether they might, in the abstract, be accounted commendable, or the reverse, must be held to be indispensable to its perfection, because they are a reflection of mental habits which have contributed to make his poetry what it is. We do not therefore object generally to his long and often somewhat intricately involved sentences, or to forms of phraseology and construction, of occasional occurrence, which are apt for a moment to perplex or startle on the first reading, or to any other deviations of a similar kind from ordinary usage or the beaten highway prescribed by our books of authority in grammar, rhetoric, and prosody, in so far as such unusual forms are the natural and unaffected product of the writer's genius, working its purposes in its own way. Such distinctive characteristics, when we have become familiar with them, and they have lost any slight repulsiveness with which they may have at first acted upon us, even acquire a power of enhancing the pleasure we receive from a composition otherwise eminently beautiful, and of riveting our love for it. We do not doubt that there are, in *Paradise Lost* for instance, many peculiar forms of phraseology which the national ear has now learned not only to tolerate but to admire, but which must have surprised more than they pleased the first readers of the poem; and even some cadences of the divine verse which now linger in all memories and all hearts, but which those who first endeavoured to catch their music probably deemed forced and dissonant. But in these cases we must suppose that true art has really been present and at work, although (nothing uncommon or wonderful) the effect may have been too new and too exquisite to be all at once understood and appreciated. The result will be very different where the peculiarity is not a real excellence, but a mere trick or whim. Then the disapproval which it may expect to meet with when the blinding influences of novelty operate no longer,—the condemnatory and decisive verdict of posterity—will be still more severe than that which may have been at first passed upon it. It may then operate as powerfully to scare away the regards of men from the genuine beauties with which it may happen to be associated, as it would help in the other case to attract and fix their admiration.

Mr Browning, like every writer who aims at an original style, would do well to keep these considerations in mind, and to beware of being seduced, while seeking to produce new and bold effects, into either slovenliness or affectation. We think there is in the present poem a slight degree occasionally of both the one and the other; and to many readers it will probably appear that there is a great deal of both. There is much both in the diction and the versification which has a harsh, awkward, and disappointing effect at first; but this, in by far the greater part, arises merely from the poem not being cast in a common mould, or formed so much as most new poems are upon the ordinary models. It is not a mere additional variation of the old air; and it cannot therefore be read off-hand so readily and smoothly as the generality of the poetical productions of the day. There is a hidden soul in its harmony which must be first unwound—a retiring grace in its unwonted forms of phraseology which must be won before the poetry can be rightly enjoyed or understood. The reader of such a work has his effort to make, as well as the writer has had his—his powers of apprehension, as the other has had his powers of production, to keep on the stretch.

An anonymous reviewer on *Sordello* (1840) in the *Dublin Review* (1840)

Sordello was to be the narrative of the 'development of a soul', specifically that of an eleventh-century poet living in the strife of northern Italy. It sank Browning's reputation for almost twenty years. The style appeared bafflingly imprecise, there was no clear narration, and it was 253 pages of rhymed couplets. The story of its publication was a tragi-comedy. The tragedy was that Browning thought he had written a popular poem. The comedy was provided by those like Douglas Jerrold and Harriet Martineau who thought they were going mad as they tried to read it. Of more than five thousand lines of the poem, Tennyson said that he understood the first, 'Who will, may hear Sordello's story told.' He also understood the last, 'Who would has heard Sordello's story told.' They were both lies, he insisted.

As it happened, there was something in the poem to appeal to a different age. There are suggestively lit descriptive passages where, for example, the eye travels through the castle of Goito with the motion of the camera in a surreal film like Jean Cocteau's La Belle et La Bête. *The interior light is subtle in its fading and changing, the objects themselves are fleeting or elusive:*

> A maze of corridors contrived for sin,
> Dusk winding-stairs, dim galleries got past,
> You gain the inmost chambers, gain at last
> A maple-panelled room: that haze which seems
> Floating about the panel, if there gleams
> A sunbeam over it will turn to gold
> And in light graven characters unfold
> The Arab's wisdom everywhere.

It would not do for the 1840s. On 14 March, the Spectator *thought the poem characterized by 'digression, affectation, obscurity'. On 28 March, the* Atlas *found all Browning's usual faults in their most pronounced form:*

the same pitching, hysterical, and broken sobs of sentences – the same excisions of words – the same *indications* of power – imperfect grouping of thoughts and images – and hurried, exclamatory and obscure utterance of things that would, probably, be very fine if we could get them in their full meaning, but which, in this bubbling and tumult of the verse, are hardly intelligible.

On 30 May, the Athenaeum *considered that Browning's obscurity had excluded* Sordello *from worthwhile criticism. The* Monthly Chronicle *for May added, 'We regard* Sordello *as a failure in toto.' The* Dublin Review, *which had wished him well, expressed the disappointment of many of his readers.*

Our perusal of *Sordello* has not renewed our early anticipation. The faults of Mr. Browning are here exaggerated and profusely displayed, to the destruction of all interest, comprehension of the narrative, sympathy with the author, or approbation of his intellectual pretensions. The story is most elliptically constructed, full of breaks and leaps; the syntax of quite an unusual character, a mass of perplexity and obscurity; the versification is harsh and knotty; the language, instead of being throughout 'English undefiled,' is larded with many fantastic and arbitrary invertions, and the whole set together in a ricketty, hysterical, capricious style, producing the most startling and repulsive effect. All this makes us fear that the defects, which we had previously fancied were ascribable to immaturity, are the result of some obstinate system which has now obtained too strong a control over the writer, ever to let him stand up a free man, to discourse of noble and regenerating themes in a mode worthy of such, or of the sublime and responsible avocation of a poet. If the critical aphorism of Coleridge be true, that the poem to which we *return* with the greatest pleasure possesses the genuine power and claims the name of *true poetry*, then is *Sordello* certainly condemned; for it is as impossible to *return* to, as to read it for the first time even with pleasure.

We regret that we have not been able to give a more recommendatory notice of Mr. Browning's work; but we have a high estimate of the aim and functions of a poet, and are jealous guardians of our country's literature. We cannot, therefore, to gratify a clever man, or to win a false character for liberality among publishers, compromise our duty and mislead our readers. He has given indication of powers, that if faithfully, diligently, and loftily cultivated, might place him in an honourable and beneficent position. The world of the beautiful is not exhausted, the number of the poets is not yet made up; there are thousands of manifestations of the good, the true, the lovely, the eternal in man, yet to be revealed. He may yet give the world assurance that he is one who has been appointed to this high calling which he aims at; if he *aspire rightly*, he will *attain*. We hope that he will do so; but let him take this warning from us, in the only quotation we shall make from his *Sordello*,—

> Change no old standards of perfection; vex
> With no strange forms *created to perplex*.

An anonymous reviewer on *Dramatic Lyrics and Romances* (1845) in the *Examiner* (1845)

Dramatic Lyrics and Romances *was the seventh of* Bells and Pomegranates, *the collective title under which Browning published eight volumes of plays and poetry between 1841 and 1846. Apart from* Pippa Passes, *these contained such individual poems as 'My Last Duchess', 'The Bishop Orders his Tomb in St Praxed's Church', and 'Soliloquy of the Spanish Cloister'. Many of them showed the first influence of Browning's Italian travels.*

But the reservations of literary critics still haunted his reputation. Memories of Sordello *were almost synonymous with his name. Browning was still far from being financially successful or even independent as an author in 1845, the year in which he met Elizabeth Barrett. But there were signs in some of the reviews that he had begun to rebuild since the collapse of his hopes in 1840. The* Examiner *provided one such portent on 15 November 1845.*

We are disposed to admire this little book of Mr. Browning's very much. Our readers know how high we have ranked his muse; and how we have grieved when she lost her way in transcendental or other fogs, and, like poor Origen's[1] fallen star, 'rayed out' only darkness. Here she has found the path again.

Mr. Browning's metaphysics have been too abundant for his poetry. That is the substance of the objection to be urged against him. And it is not a slight one. Poetry is a jealous mistress, and will have undivided homage. The analytic and the imaginative powers never yet worked well together. But it is the fault (not an inglorious one) of youth: the fault of which Shelley became conscious before he died, and from which Mr. Browning is fast freeing himself. Nothing but this retarded his advance.

His writing has always the stamp and freshness of originality. It is in no respect imitative or commonplace. Whatever the verse may be, the man is in it: the music of it echoing to his mood. When he succeeds, there have been few so successful in the melodious transitions of his rhythm. In all its most poetical and most musical varieties, he is a master; and to us it expresses, in a rare and exquisite degree, the delicacy and truth of his genius. Proctor[2] says very happily in the *Life of Ben Jonson*, that the motion of verse corresponds with the power of the poet, as the swell and tumult of the sea answer to the winds that call them up; and this is the safe test of a master in the art.

We leave several fine pieces unnamed as well as unquoted. Among them the 'Tomb at St. Praxed's,' a death-bed speech of an old Popish Prelate, which, with a grim and awful kind of humour, mixes up concerns of life and death 'in monumental mockery,'—and 'The Glove,' a French romance, given as from the recitation of Peter Ronsard, wherein the incident of the court dame flinging her glove into the den of a lion, is ingeniously and not unpleasantly turned to the lady's advantage.

These *Romances and Lyrics* form the seventh part of a collection of pieces chiefly dramatic, which Mr Browning has been publishing some years, for odd shillings and sixpences, with the title of *Bells and Pomegranates*. On the whole they are a remarkable collection, and proof of a very affluent as well as original genius. Wonderful is the saving of paper and press-work and price, in their small print and double columns. They look as though already packed up and on their way to posterity; nor are we without a confident expectation that some of them will arrive at that journey's end.

An anonymous reviewer on Browning in the *English Review* (1845)

In the following month, December 1845, the English Review *summed up Browning's progress since* Paracelsus *ten years earlier. There was no doubt that he sometimes seemed obscure, yet this was now put down to the 'modernity' of his thought and the complex skill with which he analysed character in poetry. A good many reviewers had written as if they did not know what to make of him. Now his modernism seemed to combine the more important elements of European post-romanticism.*

Mr. Browning unites within himself more of the elements of a true poet than perhaps any other of those whom we call 'modern' amongst us; yet there are few writers so little read, so partially understood. He came into the literary forum in such a mysterious guise, (that *Paracelsus* of his), and carried his great gifts about him with such a careless air, that men took but little notice of the unostentatious stranger. This first work was by no means adapted to be a 'noisy herald of his fame:' it purports to be a sort of autobiography of the great Alchemist, and is almost as obscure as the subject itself. Yet *Paracelsus* won for its author instant consideration among the few who were capable of appreciating its merits: it exhibits great power and resources; but it is perhaps the most difficult *simple* poetry in the English language. The diction is remarkable for simplicity, even when expressing the most complex thought; and the whole poem has an easy rhythmical flow that almost lulls us into forgetfulness of its deep meanings. This is in itself an evidence of the ease and mastery of his subject possessed by the writer. Moreover, notwithstanding its occasional obscurity, this work possesses rare merit: without pausing to examine our author's philosophy, we are struck by the nobleness, energy, and polish of his style, and still more by his delicate delineation of character.

Anonymous reviewers on *Christmas-Eve and Easter-Day* (1850) in the *Leader* (1850) and *Chamber's Edinburgh Journal* (1853)

The two poems in Browning's new volume joined the mid-century debate on religious faith and doubt. Browning was a convinced Christian. In Christmas-Eve, *in vivid London night-scenes, the gorgeous midnight celebration at St Peter's in Rome, and the lecture-*

room of the new criticism at Göttingen, he examines possible choices. There is Dickensian gloom and absurdity about the preacher in the plebeian Zion Chapel. There is the splendour of the Pope at Mass with 'his posturings and his petticoatings'. Last of all, in the lecture-room at Göttingen, the hawk-nosed professor talks the worst nonsense of all. New Testament history is open to question, says the professor, making Christianity acceptable as a modern moral creed, devoid of supernatural or divine content. But if the New Testament is not true, Browning argues, how can you base a moral system upon it? What, after all, was Christ's message?

> What is the point where Himself lays stress?
> Does the precept run, 'Believe in Good,
> In Justice, Truth now understood
> For the first time?' – or, 'Believe in Me,
> Who lived and died, yet essentially
> Am Lord of Life'?

In the end, it is Zion Chapel that proves to be the home of true faith. Only intellectual snobbery had blinded him to this at the start.

Easter-Day takes the form of an interior dialogue between the voices of belief and scepticism. How easy it would be to believe, if only it could be proved absolutely that 'the least Command of God's is God's indeed'. How difficult to believe when faced by the uncertainty of mortal life.

This was the first volume for whose publication Browning or his family did not pay. Chapman and Hall published it, though the initial sale was still only two hundred copies while Tennyson's In Memoriam *exhausted five editions in the same year. Despite that, Browning had sounded a theme in the debate on faith and doubt which appealed to a good many intelligent readers. Benjamin Jowett, who was later responsible for Browning's election as an honorary Fellow of Balliol, wrote:*

It is Browning's noblest work, written in his highest, though a fluctuating mood of mind. The first poem, 'Christmas-Eve,' seems to rest on the love of God, which embraces the vulgarest of human beings; the second expresses the beating of the human soul against God and nature, aspiring but unsatisfied.

On 27 April 1850, the Leader *acknowledged the force of Browning's contribution to the intellectual debate.*

On the theology of the poem we should have much to say did time and place serve; meanwhile we need only applaud in passing the sincere and earnest spirit which breathes through it. The sincerity of it will to many look like levity. Already we have heard strange objections to the 'tone', as not elevated enough. Do these critics imagine that an 'elevated' tone is difficult? Do they suppose that Browning could not have adopted it, had he thought fit? But he did *not* think fit. Instead of imitating Milton he spoke as Robert Browning; his keen sense of the ludicrous and grotesque fading into the background whenever the presence of more solemn themes overshadowed it. In the bold and artful mingling of the ludicrous with the intensely serious he reminds us of Carlyle. His style is swayed by the subject. It is a garment, not a mould; it takes the varying shapes of varied movement, and does not force its one monotone on all.

As a page out of the history of a life, the poetic confession of a troubled soul, *Christmas Eve* has a significance and a value peculiarly its own. We have read it three times, and with increasing admiration. What it wants to make it an enduring work of art is that which the author cannot give it, has not to give—the magic and the mystery of Beauty. But of its kind it is really great. The luxury of rhyme—the marvellous facility playing with difficulties as an Indian juggler plays with balls, every one will have noticed. Since Butler no English poet has exhibited the same daring propensity and facility of rhyming. If the verse is sometimes rugged it is but the better exponent of the thought Realism in Art has Truth as an aim, Ugliness as a pitfall.

Three years later, on 16 July 1853 at the end of a general review, Chamber's Edinburgh Journal, *having described Browning as 'among the most remarkable of living English poets', pondered the reason for the failure of his latest volume to win him popularity.*

We have taken no notice of Mr Browning's latest work, *Christmas-Eve and Easter-Day*; for although it contains, in fuller measure, perhaps, than any of his other writings, those evidences of strong originality to which we have already referred, the subject is one of which we cannot properly give an outline. It is a metaphysical and essentially religious poem, though partaking to a very slight degree of the character of religious poetry generally. It is too full of close and subtle reasoning ever to be popular; for while it combines much that is striking in thought and imagery, with a high tone of devotional feeling, it has depths of spiritual experience into which the ordinary reader of poetry will scarcely be inclined to go.

W. M. Rossetti on *Christmas-Eve and Easter-Day* (1850) in the *Germ* (1850)

In the 1850s, and more markedly so in the following decade, Browning began to be fashionable among a younger generation than his own. It was at a time when the appeal of Tennyson to that generation seemed to be on the wane. Among new movements in art and literature, that of the Pre-Raphaelite Brotherhood had begun in 1848. One of the first signs of the brotherhood's enthusiasm for Browning was a review in its journal, the Germ, *for May 1850.*

William Michael Rossetti was the younger brother of Dante Gabriel Rossetti. He was an Inland Revenue official at Somerset House, as well as a critic and man of letters.

Of all poets, there is none more than Robert Browning, in approaching whom diffidence is necessary. The mere extent of his information cannot pass unobserved, either as a fact, or as a title to respect. No one who has read the body of his works will deny that they are replete with mental and speculative subtlety, with vivid and most diversified conception of character, with dramatic incident and feeling; with that intimate knowledge of outward nature which makes every sentence of description a living truth; replete with a most human tenderness and pathos. Common as is the accusation of 'extravagance', and unhesitatingly as it is applied, in a general off-hand style, to the entire character of Browning's poems, it would require some jesuitism of self-persuasion to induce any to affirm his belief in the existence of such extravagance in the conception of the poems, or in the sentiments expressed; of any want of concentration in thought, of national or historical keeping. Far from this, indeed, a deliberate unity of purpose is strikingly apparent.

An anonymous reviewer on *Men and Women* (1855) in the *Athenaeum* (1855)

A good deal of Browning's posthumous reputation rested upon the view that the fifty poems in Men and Women *constituted one of the finest collections in English poetry of the last two centuries. It would be easy to suppose that the publication of the book was a turning-point in his literary career. But the book was not particularly well received and the review in the* Athenaeum *shows why.*

Browning's realism in describing a sexual love that was both physical and emotional was 'prosaic' and 'flawed by impertinences'. It was too close to the truth of life as lived between men and women. His modernity in this and in his style was not welcome. His future, the reviewer suggests, may lie in writing comic verse and simple lyrics. At the end of the review, having quoted with approval from 'The Patriot', the critic hopes that Browning's undoubted talent will be employed upon something more popular and less perverse than the present book.

There were some enthusiastic reviews, including one by the young William Morris in the Oxford and Cambridge Magazine. *But after twenty-three years of toil, Browning's anger at his rejection elsewhere was vigorously expressed. He denounced his critics privately as apes, swine, and 'grunters'. 'Don't you mind them,' he wrote to his publisher, Edward Chapman, 'and leave me to rub their noses in their own filth some fine day.' But it was many years before Chapman sold out the first edition of* Men and Women.

These volumes contain some fifty poems, which will make the least imaginative man think, and the least thoughtful man grieve. Who will not grieve over energy wasted and power misspent,—over fancies chaste and noble, so overhung by the 'seven veils' of obscurity, that we can oftentimes be only sure that fancies exist? What they are meant to typify or illustrate cannot always be detected by the eyes of even kindred dreamers. Again, in the versification of these new poems, there is an amount of extravagant licence, belonging to a superfluity of power, for which only those who have studied versification as an art will be able to account or apologize. That some among the poets having the finest musical sense have written the most irregular verses, is a fact strange and true. They have relied on the sympathy of the interpreter: they have expected him here to lean on a cadence,—there to lend accent to the rhyme, or motion to the languid phrase; in another place, to condense a multitude of syllables, so as to give an effect of concrete strength. Indeed, it may be generally declared, that for those who have not this fine artistic sense, a large proportion of modern verse is not verse at all, by reason of its licence and assumption. The artists show themselves, by their exigencies, to be less masterly than the artists of old, who had their fullest praise from the few, but their full praise also from the many,—who knew that, whereas their thoughts raised them to heights where only a limited number could bear them company, the perfection of form was such that their works, if incompletely apprehended by the ignorant, the timid, and the frivolous, had still a complete charm of their own for these,—a charm of music, a charm of imagery,—a charm which kept the idea of poetry as a separate and refined art select and holy in the popular mind. Our poets now speak in an unknown tongue,—wear whatever unpoetic garniture it pleases their conceit or their idleness to snatch up; and the end too often is pain to those who love them best, and who most appreciate their high gifts and real nobleness,—and to the vast world, whom they might assist, they bring only a mystery and receive nothing but wonder and scorn.

We fear that no one who goes through these volumes can question the justice of our remarks on their general style; no one, we are sure, can read them with understanding, and not again and again pause over thoughts, verses, pictures,—oases in the wilderness of mist and of sand,—of a bloom and freshness such as few modern magicians are able to conjure up. What—to give an instance from the second poem in the collection—can be more lyrical than the first verse of 'A Lovers' Quarrel'?—

> Oh, what a dawn of day!
> How the March sun feels like May!
> All is blue again
> After last night's rain,
> And the South dries the hawthorn-spray.
> Only, my Love's away!
> I'd as lief that the blue were grey.

But when the Lover begins to recall the happiness he enjoyed with his Lady-love in the cold winter time, ere they had quarrelled, we imagine that the most tolerant of lovers will find such reminiscences of past happiness as the following somewhat prosaic:—

What's in the 'Times'?—a scold
At the emperor deep and cold;
   He has taken a bride
   To his gruesome side,
That's as fair as himself is bold:
   There they sit ermine-stoled,
And she powders her hair with gold.

Too many of Mr. Browning's fifty poems are flawed by impertinences such as these, borne out by an audacity in Hudibrastic versification in which our author is without a rival. We do not recollect to have ever seen syllables 'tossed about' with such unhesitating legerdemain, as in the lyric called 'Old Pictures in Florence.' But in this poem the ease is too much the ease of the acrobat, who by much practice has learnt how to disjoint his limbs, and fling himself into any conceivable attitude; and the effect is dislocation—not grace. When, however, Mr. Browning is avowedly humorous, his mastery over diction and language takes forms of a quaintness which will be precious to all who relish humour.

Why one who can pour out his thoughts, fancies, stores of learning, and emotions, with an eloquent and direct sincerity such as this, should, so often as Mr. Browning has here done, prefer to rhyme the pleadings of a casuist, or the arguments of a critic, or the ponderous discoursings of some obsolete schoolman—why he should turn away from themes in which every one can answer to his sympathies, and from modes of the lyre which find their echoes wherever hearts and ears know aught of music—is an enigma no less painful than perplexing, the unriddling of which is possibly reserved for no contemporary. We had hoped that 'Men and Women' would enable us to register progress in the poet's mind (always rich to overflowing) and in the artist's hand (always able to draw whatever its owner pleased). The riches and the ability are there, but the employment and the expression of them seem to us, on the whole, more perverse, personal, and incomplete than they were formerly.

An unsigned review of *Men and Women* (1855) in the
Saturday Review (1855)

On 24 November 1855, a week after the Athenaeum *review, the*

Saturday Review *made an even more vigorous attack on the style and preoccupations of* Men and Women. *It is suggested that, though the review appeared anonymously, it may have been from the pen of Browning's friend Joseph Arnould, who had admired much of his earlier work. It seems uncharacteristic of Arnould to write in this manner. However, the review was yet one more protest of the literary conservatives against what the reviewer calls 'the false teachings of a perverted school of art'. It is as if the threat of Browning on one side and the Pre-Raphaelites on the other seemed a challenge to the established cultural order. With the appearance of Browning's darker dramas of the 1860s and 1870s, not to mention the shrill eruption of Swinburne on the literary landscape, the protests were to grow more vigorous yet.*

It is really high time that this sort of thing should, if possible, be stopped. Here is another book of madness and mysticism—another melancholy specimen of power wantonly wasted, and talent deliberately perverted—another act of self-prostration before that demon of bad taste who now seems to hold in absolute possession the fashionable masters of our ideal literature. It is a strong case for the correctional justice of criticism, which has too long abdicated its proper functions. The thing has really grown to a lamentable head amongst us. The contagion has affected not only our sciolists and our versifiers, but those whom, in the absence of a mightier race, we must be content to accept as the poets of our age. Here is Robert Browning, for instance—no one can doubt that he is capable of better things—no one, while deploring the obscurities that deface the *Paracelsus* and the *Dramatic Lyrics*, can deny the less questionable qualities which characterized those remarkable poems—but can any of his devotees be found to uphold his present elaborate experiment on the patience of the public? Take any of his worshippers you please—let him be 'well up' in the transcendental poets of the day–take him fresh from Alexander Smith[3] or Alfred Tennyson's *Maud*, or the *Mystic* of Bailey[4] —and we will engage to find him at least ten passages in the first ten pages of *Men and Women*, some of which, even after profound study, he will not be able to construe at all, and not one of which will he be able to read off at sight.

Why should a man who, with so little apparent labour, can write naturally and well, take so much apparent labour to write affectedly and ill? There can be but one of two solutions. Either he goes wrong from want of knowledge, in which case it is clear that he wants the highest institutions of genius; or he sins against knowledge, in which case he must have been misled by the false promptings of a morbid vanity, eager for that applause of fools which always waits on quackery, and which is never refused to extravagance when tricked out in the guise of originality. It is difficult, from the internal evidence supplied by his works, to know which of these two theories to adopt. Frequently the conclusion is almost irresistible, that Mr. Browning's mysticism must be of *malice prepense:*[5] on the whole, however, we are inclined to clear his honesty at the expense of his powers, and to conclude that he is obscure, not so much because he has the vanity to be thought original, as because he lacks sufficient genius to make himself clear.

George Eliot on *Men and Women* (1855) in the *Westminster Review* (1856)

For some weeks the attacks on Men and Women *continued. The* Spectator *on 22 December 1855 judged Browning as 'a fine mind enfeebled by caprice and want of discipline, and a true poet defrauding himself of fame, and the public of pleasure and enjoyment by affectations, and puerilities, and awkwardnesses that too often quite overgrow and hide the genuine power of his natural gifts'.*

In January 1856, George Eliot came to Browning's defence in the Westminster Review, *though her comments were published anonymously. She was not yet a novelist but had served as assistant editor of the* Westminster Review *for four years. Her tone was precisely the right one to answer the clamour of earlier criticism and to suggest that poetry ought not to be condemned for making demands upon the reader. Indeed, she begins by quoting the seventeenth-century commentator on Aristotle, Heinsius, who remarked that a truly majestic obscurity repels only the ignorant.*

We borrow these words to indicate what is likely to be the first impression of a reader who, without any previous familiarity with Browning, glances through his two new volumes of poems. The less acute he is, the more easily will he arrive at the undeniable criticism, that these poems have a 'majestic obscurity', which repels not only the ignorant but the idle. To read poems is often a substitute for thought: fine-sounding conventional phrases and the sing-song of verse demand no co-operation in the reader; they glide over his mind with the agreeable unmeaningness of 'the compliments of the season', or a speaker's exordium on 'feelings too deep for expression'. But let him expect no such drowsy passivity in reading Browning. Here he will find no conventionality, no melodious commonplace, but freshness, originality, sometimes eccentricity of expression; no didactic laying-out of a subject, but dramatic indication, which requires the reader to trace by his own mental activity the underground stream of thought that jets out in elliptical and pithy verse. To read Browning he must exert himself, but he will exert himself to some purpose. If he finds the meaning difficult of access, it is always worth his effort—if he has to dive deep, 'he rises with his pearl'. Indeed, in Browning's best poems he makes us feel that what we took for obscurity in him was superficiality in ourselves. We are far from meaning that all his obscurity is like the obscurity of the stars, dependent simply on the feebleness of men's vision. On the contrary, our admiration for his genius only makes us feel the more acutely that its inspirations are too often straitened by the garb of whimsical mannerism with which he clothes them. This mannerism is even irritating sometimes, and should at least be kept under restraint in *printed* poems, where the writer is not merely indulging his own vein, but is avowedly appealing to the mind of his reader.

Turning from the ordinary literature of the day to such a writer as Browning, is like turning from Flotow's[6] music, made up of well-pieced shreds and patches, to the distinct individuality of Chopin's Studies or Schubert's Songs. Here, at least, is a man who has something of his own to tell us, and who can tell it impressively, if not with faultless art. There is nothing sickly or dreamy in him: he has a clear eye, a vigorous grasp, and courage to utter what he sees and handles. His robust energy is informed by a subtle, penetrating spirit, and this blending of opposite qualities gives his mind a rough piquancy that reminds one of a russet apple. His keen glance pierces into all the secrets of human character, but, being as thoroughly alive to the outward as to the inward, he reveals those secrets, not by a process of dissection, but by dramatic painting. We fancy his own description of a poet applies to himself:[7]

> He stood and watched the cobbler at his trade,
> The man who slices lemons into drink,

The coffee-roaster's brazier, and the boys
That volunteer to help him at the winch.
He glanced o'er books on stalls with half an eye,
And fly-leaf ballads on the vendor's string,
And broad-edge bold-print posters by the wall
He took such cognizance of men and things,
If any beat a horse, you felt he saw;
If any cursed a woman, he took note;
Yet stared at nobody,—they stared at him,
And found, less to their pleasure than surprise,
He seemed to know them and expect as much.

Browning has no soothing strains, no chants, no lullabys; he rarely gives voice to our melancholy, still less to our gaiety; he sets our thoughts at work rather than our emotions. But though eminently a thinker, he is as far as possible from prosaic; his mode of presentation is always concrete, artistic, and, where it is most felicitous, dramatic.

D. G. Rossetti on *Men and Women* (1855) in his letters to William Allingham (1855–6)

Dante Gabriel Rossetti admired Browning's poems at once. He first wrote to his friend William Allingham about Men and Women *on 25 November 1855. His enthusiasm seems almost unqualified. 'The Heretic's Tragedy' was an exception until he saw how shabbily the* Athenaeum *reviewer treated it. Thereafter, Rossetti felt obliged to like that poem as well. The 'William' who read the poems to him was his brother, William Michael Rossetti.*

What a magnificent series is *Men and Women*! Of course you have it half by heart ere this. The comparative stagnation, even among those I see, and complete torpor elsewhere, which greet this my Elixir of Life, are awful signs of the times to me—'and I must hold my peace!'—for it isn't fair to Browning (besides, indeed, being too much trouble) to bicker and flicker about it. I fancy we shall agree pretty well on favourites, though one's mind has no right to be quite made up so soon on such a subject. For my own part, I don't reckon I've read them at all yet, as I only got them the day before leaving town, and couldn't possibly read them then,—the best proof to you how hard at work I was for once—so heard them read by William; since then read them on the journey again, and some a third time at intervals; but they'll bear lots of squeezing yet. My prime favourites hitherto (without the book by me) are 'Childe Roland', 'Bishop Blougram', 'Karshish', 'The Contemporary', 'Lippo Lippi', 'Cleon', and 'Popularity'; about the other lyrical ones I can't quite speak yet, and their names don't stick in my head; but I'm afraid 'The Heretic's Tragedy' rather gave me the gripes at first, though I've tried since to think it didn't on finding *The Athenæum* similarly affected.

Rossetti's second letter to Allingham, on 8 January 1856, reiterates his praise of Browning's new book and his contempt for the obtuseness or hostility of some of the reviewers.

I broke off at the last sheet in mid-Browning. Of course I've been drenching myself with him at intervals since, only he got carried off by friends, and I have him not always by me. I wish you would let me hear in a speedy answer (there's cheek for you!) all you think about his new work, and it shall nerve me to express my ideas in return; but since I have given up poetry as a pursuit of my own, I really find my thoughts on the subject generally require a starting-point from somebody else to bring them into activity; and as you're the only man I know who'd be really in my mood of receptiveness in regard to Browning, and as I can't get at you, I've been bottled up ever since *Men and Women* came out. By the bye, I don't reckon William, the intensity of fellow-feeling on the subject making the discussion of it between us rather flat. I went the other day to a penny reading-room,—a real blessing, which now occupies the place of Burford's Panorama,[8] and where all papers and reviews whatsoever are taken in. There I saw two articles on Browning: one by Masson—really thoroughly appreciative, but slow—in the *British Quarterly*; and one by a certain Brimley, of Trinity College, Cambridge, in *Fraser*, the cheekiest of human products. This man, less than two years ago, had not read a line of Browning, as I know through my brother, and I have no doubt he has just read him up to write this article; which opens, nevertheless, with accusations against R. B. of nothing less than personal selfishness and vanity, so plumply put as to be justified by nothing less than personal intimacy of many years.

William Morris on *Men and Women* (1855) in the *Oxford and Cambridge Magazine* (1856)

William Morris, twenty-one years old and an undergraduate of Exeter College, Oxford, had already won a reputation among his contemporaries. Swinburne announced soon after this that Morris's poem 'The Defence of Guenevere' was superior to anything written by Tennyson. A young and impatient movement in the arts, publicly displayed in the 1860s, was testing its strength of opinion. In this case, the enthusiasm with which Morris receives Browning's poems is set in the context of a rebellion against the critical dullness of an older generation. Though not part of the original Pre-Raphaelite Brotherhood, Morris, like Swinburne, was soon to join forces with Rossetti in a rejection of the philistinism which they perceived in the society of mid-century.

Yet a few words, and I have done. For, as I wrote this, many times angry indignant words came to my lips, which stopped my writing till I could be quieter. For I suppose, reader, that you see whereabouts among the poets I place Robert Browning; high among the poets of all time, and I scarce know whether first, or second, in our own: and it is a bitter thing to me to see the way in which he has been received by almost everybody; many, having formed a certain theory of their own about him, from reading, I suppose, some of the least finished poems among the *Dramatic Lyrics*, make all facts bend to this theory, after the fashion of theory-mongers: they think him, or say they think him, a careless man, writing down anyhow anything that comes into his head. Oh truly! 'The Statue and the Bust' shows this! or the soft solemn flow of that poem, 'By the Fireside', *Paracelsus*—that, with its wonderful rhythm, its tender sadness, its noble thoughts, must have been very easy to write, surely!

Then they say, too, that Browning is so obscure as not to be understood by any one. Now, I know well enough what they mean by obscure, and I know also that they use the word wrongly; meaning difficult to understand fully at first reading, or, say at second reading, even: yet, taken so, in what a cloud of obscurity would *Hamlet* be! Do they think this to be the case? they daren't say so at all events, though I suspect some of them of thinking so. Now, I don't say that Robert Browning is not sometimes really obscure. He would be a perfect poet (of some calibre or other) if he were not; I assert, fearlessly, that this obscurity is seldom so prominent as to make his poems hard to understand on this ground: while, as to that which they call obscurity, it results from depth of thought and greatness of subject on the poet's part, and on his readers' part, from their shallower brains and more bounded knowledge; nay, often I fear from mere wanton ignorance and idleness. So I believe that though this obscurity, so called, would indeed be very objectionable if, as some seem to think, poetry is merely a department of 'light literature'; yet, if it is rather one of the very grandest of all God's gifts to men, we must not think it hard if we have sometimes to exercise thought over a great poem, nay, even sometimes the utmost straining of all our thoughts, an agony almost equal to that of the poet who created the poem.

However, this accusation against Browning of carelessness, and consequent roughness in rhythm, and obscurity in language and thought, has come to be pretty generally believed; and people, as a rule, do not read him; this evil spreading so, that many, almost unconsciously, are kept from reading him, who, if they did read, would sympathise with him thoroughly. But it was always so; it was so with Tennyson when he first published his poems; it was so last year with 'Maud'; it is so with Ruskin; they petted him indeed at first, his wonderful eloquence having some effect even upon the critics; but as his circle grew larger and larger, embracing more and more truth, they more and more fell off from him; his firm faith in right they call arrogance and conceit now; his eager fighting with falsehood and wrong they call unfairness. I wonder what they will say to his new volume.

The story of the Pre-Raphaelites, we all know that; only here, thank Heaven! the public has chosen to judge for itself somewhat, though to this day their noblest pictures are the least popular.

Yes, I wonder what the critics would have said to *Hamlet, Prince of Denmark*, if it had been first published by Messrs. Chapman and Hall in the year 1855.

John Ruskin on Browning in *Modern Painters*, Volume IV (1856)

John Ruskin, the spiritual father of the Pre-Raphaelites, had not been an uncritical admirer of Browning's poetry. When Men and Women *first appeared, Ruskin expressed his reservations to Browning and received a brisk reply, telling him to mind his own business. But the two men remained friends and Ruskin's stock rose when he pronounced Elizabeth Barrett Browning's* Aurora Leigh *to be the greatest poem in the language, surpassed perhaps by Shakespeare's plays but not by the sonnets.*

In 1856, Ruskin published the fourth volume of his five-volume Modern Painters. *He had already won his reputation by such books as his* Seven Lamps of Architecture (1849) *and* The Stones of Venice (1851-3). *In Chapter XX of this fourth volume of* Modern Painters, *Ruskin discusses the description of the Italian middle ages and the Renaissance in English writing. His praise falls not on* Men and Women *but on an earlier poem, 'The Bishop Orders his Tomb in St Praxed's Church', from* Dramatic Romances and Lyrics (1845). *In concluding, he certainly criticizes the problem presented by such 'concentrated writing'. Yet the lustre of the praise fell upon Browning's work as a whole.*

Thus Longfellow, in the Golden Legend, has entered more closely into the temper of the Monk, for good and for evil, than ever yet theological writer or historian, though they may have given their life's labour to the analysis: and, again, Robert Browning is unerring in every sentence he writes of the Middle Ages; always vital, right, and profound; so that in the matter of art, with which we have been specially concerned, there is hardly a principle connected with the mediæval temper, that he has not struck upon in those seemingly careless and too rugged rhymes of his. There is a curious instance, by the way, in a short poem referring to this very subject of tomb and image sculpture; and illustrating just one of those phases of local human character which, though belonging to Shakespere's own age, he never noticed, because it was specially Italian and un-English; connected also closely with the influence of mountains on the heart, and therefore with our immediate inquiries. I mean the kind of admiration with which a southern artist regarded the *stone* he worked in; and the pride which populace or priest took in the possession of precious mountain substance, worked into the pavements of their cathedrals, and the shafts of their tombs.

Observe, Shakespere, in the midst of architecture and tombs of wood, or freestone, or brass, naturally thinks of *gold* as the best enriching and ennobling substance for them;—in the midst also of the fever of the Renaissance he writes, as every one else did, in praise of precisely the most vicious master of that school—Giulio Romano; but the modern poet, living much in Italy, and quit of the Renaissance influence, is able fully to enter into the Italian feeling, and to see the evil of the Renaissance tendency, not because he is greater than Shakespere, but because he is in another element, and has *seen* other things. I miss fragments here and there not needed for my purpose in the passage quoted, without putting asterisks, for I weaken the poem enough by the omissions, without spoiling it also by breaks.

The Bishop orders his Tomb in St. Praxed's Church.

"As here I lie
In this state chamber, dying by degrees,
Hours, and long hours, in the dead night, I ask,
Do I live—am I dead? Peace, peace, seems all:
St. Praxed's ever was the church for peace.
And so, about this tomb of mine.   I fought
With tooth and nail to save my niche, ye know;
Old Gandolf* cozened me, despite my care.
Shrewd was that snatch from out the corner south
He graced his carrion with. . . .
Yet still my niche is not so cramped but thence
One sees the pulpit o'the epistle side,
And somewhat of the choir, those silent seats;
And up into the aery dome where live
The angels, and a sunbeam's sure to lurk.
And I shall fill my slab of basalt there,
And 'neath my tabernacle take my rest,
With those nine columns round me, two and two,
The odd one at my feet, where Anselm** stands;
Peach-blossom marble all.
Swift as a weaver's shuttle fleet our years:
Man goeth to the grave, and where is he?
Did I say basalt for my slab, sons?   Black—
'Twas ever antique-black† I meant!   How else

---

*The last bishop.   **His favourite son; nominally his nephew.
†"Nero Antico" is more familiar to our ears; but Browning does right in translating it; as afterwards "cipollino" into "onion-stone." Our stupid habit of using foreign words without translation is continually losing us half the force of the foreign language. How many travellers hearing the term "cipollino" recognize the intended sense of a stone splitting into concentric coats, like an onion?

Shall ye contrast my frieze to come beneath?
The bas-relief in bronze ye promised me,
Those Pans and Nymphs ye wot of, and perchance
Some tripod, thyrsus, with a vase or so,
The Saviour at his sermon on the mount,
St. Praxed in a glory, and one Pan, . . .
And Moses with the tables . . . but I know
Ye mark me not!   What do they whisper thee,
Child of my bowels, Anselm?   Ah, ye hope
To revel down my villas while I gasp,
Bricked o'er with beggar's mouldy travertine,
Which Gandolf from his tomb-top chuckles at!
Nay, boys, ye love me—all of jasper, then!
There's plenty jasper somewhere in the world—
And have I not St. Praxed's ear to pray
Horses for ye, and brown Greek manuscripts. . . .
That's if ye carve my epitaph aright,
Choice Latin, picked phrase, Tully's every word,
No gaudy ware like Gandolf's second line—
Tully, my masters? Ulpian serves *his* need."

I know no other piece of modern English, prose or poetry, in which
there is so much told, as in these lines, of the Renaissance spirit,—its
worldliness, inconsistency, pride, hypocrisy, ignorance of itself, love
of art, of luxury, and of good Latin. It is nearly all that I said of the
central Renaissance in thirty pages of the "Stones of Venice" put into
as many lines, Browning's being also the antecedent work. The worst
of it is that this kind of concentrated writing needs so much *solution*
before the reader can fairly get the good of it, that people's patience
fails them, and they give the thing up as insoluble; though, truly, it
ought to be the current of common thought like Saladin's talisman,
dipped in clear water, not soluble altogether, but making the element
medicinal.

An anonymous reviewer on 'A poet without a public' in *Chamber's Journal* (1863)

The publication of Selections from the Poetical Works of Robert
Browning *in 1863 was hardly an encouraging experience for their*

author. He had returned from Italy two years earlier on the death of Elizabeth Barrett Browning. Fifty-one years old, after thirty years of writing poetry, his sales were still small and reviews were often unenthusiastic. His contemporary, Tennyson, had been a household literary god for a dozen years. None of Browning's individual volumes had even sold well enough to need reprinting. But he worked with pertinacity and resolve, remarking that 'the horse goes round the mill'. He seemed indifferent to his predicament as Chamber's Journal *described it.*

It is probable that no man of our times has written so much and so well without general acknowledgment as Robert Browning. The poet whom poets love best often lacks the favourable voice of the public; but although his more ambitious efforts may be unknown to them, some song, or graceful line, at least, of his, is usually familiar in many a mouth that cannot tell from whom they come. It very rarely happens that *everything* a writer of genius pens is *'caviare* to the multitude,' but it happens sometimes, and it has done so in the case of the author we have mentioned. Mr. Browning is the poetic idol of men who give law to cliques and coteries. *The Athenæum* 'kotows' to him. Mr. Ruskin quotes from him at length in obvious admiration. Even at the university, where new poets find little acceptance, his exquisite verses are set by enthusiastic professors to be rendered into Greek by the candidates for the Classical Tripos. And yet we are afraid that not one in ten of the people who subscribe to *Mudie's*[9] have ever read a word of his writings. The reason of this is certainly not that they are not worth reading. They have great beauty, undoubted originality, and a dramatic vigour that is equalled by no poet living. The obstacles to his popularity are, on the other hand, manifold. He has chosen to make his dwelling in Italy, and to select from thence the subjects of his muse. His preference for that spot is undisguised, and, to Englishmen, almost repulsive. At all events, under such circumstances, a poet can scarcely expect to be accepted in his own country.

His topic being thus alien, to begin with, he takes pains to deprive it still more of interest by selecting the period of action two or three hundred years back or so, his favourite century being the sixteenth. Finally, he strains off his possible audience—select enough already— by writing in as involved a style as he can, with passing allusions to the most recondite matters—after the manner of Carlyle in his *French Revolution*—which he chooses to take for granted everybody must know all about.

E. P. Hood on Browning in the
Eclectic and Congregational Review (1863)

Despite the difficulty which many readers experienced in reading some of Browning's poems, he made headway by means of selections from – or collections of – his poetry. There had been one of these as early as 1849 and two were made in 1863. He doubted the success of them at first, as he wrote to the sculptor William Wetmore Story:

There's printing a book of 'Selections from R. B.' (SCULPTOR and poet) which is to popularize my old things; and So-and-so means to review it, and Somebody-or-other was always looking out for such an occasion, and What's-his-name always said he admired me, only he didn't say it, though he said something else every week of his life in some journal. The breath of man!

It was not the reviews that saved him. He returned to England as a widower and was cultivated by London society. He became something of a public figure, in part by association with the reputation of Elizabeth Barrett Browning. He was elected through Jowett's influence to an honorary Fellowship at Balliol. Whatever the critics might say of him, the sales of his books increased. 'Chapman says, "The new orders come from Oxford and Cambridge," and all my cultivators are young men.' There was a new mood among them, perhaps suggesting that Browning's moment had come. Edmund Gosse, a young man at the time, recalled the sentiment of the day:

There was an idea abroad, and it was not ill-founded, that in matters of taste the age in England had for some time been stationary, if not stagnant. It was necessary to wake people up.

Browning seemed like a newly discovered poet. E. P. Hood put the matter well in his review of May 1863, praising Browning while admitting his lack of popular appeal:

Robert Browning is one of the least known of our great modern writers, although his name has been now so long before the world; yet it may perhaps be questioned whether, with all his native prodigality and munificent endowment of thought,

scholarship, and genius, he is not better known as the husband
of Mrs Browning than by the productions of his own pen.

*Here and there Hood showed reservations about Browning's
approach to poetry and subject-matter. But at last the poet of* Men and
Women *had been publicly classed among 'our great modern writers'.
Much might be forgiven a reviewer who saw the truth of that. Hood
went on to point out the problems presented by Browning's poetry
but there was no mistaking a new sympathy in the tone of the
criticism.*

And here we touch at once the most prominent of those obstacles
interfering with the fame of Robert Browning. He writes for men—
for men and women—but not for Englishmen. He unconditions
himself from those circumstances which would attract English
readers, lives in other ages, and other countries, and with a power we
believe to be felicitously transparent and clear he seems to determine
on making himself obscure. In this particular there is a contradiction
between the essentially dramatic structure of his scenery and the
magnificent dramatic grandeur of the passions he portrays and
embodies, and the frequently involved tortuousness of his versification. A second thought shows us that this is indeed very natural to
his peculiar genius. How he delights to work and worm and wind his
way to the subtlest places of the soul, and to the mazy problems which
the soul is perpetually seeking to solve! His knowledge is most
recondite. Out-of-the-way magnificent scenes attract and claim and
charm him—great historic incidents and historical characters, though
great not by the rustle of the robe, or the clash of the armour along
the chief streets of history, but by the exhibition they have made of
the greatness of souls. He is a dramatist in all that we usually imply by
that word, entering into the innermost arena of the being. His poems
are, to quote the title of one of his dramas, *Soul tragedies*. We trust we
shall not be misunderstood when we say they present an order of
tragedy differing from Shakspeare's—the agony, the strife, the
internal stress are more internalised. He transfers the circumstances
of our being from the *without* to the *within*. In this way they all
become noble pictures of the striving and the attaining soul.

Walter Bagehot on *Dramatis Personae* (1864) in the *National Review* (1864)

Dramatis Personae *was Browning's first new book for nine years. It was dominated by three long poems, 'A Death in the Desert', 'Caliban upon Setebos', and 'Mr Sludge, "The Medium" '. The first of these is a dramatic monologue by St John, sixty-four years after the Crucifixion. He is the last man alive to have witnessed the events of the Gospels. 'How will it be when none more saith, "I saw"?' The question was of direct relevance to the Victorian debate on faith and doubt. Only at the end of the poem do we realize that even the follower who has preserved the saint's last words is to die next day in the Roman arena – 'Seeing that I to-morrow fight the beasts' – and must pass the manuscript on to someone else. The poem describes the events of the Gospels as historical truth. But how hard it will be in future for anyone to accept the documentary evidence, handed down through so many centuries.*

'Caliban upon Setebos; or, Natural Theology in the Island' reflects Browning's attempt to reconcile the idea of a benevolent Christian God with the evil and suffering that afflict humanity. But to treat the topic in the quirky childish babble of Shakespeare's monster wallowing in mud was hardly to the taste of Victorian 'High Seriousness'. Caliban talks of himself, like a small child, as 'he' rather than 'I'. In the end, he cowers at the thunder and lightning with which the island god Setebos punishes the monster's rebellion of the heart:

> White blaze –
> A tree's head snaps – and there, there, there, there, there,
> His thunder follows! Fool to gibe at him!
> Lo! 'Lieth flat and loveth Setebos!

'Mr Sludge, "The Medium" ' is a self-justification by a spiritualist medium who has been caught out as a cold and deliberate cheat:

> Now, don't, sir! Don't expose me! Just this once!
> This was the first and only time, I'll swear, –
> Look at me, – see, I kneel . . .

Even without Browning's enthusiastic visit to the Paris morgue in 'Apparent Failure', there was enough in this book to show, despite the power and modernity of the writing, that it scarcely conformed to any genteel Victorian idea of the 'poetical'. This was the world of Hugo, post-romanticism as the grotesque, or the Baudelaire of Fleurs du Mal. *Tennyson might safely be read aloud in the family groups of the drawing-room or the deanery. Mr Sludge's description of himself as a prostitute despising her customers and pimps was not likely to be the stuff of family entertainment:*

> Gratitude to these?
> The gratitude forsooth of a prostitute
> To the greenhorn and the bully-friends of hers.

To the young men, however, it was Browning who was sweeping forward to the future in subject-matter and treatment. Tennyson remained lost somewhere in the idyllic world of King Arthur, alias the late Prince Albert.

Walter Bagehot reviewed Dramatis Personae *in the* National Review *for November 1864. He admired Browning's skill but it was the skill of the grotesque. 'Grotesque', he wrote, 'shows you what ought to be by what ought not to be, when complete it reminds you of the perfect image, by showing you the distorted and imperfect image. Of this art we possess in the present generation one prolific master. Mr Browning is an artist working by incongruity.'*

Possibly hardly one of his most considerable efforts can be found which is not great because of its odd mixture. He puts together things which no one else would have put together, and produces on our minds a result which no one else would have produced, or tried to produce. He not only possesses superficial usable talents, but the strong something, the inner secret something which uses them and controls them; he is great, not in mere accomplishments, but in himself. He has applied a strong intellect to real life; he has applied the same intellect to the problems of his age. He has striven to know what *is*: he has endeavoured not to be cheated by counterfeits, not to be infatuated with illusions. His heart is in what he says. He has battered his brain against his creed till he believes it. He has accomplishments too, the more effective because they are mixed. He is at once a student of mysticism, and a citizen of the world. He brings to the club sofa distinct visions of old creeds, intense images of strange thoughts: he takes to the bookish student tidings of wild Bohemia, and little traces of the *demi-monde*. He puts down what is good for the naughty and what is naughty for the good. Over women his easier writings exercise that imperious power which belongs to the writings of a great man of the world upon such matters. He knows women, and therefore they wish to know him. If we blame many of Browning's efforts, it is in the interest of art, and not from a wish to hurt or degrade him. Mr. Browning has undertaken to describe what may be called *mind in difficulties*—mind set to make out the universe under the worst and hardest circumstances.

Mr. Browning possibly, and some of the worst of Mr. Browning's admirers certainly, will say that these grotesque objects exist in real life, and therefore they ought to be, at least may be, described in art. But though pleasure is not the end of poetry, pleasing is a condition of poetry. An exceptional monstrosity of horrid ugliness cannot be made pleasing, except it be made to suggest—to recall—the perfection, the beauty, from which it is a deviation. Perhaps in extreme cases no art is equal to this; but then such self-imposed problems should not be worked by the artist; these out-of-the-way and detestable subjects should be let alone by him. It is rather characteristic of Mr. Browning to neglect this rule. He is the most of a realist, and the least of an idealist of any poet we know.

R. W. Buchanan on *The Ring and the Book* (1868–9) in the *Athenaeum* (1869)

In March 1869, when he was already fifty-seven, Robert Browning emerged at last as the great English poet of his day and perhaps the greatest of the moderns anywhere. Publication of The Ring and the Book *was complete. It was his masterpiece. As if by some subconscious literary chemistry, he had fused all those elements in which he excelled. The story of this 'Roman murder' was based on a trial of 1698. Guido Franceschini, a middle-aged patrician of Arezzo, bought the twelve-year-old Pompilia from her parents as his bride. After five years of marital tyranny, she begged a young clergyman, Caponsacchi, to help her escape. Guido, cheated of his bargain, at length went to Rome with his 'bravoes'. They killed Pompilia's parents and inflicted fatal wounds on the girl herself. When charged with murder, Guido insisted that the law permitted a man to kill his adulterous wife. But Pope Innocent XII, the supreme arbiter and a figure of great humanity, decided in favour of Pompilia's innocence. Guido is dragged to his death:*

Abate, – Cardinal, – Christ, – Maria, – God, . . .
Pompilia, will you let them murder me?

*The poem presents the story through the words of the participants,
murderer and victim, onlookers and pontiff, rescuer and trial lawyers.
The drama and description are so intense that one can almost smell
and taste Browning's Rome, the burning tapers and the incense
smoke, the waxed wood and the hot streets. High society and common
crime, political intrigue and self-righteous sadism, mingle with
innocence and humanity. The crowds jostle for a sight of the
murdered corpses on the altar steps and take sides, for and against the
killers. Guido is one of Browning's best psychopaths since 'Porphyria's Lover'. He admits his fault to his judges. What he should have
done was to take steps earlier in training Pompilia to his will:*

If I, – instead of threatening, talking big . . .
Had, with the vulgarest household implement,
Calmly and quietly, cut off, clean thro' bone,
But one joint of one finger of my wife . . .

*Had he cut off a finger joint every time Pompilia looked at another
man, says Guido, she might now be a little awkward at needlework.
But she would still be alive – surely better than being dead with
fingers intact. Guido talks – like Porphyria's lover – with the
unanswerable logic of the morally insane:*

Why, there had followed a quick sharp scream, some pain,
Much calling for plaster, damage to the dress,
A somewhat sulky countenance next day,
Perhaps reproaches, – but reflections too!

*The Ring and the Book showed the brilliance and corruption of
Roman society, mental analysis worthy of great fiction, and the
sweeping genius of a writer in total command of his art. A modern
reviewer might simply call it a page-turner. Browning's contemporaries were more eloquent in their praise. Swinburne wrote to his friend
Richard Monckton Milnes, Lord Houghton:*

What a wonderful work this is of Browning's. I tore through the
first volume in a day of careful study, with a sense of absolute
possession. I have not felt so strongly that delightful sense of
being mastered – dominated – by another man's work since I
was a small boy. I always except, of course, Victor Hugo's which
has the same force and insight and variety of imagination

together with that exquisite bloom and flavour of the highest poetry which Browning's has not: though it has perhaps a more wonderful subtlety at once and breadth of humorous invention and perception. As for the interest, it simply kills all other matters of thought for the time. This is his real work – big enough to give him breathing-space, whereas in play or song he is alike cramped. It is of the mixed-political composite-dramatic order which alone suits him and serves him.

Browning was used to hostility and said so in the first book of his poem:

> Well, British Public, ye who like me not,
> (God love you!) and will have your proper laugh
> At the dark question, laugh it! I laugh first.

Instead, there was praise on all sides. The American poet Sidney Lanier wrote in 1870 that Browning caught and held his reader with the skill of a lasso. Even the Athenaeum, *which had never found much good in him, made amends.*

At last, the *opus magnum* of our generation lies before the world— the 'ring is rounded'; and we are left in doubt which to admire most, the supremely precious gold of the material or the wondrous beauty of the workmanship. The fascination of the work is still so strong upon us, our eyes are still so spell-bound by the immortal features of Pompilia (which shine through the troubled mists of the story with almost insufferable beauty), that we feel it difficult to write calmly and without exaggeration; yet we must record at once our conviction, not merely that *The Ring and the Book* is beyond all parallel the supremest poetical achievement of our time, but that it is the most precious and profound spiritual treasure that England has produced since the days of Shakspeare. Its intellectual greatness is as nothing compared with its transcendent spiritual teaching. Day after day it grows into the soul of the reader, until all the outlines of thought are brightened and every mystery of the world becomes more and more softened into human emotion. Once and for ever must critics dismiss the old stale charge that Browning is a mere intellectual giant, difficult of comprehension, hard of assimilation. This great book *is* difficult of comprehension, *is* hard of assimilation; not because it is obscure— every fibre of the thought is clear as day; not because it is intellectual,—and it is intellectual in the highest sense,—but because the capacity to comprehend such a book must be spiritual; because, although a child's brain might grasp the general features of the picture, only a purified nature could absorb and feel its profoundest meanings. The man who tosses it aside because it is 'difficult' is simply adopting a subterfuge to hide his moral littleness, not his mental incapacity. It would be unsafe to predict anything concerning a production so many-sided; but we quite believe that its true public lies outside the literary circle, that men of inferior capacity will grow by the aid of it, and that feeble women, once fairly initiated into the mystery, will cling to it as a succour passing all succour save that which is purely religious.

H. B. Forman on 'Browning's poetry' in the *London Quarterly Review* (1869)

If confirmation of Browning's new literary fame were needed, it came from the ungrudging praise of The Ring and the Book *by such critics as Henry Buxton Forman, a senior civil servant in the Post Office who was also an editor of Keats and Shelley. He was later a party to the notorious literary forgeries of Thomas James Wise. Ironically, the first of these was a bogus edition of Elizabeth Barrett Browning's* Sonnets from the Portuguese, *which was apparently three years earlier than the accepted first edition. Buxton Forman and Wise had no scruples about cheating wealthy book-collectors and dealers, but their enthusiasm for Browning's poetry seems entirely genuine.*

The idea that epics have 'died out with Agamemnon and the goat-nursed gods', is one which is obviously absurd, even without practical evidence to the contrary, and has arisen from the false notion that 'heroic' is a term applicable only to wars and large actions. Now that Walt Whitman[10] has written the Epic of Democracy on the other side of the Atlantic, and Browning, on this side, has furnished what may be fitly termed the Epic of Psychology, the idea of the decease of the epic is more than ever a dead idea. The day has long gone by when heroism meant pugilism, and the might of man was measured by magnitude of muscle. Breadth of mind and width of heart

come first now, and the largest action is not that which covers the
greatest area and deploys the largest aggregate of physical powers,
but that which involves most disinterestedness, philanthropy, purity
of heart, power of thought—in short, the maximum of intellectual
and moral force. For such a display, one set of modern men and
women serves as well as another for types; and the Roman murder
case of 150 years ago, which has so strongly taken hold of Browning,
was the germ of what is more essentially modern than any great
poetic production of these latter centuries.

That we have not done critical justice to *The Ring and the Book*
we are sensible. The value of a work of this magnitude from a poet
with the wide artistic powers, and the 'intellectual equipment' which
we find in Browning, is not easy to estimate, when we take into
consideration the range of a powerful poet's influence, not only on
his contemporaries, but also on those to come in the long roll of the
onward centuries.

An anonymous reviewer on *Red Cotton Night-Cap Country* (1873) in the *Spectator* (1873)

*Browning's fame was secure after 1869 but this did not prevent him
from coming under attack for his choice of subject-matter and
treatment in later poems.* Red Cotton Night-Cap Country *was his
story of the jeweller, Mellerio (Miranda in the poem), who burnt his
hands off in an act of remorse for an illicit love affair, then went back
to his mistress and finally threw himself off the tower of his country
house, convinced that the Virgin would bear him up and restore the
age of faith by a public miracle in the skies of Normandy.*

*It is hard to read the poem without thinking of Zola, Maupassant,
and the new French fiction. The work was condemned for much the
same reasons as those two writers. The American novelist and tourist
William Dean Howells dismissed it in the* Atlantic Monthly *for July
1873 as a story that was:*

horrible and revolting in itself; and it is so told as to bring out its
worst with a far-reaching insinuation, and an occasional frantic
rush at expression of its unseemliness for which the manure-
heap offers the proper imagery of 'dung' and 'devil's dung'. We

suppose we shall be told of power in the story; and power there undeniably is, else no one could be dragged through the book by it. . . . The poem – if it is a poem – is as unhandsome as it is unwholesome; it is both bad art and bad taste, and it is to be defended, it seems to us, neither as a lesson from a miserable fact, nor as a successful bit of literary realism.

In the following month, the reviewer in Harper's Magazine *made a point of not having read the book through. It was not necessary, in his opinion:*

We have read enough to know both the story and the manner in which it is told, and to enter our strong protest against the endeavour to glorify an illicit love with one who had been in succession a profligate woman and an unfaithful wife. . . . It can only be characterized as harmless because the class of people who would be liable to be harmed by it will not understand it nor even read it.

Browning ignored such prudery, which insists on the one hand that a book is utterly tedious and unreadable, on the other that it is scandalous and dangerous. In this case an American Mrs Grundy tried to have her cake and eat it. Moreover, profligate women and unfaithful wives had been a mainstay of literature from Helen of Troy and Clytemnestra down to Emma Bovary. Clara, in Browning's poem, is a mere amateur in sin compared with certain ladies who adorned the classical curriculum of Victorian schools. But reviews like these stamped Browning as the author who chose 'morbid anatomy' as his profession. This was and always had been true, since Madhouse Cells *in 1834. But a new moral righteousness began to gather in the 1870s and 1880s which, for example, sent Henry Vizetelly to prison for daring to publish Maupassant and Zola in English. The rebellion of the young in the 1860s – as, indeed, in the 1960s – had given way to a more sanctimonious middle age. Even the relatively urbane review in the* Spectator, *on 10 May 1873, confirmed this.*

As to style, we must add that there is far less of obscurity, but also far less of fitful eloquence, than usual with Mr. Browning. There is the same faulty, short-hand, article-eliminating hurry of style, as if the poet had to get his story told within a certain number of minutes, and every superfluous word, and many words by no means superfluous, must therefore be left to the reader to guess at. But there are very few passages the meaning of which is not quite clear at the second reading, and as our extract will have shown, there are some of great subtlety and intellectual vivacity. Still Mr. Browning has not succeeded in giving any true poetic excuse for telling a story so full of disagreeable elements. When told, it fails to purify, as tragedy should, 'by pity and by fear'.

G. K. Chesterton on 'Browning in later life' and 'The philosophy of Browning' in *Robert Browning* (1903)

Henry James's comment at the time of Browning's death in 1889, 'none of the odd ones have been so great and none of the great ones so odd' was not a general view. To the world, Browning was the optimist of the poker-work motto, insisting that God's in His heaven all's right with the world, or that a man's reach should exceed his grasp, or urging his readers to grow old along with me the best is yet to be. Perhaps it is enough to say that 'God's in His heaven' is something of an irony, taken from Pippa Passes, *whose principal topics are murder, adultery, prostitution, and political assassination.*

G. K. Chesterton went beyond mottoes and recitation pieces. He found the prime theme of Browning's poetry to be the anatomy of human nature and conduct, by a poet who worked among the debris like a cheerful and unperturbed pathologist in his private mortuary.

If the heavens had fallen, and all the waters of the earth run with blood, he would still have been interested in existence, if possible a little more so. He is a great poet of human joy for precisely the reason of which Mr. Santayana complains: that his happiness is primal, and beyond the reach of philosophy. He is something far more convincing, far more comforting, far more religiously significant than an optimist: he is a happy man.

This happiness he finds, as every man must find happiness, in his own way. He does not find the great part of his joy in those matters in which most poets find felicity. He finds much of it in those matters in which most poets find ugliness and vulgarity. He is to a considerable extent the poet of towns. "Do you care for nature much?" a friend of his asked him. "Yes, a great deal," he said, "but for human beings a great deal more." Nature, with its splendid and soothing sanity, has the power of convincing most poets of the essential worthiness of things. There are few poets who, if they escaped from the rowdiest waggonette of trippers, could not be quieted again and exalted by dropping into a small wayside field. The speciality of Browning is rather that he would have been quieted and exalted by the waggonette.

Chesterton's curiosity extended to Browning's success in avoiding censorship or restriction of his work. He had, of course, received unfavourable reviews and a few moral rebukes. But he had escaped the kind of clamour that papers like the Methodist Times *directed against Zola and Henry James. The National Vigilance Association set up in 1886, in succession to the Society for the Suppression of Vice, was dedicated to cleaning up English life and literature. Prosecutions had been brought by both organizations on the most trivial grounds. Browning had slipped by without so much as a comment. To Chesterton that seemed most remarkable. Even in 1903, he prudently declines to quote the poems whose coarseness might have given such offence.*

The same peculiarity ought, as I have said, to have been apparent to any one who knew anything of Browning's literary work. A great number of his poems are marked by a trait of which by its nature it is more or less impossible to give examples. Suffice it to say that it is truly extraordinary that poets like Swinburne (who seldom uses a gross word) should have been spoken of as if they had introduced moral license into Victorian poetry. What the Nonconformist conscience has been doing to have passed Browning is something difficult to imagine. But the peculiarity of this occasional coarseness in his work is this—that it is always used to express a certain wholesome fury and contempt for things sickly, or ungenerous, or unmanly. The poet seems to feel that there are some things so contemptible that you can only speak of them in pothouse words. It would be idle, and perhaps undesirable, to give examples; but it may be noted that the same brutal physical metaphor is used by his Caponsacchi about the people who could imagine Pompilia impure and by his Shakespeare in "At the Mermaid," about the claim of the Byronic poet to enter into the heart of humanity. In both cases Browning feels, and perhaps in a manner rightly, that the best thing we can do with a sentiment essentially base is to strip off its affectations and state it basely, and that the mud of Chaucer is a great deal better than the poison of Sterne.

Donald Thomas on 'The madhouse and the shrine' in *Robert Browning: A Life within Life* (1982)

To explain the poetry of a writer of Browning's type by 'practical criticism' would be self-defeating. The key to it, as Henry James suggested, lay in the possession of its author. That he lived a double life was the general opinion of those who knew him. He was sometimes the hearty dinner-guest and sometimes the poet of solitary, often macabre preoccupations. Those who met him in society sometimes found it hard to believe that this could be the same man as the creator of the poems.

It is not always the case that the illumination of poetry comes from the life of its author. We know too little of Shakespeare, let alone Homer or Virgil. But in Browning's case biography is the principal means of literary investigation. Conversely the life of such a literary figure, as opposed to a politician or a man of action, is revealed far more through his art than in letters or public achievements. The following passage endeavours to characterize the private Browning – the poet – as opposed to the booming guest of house-party and dinner-table, who complained jokingly that he had 'dinnered' his life away.

It was not remarkable that a poet should keep his private creative life and his public appearances well separated. What caused the comments in Browning's case, during his last thirty years, was the absolute distinction between the interior world of his days and the embarrassment of the bonhomous philistinism with which he 'dinnered himself away' in fashionable society, night after night. Henry James devised a theory of two Brownings, as if he were a literary Jekyll and a philistine Hyde. Gladstone's daughter Mary, meeting him at dinner, knew that this could not be the poet Browning. 'He talks everybody down with his dreadful voice, and always places his person in such disagreeable proximity with yours and puffs and blows and spits in yr. face. I tried to think of Abt Vogler but it was of no use – he couldn't ever have written it.'

There could have been no more fascinating subject for a dramatic monologue than Browning's own account of the two conflicting dispositions which he bore within him. Yet, if Burne-Jones was to be believed, the truth was clear enough. According to Mary Gladstone, Burne-Jones reassured her when he 'called Browning's outside "moss", and said the works of a man were his real self'.

However, the resolution of that psychological conflict merely lays the way open to a moral one, of which 'Madhouse Cells' was the first example. Browning was the public Liberal and the anti-vivisectionist, nobly abhorrent of cruelty towards human beings or animals: but the human potentiality for cruelty and oppression in its most bizarre forms fascinated him as strongly as it had Nathaniel Wanley two centuries before and perhaps more than any other single theme in his own work. As Alfred Domett reported, Browning collected those instruments which were devised for the infliction of pain or death. Humanitarianism did not inhibit him, for instance, from allowing Half-Rome in *The Ring and the Book* to discuss with relish the brutal refinements of the dagger which stabbed Pompilia and her parents, the wounds now on display upon the chancel steps. That Genoese weapon is equipped with tiny hook-teeth which spring open as the blade enters the flesh and rip wide the wound as it is drawn out again.

The deeper fascination for Browning lay in the moral incongruity of such horrors, and the problems which they posed about the aberrations of the human mind. In his poem 'A Forgiveness', in *Pacchiarotto and How he Worked in Distemper* (1876), he combines the study of mentality and morality, as if to encompass all mankind in a madhouse cell. The poem meditates on one of the oddest works of man's hand. Knives, guns, whips, daggers, are employed to cause death or suffering. Why, then, are they made with such loving and decorative art, as if they were the finest expression of the human spirit?

> I think there never was such – how express? –
> Horror coquetting with voluptuousness,
> As in those arms of Eastern workmanship –
> Yataghan, kandjar, things that rend and rip,
> Gash rough, slash smooth, help hate so many ways,
> Yet ever keep a beauty that betrays

Love still at work with the artificer
Throughout his quaint devising. Why prefer,
Except for love's sake, that a blade should writhe
And bicker like a flame?

Browning devoted some fifty years to considering that last question in one form or another. In doing so he touched upon a most sensitive nerve of moral philosophy in the world of new philanthropic pretensions. Was it not enough, in the course of war or crime, that men and women should be put to death or tortured? Why was it necessary that the implements used should be embellished with such affection by the artist or craftsman?

It was a distinctively modern misgiving. The shield of Achilles and the weapons of the besieging Greeks had not caused Homer such moral qualms: nor could there be equivocation on the part of those who abominated such devices altogether. The terms in which Browning writes are those of a post-romantic age. Yet what is 'Horror conquetting with voluptuousness,' in 'Porphyria's Lover' or *The Ring and the Book*, but the literal counterpart to Hugo's metaphor of *Beauty and the Beast*?

In the closed world of his poetic imagination, the moral beauty of sexual love and the moral bestiality of the psychopath drew Browning's most powerful responses. That this should be the case was in part a matter of personality, in part the romantic inheritance. The decades before Browning's birth, no less than those of his youth, had been a period of philanthropic aspiration in European culture and society alike. Yet the moral disturbance which the Marquis de Sade provoked in literature was seen no less in the great canvases of Delacroix or a painting like Goya's *The Throat-Slitting* of 1810–12. Beauty or voluptuousness, in Goya's painting, for example, is represented by the captured woman in the cave, kneeling bound and naked but for her stockings. The two bandits are naked too and the events preceding this moment are powerfully suggested. The horror or brutality is summed up by the dead body of the woman's husband or companion, and the bandit who drags back her head by the hair, the better to apply his knife to her throat now that he has no further use for her.

To an earlier or a later age, such scenes (whether by Goya or Browning) were better not depicted. A gentler age would find them unendurable, a more barbaric age might think them mundane. It was in the romantic period and its aftermath that the moral conjunction of philanthropy and savagery fused with such power in the darker dramas of poetry or visual art.

Browning did not seek to justify his preoccupation with the tyrant, the cheat, or the psychopath in such terms. He shared with the romantics a curiosity about the odder freaks and motives of personality, the deviant paths that led by one route to love or holiness, by another to righteous cruelty or moral cynicism. Yet he saw himself no less as a beneficiary of the great Puritan tradition which endorsed his enthusiasms with the theological imperative of Original Sin. By his own account, it was this that gave the impetus to his religious and literary creeds. Puritanism offered an intellectual framework to a study of human oddity which might otherwise have seemed merely the inquisitiveness of the dilettante. At the heart of such faith was a central tenet. In 'Gold Hair: A Story of Pornic' from *Dramatis Personae* (1864), he describes it simply and specifically.

Original Sin.
The Corruption of Man's Heart.

Browning was not a formally religious poet any more than he was a pure romantic idealist. His role was to diagnose the corruption or the moral incongruity of human conduct, to be the pathologist rather than the healer. To that extent he had more in common with Sade than with Wordsworth, a greater affinity with Nathaniel Wanley than with Bunyan.

In 'Ned Bratts', published in *Dramatic Idylls* (1879), Browning elaborates the moral paradox about the beauty of implements designed to cause death or pain. As a dispassionate observer he describes men and women crowding eagerly to watch seventeenth-century Puritans branded on the face, or flogged, or having their noses slit off, 'just leaving enough to tweak'. He calls the occasion 'things at jolly high-tide, amusement steeped in fire'.

A reader of his poetry might reasonably wonder whether such ferocity appealed only to the figures of the poetry and not to the author. Observers of his impatient energy and bitter invective noted how hostility was apt to be expressed in images of physical violence. In imagination, if not in reality, it was Browning himself who appeared to prefer his excitement 'steeped in fire'.

NOTES

1 Origen, AD 185-253, Christian thinker of the Alexandrian school who was subsequently held to be heretical. He suggested that the stars are

living beings to whom God has given souls which were already in existence.

2 Bryan Walter Proctor (1787-1874) wrote under the pseudonym of Barry Cornwall. In 1838 he published an edition of the works of Ben Jonson with a memoir.

3 Alexander Smith (1830-67), Scottish poet whose *Life Drama* (1853) caused him to be satirized as one of 'The Spasmodic School' by W. E. Aytoun in the mock-tragic *Firmilian: or, The Student of Badajoz* (1854).

4 Philip James Bailey (1816-1902), author of *Festus*, 1839-93, regarded as the father of 'The Spasmodic School', published *The Mystic* in 1855 and made it part of his larger poem.

5 *malice prepense* – intent to injure.

6 Friedrich Freiherr von Flotow (1812-83), German composer of tuneful opera: *Le Naufrage de la Méduse* (1839); *Stradella* (1844); *Martha* (1847).

7 'He stood and watched the cobbler at his trade ...' The passage is quoted from Browning's poem, 'How It Strikes a Contemporary'.

8 Robert Burford (1792-1861), painter and proprietor of panoramas in Leicester Square and the Strand from 1827, often painted from scenes sketched by him in other European capitals.

9 Charles Mudie (1818-90), stationer and bookseller, was the founder of Mudie's Lending Library in 1842. Its power to impose literary taste through its choice of books was attacked by George Moore in *Circulating Morals: or, Literature at Nurse* (1885).

10 Walt Whitman's *Leaves of Grass* first appeared in 1855 but was subsequently expanded.

3

Arnold

Matthew Arnold's poetry spanned a period of twenty years, from *The Strayed Reveller* in 1849 until the appearance of *Poems* in 1869. Thereafter, he was known as the Arnold of *Culture and Anarchy* (1869) and two series of *Essays in Criticism* (1865 and 1888). He came to poetry with all the qualifications of a scholar and a gentleman. Indeed, when Charles Kingsley reviewed *The Strayed Reveller and Other Poems* in 1849, he remarked that the book, whose author was known only as 'A', was 'evidently the work of a scholar, a gentleman, and a true poet. The short pieces which it contains show care and thought, delicate finish, and an almost faultless severity of language and metre.'

This comment illuminated the strength and weakness of Arnold's poetry. His education at Rugby and Balliol left him with every classical verse-form and metre at his disposal. He won the Newdigate Prize for poetry at Oxford as an undergraduate in 1843. But criticism of his poetry often hovered close to the two fatal descriptions, 'academic' and 'dilettante'. He was correct and meticulous, neither extravagant nor vulgar. Mr. Sludge, 'The Medium' or Guido Franceschini would never have got into one of Arnold's poems.

His greatest gift was for subtle resonance of mood and landscape. He was wistfully elegiac and evocative in his poetry. But the sales of his early work were even worse than those of Browning's *Sordello*, numbering only a few dozen copies of the five hundred printed. Arnold withdrew *The Strayed Reveller* from circulation. He did the same with his second book, *Empedocles on Etna and Other Poems* (1852).

In 1853 he published a selection from the two withdrawn books as *Poems*, including two new pieces, 'Sohrab and Rustum' and 'The Scholar-Gipsy'. J. A. Froude, who was no admirer of the pastiche classicism of *Empedocles on Etna*, wrote in the *Westminster Reveiw* that 'Sohrab and Rustum' alone 'would have settled the position which Mr Arnold has a right to claim as a poet'. At the same time, Coventry Patmore commended 'The Scholar-Gipsy' to his readers.

'We would ask all lovers of poetry to read it and see whether it does not touch their hearts with a sense of fresh beauty, such as one feels on first looking over a new kind of country.' It did. With a handful of Arnold's other individual pieces, it remained a truly popular poem among English readers.

By no means all the poetry which Arnold had written at this time was in print. 'Dover Beach', one of the most natural and eloquent statements of personal doubt, was held back until *New Poems* in 1867. Nevertheless, the volumes of shorter poems in the 1850s were generally well received. Formal works like the tragedy *Merope* (1857) were not. *Fraser's Magazine*, in June 1858, complained that it was too much a mere imitation of the Greeks. George Lewes in the *Leader* liked the poetry but thought the tragic form a 'mistake'.

New Poems (1867) and *Poems* (1869) were well received by critics like Leslie Stephen, who noted Arnold's harmony, noble manner, and 'sombre yet elevated pathos'. With ambiguous generosity, he remarked, 'The poetic light shines in a tranquil air.' That was both the appeal and the limitation of Arnold's verse.

Like most Victorians, Arnold suffered at the hands of his critics in the early twentieth century. The less formal poems, elegiac, pastoral, idyllic, never lost their popularity in anthologies of English verse. But F. R. Leavis cut him dead in 1932. In the following year, T. S. Eliot wrote of him as a man who 'had neither walked in hell nor been rapt to heaven'. His poetry 'is academic poetry in the best sense; the best fruit which can issue from the promise shown by the prize-poem'. But Eliot, more characteristically generous than Leavis, saw the intimate and reflective virtues of Arnold's writing. Such appreciations stimulated a new discrimination between the formal classical exercise and the true poetry.

In 1939, the publication of Lionel Trilling's *Matthew Arnold*, written with a strong sense of the historical and social context of the subject, opened the way for both appreciation and enjoyment of Arnold's poetry in the new enthusiasm for Victorian literature that developed after the Second World War.

Charles Kingsley on *The Strayed Reveller and Other Poems* (1849) in *Fraser's Magazine* (1849)

Kingsley's review of Arnold's first collection of poems is by no means all hostile. But Kingsley's sense of moral purpose was a match for

Arnold's own. He admires the 'simple naturalness' of 'The Forsaken Merman'. But he finds Arnold's best poetry buried among a welter of imitation classicism and intellectual self-indulgence. What is the use of it? What do we want, Kingsley asks, with an aimless piece like 'Resignation, to Fausta', which he later describes as 'a yawn thirteen pages long, with which the volume finally falls fast asleep, and vanishes in a snore'?

But he begins with 'The Forsaken Merman', a fine poem and a haunting fable, in which a merman and his children lament for their mermaid who has been enticed ashore at Easter by the religion of humankind and will never return. Compared with this, the classical imitations are cold and dead.

We are not ashamed to confess that this poem 'upset' us. We have seldom read deeper or healthier pathos in the English language. The half-human, simple affection of the husband, the wonderful church-yard scene, the confusion of feeling and arrangement in the former part of the poem, and the return to the simple and measured melody of resignation in the close, are all perfect. And consciously or unconsciously, probably the latter, there is in it 'godly doctrine, and profitable for these days,' when the great heresy of 'Religion *versus* God' is creeping on more subtilly than ever: by which we mean the setting up of forms of worship and systems of soul-saving in opposition to the common instincts and affections of humanity, divine, because truly human; in opposition to common honesty and justice, mercy and righteousness; in short, in opposition to God. Any one who opens just now the leading religious periodicals on any side of the question, and has human eyes to see and a human heart to feel, will not be at a loss to understand our drift. The poet may have had no such intentional meaning; but no man can write true poetry, that is true nature, without striking on some eternal key in harmony with the deepest laws of the universe.

But having praised thus far, we must begin to complain. To what purpose all the self-culture through which the author must have passed ere this volume could be written? To what purpose all the pure and brilliant imagination with which God has gifted him? What is the fruit thereof? When we have read all he has to say, what has he taught us? What new light has he thrown on man or nature, the past awful ages or this most awful present one, when the world is heaving and moaning in the agonies, either of a death-struggle, or a new birth-hour more glorious than that which the sixteenth century beheld? Is he, too, like our friends the fashionable novelists, content to sit and fiddle while Rome is burning? Can he tell us no more about the French Revolution than—

> Yet, when I muse on what life is, I seem
> Rather to patience prompted, than that proud
> Prospect of hope which France proclaims so loud;
> France, famed in all great arts, in none supreme.
> Seeing this vale, this earth, whereon we dream,
> Is on all sides o'ershadow'd by the high
> Uno'erleap'd mountains of Necessity,
> Sparing us narrower margin than we deem.
> Nor will that day dawn at a human nod.
> &c. &c.?

Who ever expected that it would? What does the age want with fragments of an Antigone? or with certain 'New Sirens?'—little certainly with these last, seeing that the purport of them is utterly undiscoverable (as is, alas! a great deal more of the volume)—or with sleepy, melancholy meditations, not really on a 'Gipsy-Child,' but on his own feelings about the said child? or with *fainéant* grumblings at the 'credulous zeal' of one Critias, who reasonably enough complains:—

> Why in these mournful rhymes,
> Learn'd in more languid climes,
> Blame our activity,
> Who with such passionate will
> Are what we are meant to be?

What, indeed, do we want with the 'Strayed Reveller' itself, beautiful as it is, a long line of gorgeous and graceful classic sketches, with a moral, if any, not more hopeful than that of Tennyson's 'Lotos-Eaters'? We say if any, for, in too many of these poems, it is very difficult to get at any clear conception of the poet's idea. The young poets, now-a-days, are grown so wondrous wise, that our weak brains have to flee for the intelligible to Shakespeare and Milton, Bacon and Kant. Would that the rising generation would bear in mind that dictum of Coleridge's (which he did not, alas! always bear in mind himself in his prose), that perplexed words are the sure index of perplexed thoughts, and that the only reason why a man cannot express a thing plainly, is, that he does not see it plainly.

W. E. Aytoun on *The Strayed Reveller and Other Poems* (1849) in *Blackwood's Magazine* (1849)

W. E. Aytoun was an Edinburgh barrister, a dramatic poet and editor of ballads, and Professor of Rhetoric at Edinburgh University in 1845. He was a regular contributor to Blackwood's Magazine, *started in 1817 to rival the* Edinburgh Review. *In September 1849 he contributed a critique of Matthew Arnold's first book. He discusses more dispassionately than Charles Kingsley the difficulties and restrictions faced by a modern poet who takes classical antiquity as his model. The public school curriculum included the composition of Latin and Greek verse. There is, Aytoun hints, still too much of this exercise about Arnold's poetry, while Tennyson in his Hellenic subjects avoids it.*

The *Strayed Reveller* is rather a curious compound of imitation. He claims to be a classical scholar of no mean acquirements, and a good deal of his inspiration is traceable to the Greek dramatists. In certain of his poems he tries to think like Sophocles, and has so far succeeded as to have constructed certain choric passages, which might be taken by an unlettered person for translations from the antique. The language, though hard, is rather stately; and many of the individual images are by no means destitute of grace. The epithets which he employs bear the stamp of the Greek coinage; but, upon the whole, we must pronounce these specimens failures. The images are not bound together or grouped artistically, and the rhythm which the author has selected is, to an English ear, utterly destitute of melody. It is strange that people cannot be brought to understand that the genius and capabilities of one language differ essentially from those of another: and that the measures of antiquity are altogether unsuitable for modern verse. It is no doubt possible, by a Procrustean operation, to force words into almost any kind of mould; a chorus may be constructed, which, so far as scanning goes, might satisfy the requirements of a pedagogue, but the result of the experiment will inevitably show that melody has been sacrificed in the attempt. Now melody is a charm without which poetry is of little worth; we are not quite sure whether it would not be more correct to say, that without melody poetry has no existence. Our author does not seem to have the slightest idea of this.

Mr Tennyson, to whom, as we shall presently have occasion to observe, this author is indebted for another phase of his inspiration, has handled classical subjects with fine taste and singular delicacy; and his 'Ulysses' and 'Œnone' show how beautifully the Hellenic idea may be wrought out in mellifluous English verse. But Tennyson knows his craft too well to adopt either the Greek phraseology or the Greek rhythm. Even in the choric hymns which he has once or twice attempted, he has spurned halt and ungainly metres, and given full freedom and scope to the cadence of his mother tongue.

G. D. Boyle on *Empedocles on Etna* (1852) in the *North British Review* (1853)

Arnold's second book, also published under the monogram 'A', was received in much the same way as The Strayed Reveller. *By no means all the comments of reviewers were unappreciative. Arnold appeared capable of fine poetry but he was too self-centred and indifferent to the real world. His imitations of classical antiquity, graceful in parts, lacked any true animating spark. The present review, in March 1853, says bluntly of the long dramatic poem which gives the volume its title: ' "Empedocles on Etna" is an utter mistake.' The question was whether Arnold could break free of such self-imposed constraint. G. D. Boyle sums up this concern:*

'A' constantly disappoints us. We are in hopes all throughout his volumes that we are about to be delighted with a flow of melody, or a noble train of sentiment. He is often on the verge of excellence. He has been astride Pegasus. We can hardly venture to assert that he has ridden him.

Boyle's review also reflects the dominant influence of Tennyson in English poetry by 1853, which even Arnold cannot avoid. But there is a suggestion at the end that the philosophic and reflective qualities of Arnold's poems, with their subtle evocation of landscape, are more plausibly derived from Wordsworth.

It would be ungenerous to omit mention of an improvement which has taken place in the tone of many of our writers of verse. That there is often a delicacy and purity of feeling, a desire after noble objects of ambition, and what is better than either, an earnest and sometimes pathetic expression of sympathy for the wants of the poor, few of those who are in the habit of bestowing attention on the literature of the day will feel inclined to deny. For the higher attributes and mysterious qualities of song, we look in vain. But at least let us be grateful for the absence of misanthropical monodies, and voluptuous love songs. There is another peculiarity in many of the recently published volumes of verses, which can hardly fail to force itself on the notice of every reader. We mean the unmistakable traces which they bear of the influence exercised on his age and contemporaries by Mr. Tennyson. When the earlier poems of Tennyson first made their appearance, the admirers and disciples of the sensational school claimed their author for themselves. In his more recent productions, however, the poet has shown himself in an entirely new light. The debatable land that lies between the regions of sensation and the regions of thought, Mr. Tennyson has fairly claimed to hold. Where a great genius walks securely, how few there be that can follow! In the efforts of the pupils there is a want of proportion, and an absence of harmony which render the varied ease and facile gracefulness of the master only more apparent. It is far from unnatural that the younger portion of the community should fix their admiration on the poet who is nearest them. Grave seniors may hint at the propriety of rigid adherence to classic models, and point to 'the pure well of English undefiled,'—but in spite of all that has been, or that can be said, the poet whose verse comes bounding over the soul, who is continually in the thoughts and language of youth, must be he who has felt the difficulties, and perhaps solved the problems of the present time. There is one, it is true, who is for all ages and for all times, but it is rare to discover that the first affections of male or female students of poetry centre in Shakespeare. 'Knowledge comes, but wisdom lingers.'

But it is time to turn from our somewhat desultory reflections and introduce our readers to 'A.'

The Strayed Reveller has been before the world for some time, and was, we believe, favourably noticed by more than one journal, on its first appearance. It is in all respects a pleasing and interesting collection. The writer, evidently a man of high culture, gave in this volume a promise of excellence which, we regret to say, his last production, *Empedocles on Etna*, has not fulfilled. The poems in the first volume, as regards smoothness of rhythm, and elaboration of style, are strikingly superior to those of the second. Nor is the philosophy and general tone of the *Reveller* improved in *Empedocles*. An indolent, selfish quietism pervades everything that 'A.' has written, mars the pleasure of the reader, and provokes him into thinking severe thoughts about the poet. But 'A.' is a poet. He has held deep communion with nature. He has studied in a way that we wish was more common than it is. From the works of Sophocles, and Homer, Goethe, and Wordsworth, he has gathered fruits, and he has garnished his gains with fresh blooming flowers of his own. The *Strayed Reveller* is an imitation of the antique. Though containing some fine imagery, there is little which we care to extract. A 'Fragment from an Antigone' is well executed, but hardly worth the trouble which must have been bestowed upon it.

There are indications throughout these volumes that the glorious scenery which surrounds the English lakes has especial attraction for 'A.' When we next meet with him, we trust that his poetry will exhibit more than it does at present of the severe manliness and exalted tone which must ever be associated in the minds of lovers of poetry with the hills and dales of Westmoreland. Less of aversion to action in all its forms,—greater sympathy with the wants of the present generation, will endear him to many who would now turn away contemptuously from the self-complacent reverie, and refined indolence, which too often disfigure his pages. It is not merely as an artist that men love to regard a favourite poet. He must not only himself obey the dominion of moral and religious ideas, he must do more—he must teach others to go and do likewise. But, when all deductions have been made, and every critical objection has been stated, there still remains enough in the poetry of 'A.' to justify a warm eulogy, and to entitle us to hope that he may yet produce poems worthy of a higher praise.

Matthew Arnold in his Preface to *Poems* (1853)

When Arnold withdrew his first two books and published a selection from them with additional poems in 1853, 'Empedocles on Etna' was omitted. This time his name appeared on the title-page and he wrote a Preface defending himself against what he regarded as unjustified attacks. If it did nothing else, the Preface showed that he could argue powerfully and directly as a critic with something of the cut-and-dried assurance of Aristotle's Poetics. *At the same time, he misses or evades the true point at issue. Arnold insists that subjects from the ancient world, if they have sufficient significance, are as proper for modern poetry as any other. This had not been denied. Indeed, Boyle cited Tennyson as an example of its truth. The objection to Arnold had been the manner in which he treated such subjects.*

But Arnold suggests that the subject is of greater importance than the 'treatment', if treatment means the superficial beauty, imagery, or melody of the verse:

> This the Greeks understood far more clearly than we do. The radical difference between their poetical theory and ours consists, as it appears to me, in this: that, with them, the poetical character of the action in itself, and the conduct of it, was the first consideration; with us, attention is fixed mainly on the value of the separate thoughts and images which occur in the treatment of an action. They regarded the whole; we regard the parts. With them, the action predominated over the expression of it; with us, the expression predominates over the action.

Presently, in what might almost be an echo of his lament over 'this strange disease of modern life' in 'The Scholar-Gipsy', Arnold comments on the present as 'an age wanting in moral grandeur', and 'an age of spiritual discomfort'. In this he gave ammunition to those who belittled him for turning away from the reality of his time.

There is one other comment, quoted without enthusiasm by Arnold, that stands out in the Preface. Critics, he writes, urge the poet to offer 'a true allegory of the state of one's own mind in a representative history'. The first half of that phrase is actually a description of Arnold's best poetry. His elegies and idylls presented scene and atmosphere as allegorical impressions of his inner struggle. Much of the rest of his poetry tended towards representative history, as described in the second half of the phrase, in poems like 'Sohrab and Rustum'.

In the following passage, he defends the choice of subject in his first published volumes.

'The poet', it is said,* and by an intelligent critic, 'the poet who would really fix the public attention must leave the exhausted past, and draw

ARNOLD

his subjects from matters of present import, and *therefore* both of interest and novelty.'

Now this view I believe to be completely false. It is worth examining, inasmuch as it is a fair sample of a class of critical dicta everywhere current at the present day, having a philosophical form and air, but no real basis in fact; and which are calculated to vitiate the judgment of readers of poetry, while they exert, so far as they are adopted, a misleading influence on the practice of those who make it.

What are the eternal objects of poetry, among all nations, and at all times? They are actions; human actions; possessing an inherent interest in themselves, and which are to be communicated in an interesting manner by the art of the poet. Vainly will the latter imagine that he has everything in his own power; that he can make an intrinsically inferior action equally delightful with a more excellent one by his treatment of it. He may indeed compel us to admire his skill, but his work will possess, within itself, an incurable defect.

The poet, then, has in the first place to select an excellent action; and what actions are the most excellent? Those, certainly, which most powerfully appeal to the great primary human affections: to those elementary feelings which subsist permanently in the race, and which are independent of time. These feelings are permanent and the same; that which interests them is permanent and the same also. The modernness or antiquity of an action, therefore, has nothing to do with its fitness for poetical representation; this depends upon its inherent qualities. To the elementary part of our nature, to our passions, that which is great and passionate is eternally interesting; and interesting solely in proportion to its greatness and to its passion. A great human action of a thousand years ago is more interesting to it than a smaller human action of to-day, even though upon the representation of this last the most consummate skill may have been expended, and though it has the advantage of appealing by its modern language, familiar manners, and contemporary allusions, to all our transient feelings and interests. These, however, have no right to demand of a poetical work that it shall satisfy them; their claims are to be directed elsewhere. Poetical works belong to the domain of our permanent passions; let them interest these, and the voice of all subordinate claims upon them is at once silenced.

Achilles, Prometheus, Clytemnestra, Dido,—what modern poem presents personages as interesting, even to us moderns, as these personages of an 'exhausted past'? We have the domestic epic dealing with the details of modern life which pass daily under our eyes; we

123

have poems representing modern personages in contact with the problems of modern life, moral, intellectual, and social; these works have been produced by poets the most distinguished of their nation and time; yet I fearlessly assert that *Hermann and Dorothea, Childe Harold, Jocelyn, The Excursion*,[1] leave the reader cold in comparison with the effect produced upon him by the latter books of the *Iliad*, by the *Oresteia*, or by the episode of Dido. And why is this? Simply because in the three last-named cases the action is greater, the personages nobler, the situations more intense: and this is the true basis of the interest in a poetical work, and this alone.

It may be urged, however, that past actions may be interesting in themselves, but that they are not to be adopted by the modern poet, because it is impossible for him to have them clearly present to his own mind, and he cannot therefore feel them deeply, nor represent them forcibly. But this is not necessarily the case. The externals of a past action, indeed, he cannot know with the precision of a contemporary; but his business is with its essentials. The outward man of Oedipus or of Macbeth, the houses in which they lived, the ceremonies of their courts, he cannot accurately figure to himself; but neither do they essentially concern him. His business is with their inward man; with their feelings and behaviour in certain tragic situations, which engage their passions as men; these have in them nothing local and casual; they are as accessible to the modern poet as to a contemporary.

*In the *Spectator* of April 2, 1853. The words quoted were not used with reference to poems of mine.

G. H. Lewes on *Poems* (1853) in the *Leader* (1853)

The response of critics like G. H. Lewes, biographer and critic, friend and lifelong companion of George Eliot, raised Arnold's reputation considerably. 'Study the Classics and the Moderns too,' wrote Lewes in his review at the end of the year, 'but beware of the rudeness and baldness of the one, no less than of the rhetoric and glitter of the other!' With this 'text', as he called it, he examined the volume of 1853 and found much to admire. A good deal of the review was spent in quoting and doing justice to Arnold's own Preface. But when Lewes discussed 'Sohrab and Rustum', he indicated the promise that might soon bear fruit.

Mr. Arnold, as a scholar, and one of poetical tendencies rather than of poetical genius, a man of culture, reflection, and sensibility, but not forming one of that small band of Singers who 'sing as the birds sing,' naturally looks towards Greece for inspiration. His poems will delight scholars, who will with curious pleasure follow him in his undisguised imitations of works which long have been their ideals; they will note his curiosities of verse, and his Græcism of imagery. Nor will the larger public read without delight. Poems such as these are not common. Some of the qualities most easily appreciable these poems possess, and they will secure an audience. But the fit audience is that of the cultured few. The longest poem in the volume, *Sohrab and Rustum*, will be the greatest favourite, for it tells an intelligible and interesting story, and the story moves through pictures and pathos such as we rarely meet in 'volumes of poetry.' It has its Græcisms, but they are little more than ornaments of questionable taste; the real attractiveness lies in the qualities just named.

J. A Froude on *Poems* (1853) in the *Westminster Review* (1854)

On 1 Janury 1854, the Westminster Review *published an enthusiastic article on Arnold's poetry by the English historian J. A. Froude, friend of Kingsley and Carlyle, author of a controversial novel,* The Nemesis of Faith *(1849), and long afterwards to be Regius Professor of History at Oxford in 1892, two years before his death.*

Froude goes straight to the main difficulty of Arnold's poetry. The major poems, 'The Strayed Reveller' or 'Empedocles on Etna', are weak. The strength and beauty lie in the shorter pieces. Get rid of the large formal structures and what you have left is among the best poetry of the age. That is much clearer to Froude in the new selection than when the first two volumes appeared with their self-consciously important title-poems. He quotes a long passage from 'A Summer Night', from line 34, 'And I, I know not if to pray' and adds, 'In these lines, in powerful and highly sustained metaphor, lies the full tragedy of modern life.' The true qualities of Arnold's poetry seem to Froude to be precisely those which other critics found lacking.

So far we have spoken with reserve, for we have simply stated the feelings with which we regarded this little volume on first reading it; but the reserve is no longer necessary, and the misgivings which we experienced have not been justified. At the close of last year another volume was published, again of miscellaneous poems, which went beyond the most sanguine hopes of A.'s warmest admirers. As before with 'The Strayed Reveller,' so again with 'Empedocles on Etna,' the *pièce de résistance* was not the happiest selection. But of the remaining pieces, and of all those which he has more recently added, it is difficult to speak in too warm praise. In the unknown A., we are now to recognise a son of the late Master of Rugby, Dr. Arnold. Like a good knight, we suppose he thought it better to win his spurs before appearing in public with so honoured a name; but the associations which belong to it will suffer no alloy from him who now wears it. Not only is the advance in art remarkable, in greater clearness of effect, and in the mechanical handling of words, but far more in simplicity and healthfulness of moral feeling. There is no more obscurity, and no mysticism; and we see everywhere the working of a mind bent earnestly on cultivating whatever is highest and worthiest in itself; of a person who is endeavouring, without affectation, to follow the best things, to see clearly what is good, and right, and true, and to fasten his heart upon these. There is usually a period in the growth of poets in which, like coarser people, they mistake the voluptuous for the beautiful; but in Mr. Arnold there is no trace of any such tendency; pure, without effort, he feels no enjoyment and sees no beauty in the atmosphere of the common passions; and in nobleness of purpose, in a certain loftiness of mind singularly tempered with modesty, he continually reminds us of his father. There is an absence, perhaps, of colour; it is natural that it should be so in the earlier poems of a writer who proposes aims such as these to himself; his poetry is addressed to the intellectual, and not to the animal emotions; and to persons of animal taste, the flavour will no doubt be over simple; but it is true poetry—a true representation of true human feeling. It may not be immediately popular, but it will win its way in the long run, and has elements of endurance in it which enable it to wait without anxiety for recognition.

Among the best of the new poems is 'Tristram and Iseult.' It is unlucky that so many of the subjects should be so unfamiliar to English readers, but it is their own fault if they do not know the 'Morte d'Arthur.' We must not calculate, however, on too much knowledge in such unpractical matters; and as the story is too long to tell in this place, we take an extract which will not require any. It is a picture of sleeping children as beautiful as Sir Francis Chantrey's. . . .[2]

This is very beautiful; a beautiful description of one of the most beautiful objects in nature; but it is a description which could never have been composed except by a person whose mind was in tune with all innocent loveliness, and who found in the contemplation of such things not merely a passing emotion of pleasure but the deepest and most exquisite enjoyment.

Besides Tristram and Iseult, we select for especial mention out of this second volume, 'A Farewell,' 'Self-Dependence,' 'Morality;' two very highly-finished pieces called 'The Youth of Nature' and 'The Youth of Man,' expressing two opposite states of feeling, which we all of us recognise, and yet which, as far as we know, have never before found their way into language; and 'A Summer Night,' a small meditative poem, containing one passage, which, although not per-fect—for, if the metre had been more exact, the effect would, in our opinion, have been very much enhanced—is, nevertheless, the finest that Mr. Arnold has yet written.

Coventry Patmore on *Poems* (1853) in the *North British Review* (1854)

Though unsigned, the North British Review *of Arnold's* Poems *is attributed to Coventry Patmore, whose popularity as the poet of* The Angel in the House *began that year with the publication of its first part, 'The Betrothal'. Patmore was also well disposed towards the new Pre-Raphaelite movement and had contributed to its magazine, the* Germ. *Though Arnold's classicism was not much to his taste, he found a major poetic talent in 'Tristram and Iseult', 'The Church of Brou', 'The Scholar-Gipsy', and those pieces whose pictorial romanticism had something in common with the Pre-Raphaelites themselves.*

Leaving the classic poems, we might pause over the romantic ones, 'Sir Tristram and Iseult,' and the 'Church of Brou,' or might express once more admiration of 'The Forsaken Merman,'—on the whole, the most universal favourite of all that Mr. Arnold has yet given to the world. But from these let us turn to 'The Scholar Gipsy,' one of the fresh additions which this volume contains. We would ask all lovers of poetry to read it, and see whether it does not touch their hearts with a sense of fresh beauty, such as one feels on first looking over a new kind of country. And we would ask Mr. Arnold to consider whether the acceptance this poem is sure to win, does not prove to him that it is better to forget all his poetic theories, ay, and Homer and Sophocles, Milton and Goethe too, and speak straight out of things which he has felt and tested on his own pulses. It may be that it derives some of its charm from the vividness with which it brings back old scenes and dear recollections; yet we cannot but think that every one with an open heart for nature, whether he has seen the neighbourhood of Oxford or not, will welcome its delightful pictures.

Leslie Stephen on *New Poems* (1867) in the *Saturday Review* (1867)

In an unsigned review which was probably the work of Leslie Stephen, the last collection of Arnold's major poems prompted a survey of his work as a whole. By this time his career as a poet was virtually at an end. The last of his more famous poems, 'Thyrsis', the elegy for his friend A. H. Clough, had appeared in Macmillan's Magazine *the previous year.*

Arnold had dismissed Swinburne as a 'pseudo-Shelley' and Swinburne denounced Arnold as a 'pseudo-Wordsworth'. But Stephen remarks astutely that, despite their apparent differences, Arnold and Swinburne had one thing in common. Both were rebels against 'the sovereignty of the drawing-room school of poetry. . . . Mr Swinburne rises in hot rebellion against it from the side of Sense, and Mr Arnold surveys it with cold displeasure from the remote altitudes of Reason.' The young lady and her mama were equally puzzled by the topics of lesbianism or sado-masochism in Swinburne's poems and by the Greek allusions of Arnold.

Yet Stephen is more ready than Kingsley or Aytoun to see that even Arnold's classicism is not without strong merits. 'Empedocles on Etna' is 'incurably faulty as a tragedy', and yet it is 'a poem that nearly every verse-writer of our time might study with high advantage'. Arnold's weakness is that 'He overweights his poetry with thought. And that is precisely the quality in which most modern English poetry is thoroughly wanting.'

So far as Arnold's poetic tone is concerned, Stephen describes it with characteristic discrimination and sensitivity.

The poetic light shines in a tranquil air. There are natures, it is true—Shelley's for example—in which the rush and bound of the thought, in spite of intellectual distractions, seems to kindle light and heat by its own course. But Mr. Arnold is of another calibre. He is one of the poets who are made, who are not born. He is never impetuous, never ebullient. Nowhere even for a moment are we impressed with a sense of spontaneousness. And it is easy to see that this is the genuine result of an original want, and not of the discipline to which he has subjected himself in the severer forms of his favourite classics. Not to speak of the ancients, it is impossible to read pieces like *Athalie* or *Cinna*,[3] whatever we may think of their dramatic merits, without being alive to the broad current of poetic feeling spontaneously flowing within the too rigid channels prescribed for it. If we remember how many poems which the world would not willingly let die have been the products of natures that, like Wordsworth's for example, became deeply poetic by culture and serene meditation, added to fine original susceptibilities, though not the finest, it is no too grievous disparagement to say of a poet that his verse is not the outcome of a spontaneously and ebulliently poetic mind. But it is a serious thing for such a mind to get into the distracting eddies of an epoch like ours, the critical hour of a great spiritual and intellectual interregnum. It is a serious thing for a mind not endowed with an ever-flowing fountain of poetic brightness, its own and inextinguishable, to fall among the shadows of a dim-believing age. We may get, as we do get in the present volume, gracious harmony of verse, delicately pensive moods, stately and grave thoughts, but of light and brightness we get too little, and of the cheerful inspiration of poetic joy scarcely any. There are occasional pieces and stanzas which must be excepted from this criticism, where we have glimpses of the old calmness and luminous objectivity. 'Thyrsis' is a poem of perfect delight, exquisite in grave tenderness of reminiscence, rich in breadth of western light, and breathing full the spirit of grey and ancient Oxford—

That sweet city, with her dreaming spires.

It is admirable, not merely for single touching lines and for single happy expressions and delicate strokes. Like 'The Scholar Gipsy', its companion-piece, in a former volume, it is remarkable for unity and completeness of conception—for that harmoniousness of composition which at once stirs and soothes, excites and satisfies the reader's mind, and which is the object and criterion of art. In 'Thyrsis' the poet projects his mind into the outer world with an effect that contrasts but too vividly with the self-brooding tone of the rest of the volume. One can only regret that the mood did not last longer, and has not been more frequent.

Isidore G. Ascher on *New Poems* (1867) in the *St James's Magazine* (1868)

'Nowadays one meets with so much that is turgid and commonplace in thought and expression, that a volume like the one we propose noticing is a positive bonne bouche.' *Despite a certain 'gush', Isidore Ascher's article was, of course, calculated to promote Arnold's reputation among a more general middle-class audience who might nowadays be found reading Sunday quality papers and colour supplements. Arnold, weeded of his more ambitious classical imitations, was becoming a poet for the bourgeois romantic. 'Sohrab and Rustum' was taught to schoolchildren who would not have read Homer in Greek or English. Oxford, until the advent of the motor-car, became:*

> that sweet city with her dreaming spires,
> She needs not June for beauty's heightening.

Some of Arnold's lines in 'Thyrsis' had less to do with Clough or his poetry than with the homely world of the scrapbook-screen and pressed flowers, summer evenings, and the domestic romance of villa gardens in St John's Wood or Dulwich to which the Forsytes of the real world returned from 'Change. It was the stuff of sentimental paintings in which young lovers met or parted with quiet earnestness:

> Too quick despairer, wherefore wilt thou go?
>> Soon will the high Midsummer pomps come on,
>>> Soon will the musk carnations break and swell,
>> Soon shall we have gold-dusted snapdragon,
>>> Sweet-William with his homely cottage-smell,
>>>> And stocks in fragrant blow;
>> Roses that down the alleys shine afar,
>>> And open jasmin-muffled lattices,

And groups under the dreaming garden-trees,
And the full moon, and the white evening star.

*How could such verse not be popular? It was every tourist's dream of
English summer. Ascher, himself a Canadian, put a respectable
intellectual gloss upon Arnold's achievement.*

The limited space of a magazine paper does not permit us to enter
more fully in detail into the characteristics of Mr. Arnold's new
poems, which are well worth studying, specially on account of their
peculiar thought—thought which to some extent reflects and inter-
prets some of the tendencies of the day. Pervaded as they are with
doubt, which sometimes borders on scepticism; with a cold questioning, which now and then touches on infidelity, the doubt is always
real, never assumed, and the questions are poignant, and always
suggestive; and even the gloom which haunts the thoughts never
obscures them. Like Milton's 'visible darkness,' it is a very clear
shadow, taking its rise, not always from the problems and mysteries
of wretched and unfortunate lives, like the darkness lurking in Mr.
Buchanan's writings, but, instead, emanates from the perturbed spirit
of the writer. Such a book as the one we have attempted to notice
hardly inspires hopefulness; but, on the other hand, it awakens
reflection. The brightness and beauty of external nature do not often
find their counterpart in human nature. The loveliness of the external
world contrasts, alas, too often, with the terrible glooms of the world
around us, and it is only right that in rendering the veil of self-
complacency, which so often blinds our vision to the drear realities in
our midst, we should look at life as it is, instead of dreaming of it as we
should like it to be. The truths which our glance may reveal to us may
be sad enough, Heaven knows; still better be alive to them than to the
bright falsehoods of the optimist.

R. H. Hutton on 'The poetry of Matthew Arnold' in the *British Quarterly Review* (1872)

---

*Arnold died in 1888. The last of the critics quoted to have written
during his lifetime was Richard Holt Hutton who was later to
commend Tennyson for the maturity of thought in his poetry rather*

than for mere aesthetic charm. Soon after Hutton published his 1872 essay, Benjamin Jowett was privately dismissing Arnold as 'too flippant to be a prophet' and 'a master in the art of plausibility'. These comments had been provoked by Arnold's Literature and Dogma. *But Hutton, in his survey of Arnold the poet, found authority and consistency. Arnold, the child of Wordsworth and Goethe, sustained a 'lofty didactic impulse'.*

Hazlitt, writing of one of Wordsworth's latest and more classical poems, 'Laodamia,' describes it as having 'the sweetness, the gravity, the strength, the beauty, and the languor of death: calm contemplation and majestic pains.' There also, we have, in one of Hazlitt's terse and sententious criticisms, the aroma of the finest poems of Wordsworth's greatest poetical disciple—one, too, who is the disciple of Wordsworth, emphatically in his later rather than in his earlier phase; Wordsworth schooled into a grace and majesty not wholly meditative, but in part, at least, critical; Wordsworth the conscious artist as well as poet; not Wordsworth the rugged rhapsodist of spiritual simplicity and natural joy. 'The sweetness, the gravity, the strength, the beauty, and the languor of death,—calm contemplation and majestic pains,'—all these may be found in the most characteristic and most touching of Mr. Arnold's poems; in the melancholy with which the sick King of Bokhara broods over the fate of the wretch whom his pity and power could not save from the expiation he himself courted; in the gloomy resentment of Mycerinus against the unjust gods who cut short his effort to reign justly over his people; in the despair of Empedocles on Etna, at his failure to solve the riddle of the painful earth—his weariness of 'the devouring flame of thought,' the naked, eternally restless mind whose thirst he could not slake; in those fine lines written by a deathbed, in which Mr. Arnold contrasts the hopes of youth with what he deems the highest gain of manhood, 'calm'; in the noble sonnet which commemorates Sophocles as one whom 'business could not make dull nor passion wild'; in the graphic 'Memorial Verses,' wherein he praises Wordsworth for assuaging that dim trouble of humanity which Goethe could only dissect and describe; in the melodious sadness of the personal retrospects in 'Resignation,' 'A Southern Night,' and 'Self-Dependence'; in the large concessions to Heine's satiric genius, made in the verses composed at his tomb at Montmartre; in the consciously hopeless cravings of 'The Scholar Gipsy' and 'Thyrsis' after a reconciliation between the intellect of man and the magic of Nature; and, most characteristically of all, in the willing half-sympathy given by Mr. Arnold to those ascetics of the Grande Chartreuse, whom his intellect condemns, and in the even deeper enthusiasm with which he addresses, in the midst of melancholy Alpine solitudes, that modern refugee from a sick world, the author of 'Obermann,' delineates the intellectual weakness and dejection of the age, and feebly though poetically shadows forth his own hopeless hope of a remedy. In all these poems alike, and many others which I have not space to enumerate—in all, indeed, in which Mr. Arnold's genius really gains a voice—there is 'the sweetness, gravity, strength, beauty, and the languor of death,' blended in the spirit of a calm contemplativeness which takes all the edge off anguish and makes the poet's pains 'majestic'; for Mr. Arnold's poems are one long variation on a single theme, the divorce between the soul and the intellect, and the depth of spiritual regret and yearning which that divorce produces. Yet there is a didactic keenness with the languor, an eagerness of purpose with the despondency, which give half the individual flavour to his lyrics. A note of confidence lends authority to his scepticism; the tone of his sadness is self-contained, sure, and even imperious, instead of showing the ordinary relaxation of loss; and the reader of his poetry is apt to rise from it with the same curious questioning in his mind which Mr. Arnold has put into the mouth of Nature, in the verses called 'Morality,'—a questioning after the origin of 'that severe, that earnest air,' which breathes through poetry of all but hopeless yearning and all but unmixed regret.

No doubt one kind of answer to this question is, that Mr. Arnold has inherited from the great teacher of Rugby and historian of the Punic War the lofty didactic impulse which marks all his prose and poetry alike, although the substance of the lessons he is so eager to give has sadly dwindled in the descent from father to son. But that is but one sort of answer, explaining rather the source of the peculiar strain in his temperament which has impressed a certain nervous depth and moral 'distinction' upon poetry of which the drift is uniformly a realistic melancholy, than the source from which he has fed the flame of his genius, and justified the calm egotism of its literary rescripts. Intellectually, Mr. Arnold's descent, as he himself is always foremost to acknowledge, is to be derived in almost equal degree from Goethe the critic and artist, and from Wordsworth the poet; both of them, observe, marked by the same character of clear, self-contained, thoughtful, heroic egotism. I say Goethe the critic and artist—for I recognise but little, in Goethe's deepest and most perfect vein of poetry, of that conscious self-culture and that lucidity of enthusiastic self-study, which lend the charm to his conversations, his novels, and his criticisms. And Mr. Arnold, even in his capacity of poet—I am not about to touch his essays, except so far as they throw a light on his poetry—is always aiming at self-culture; and singing, not songs of involuntary melody, but of carefully-attuned aspiration or regret. From both Goethe and Wordsworth, again, he has learned to treat his own individuality with a certain exaltation of touch, an air of Olympian dignity and grace, which lends the fascination of 'the grand style' to lyrics so sad that they might otherwise trail upon the earth too slack and limp a growth.

Lionel Johnson on Matthew Arnold in *Post Liminium* (1912)

Arnold held his own in the anthologies of poetry published early in the twentieth century, largely by virtue of those shorter elegiac poems that reviewers of his own day had most admired. He was also in demand for his prose writings on education, society, and literature.

By the 1930s his poetry stimulated new critical interest, by no means all of it favourable and some of it, though favourable, not likely to do much for Arnold's fame. H. W. Garrod, writing about him in Poetry and the Criticism of Life *(1931) sometimes seemed like one dilettante writing about another. He liked Arnold because Arnold was 'enjoyable', and almost seemed to like him just because he thought no one else did. F. R. Leavis, in the following year, in* New Bearings in English Poetry, *devoted more space to Arnold than to any other Victorian. But this was largely to prove the case that Arnold had turned his back upon the society and its problems which he professed to discuss, and was guilty of escapism or 'evasion'. Arnold, however, is more honest in Leavis's judgment in renouncing the world for myth or idyll than the other poets who did so without admitting it.*

In the year after this, 1933, T. S. Eliot in The Use of Poetry and the Use of Criticism *suggested that Arnold seemed most at ease 'in a master's gown'. Unlike most of Arnold's contemporaries, Eliot thought 'Empedocles on Etna' one of the finest academic poems ever written but regarded more romantic poems like 'The Forsaken Merman' or 'Tristram and Iseult' as no more than charades.*

It was not until the studies by Lionel Trilling (1939), C. B. Tinker and H. F. Lowry (1940), and E. K. Chambers (1947) that Arnold's work began to receive the kind of thorough discussion that it merited. Biography had a direct relevance to this when, for instance, Chambers suggested that the end of an early love affair recorded by Arnold in the Marguerite poems led to a colder and more impersonal style in the immediate aftermath. Chambers also suggested that the end of Arnold's career as a poet, occurring in his forties, resulted quite simply from the competing demands made upon him in public life and government service, and as the author of a growing quantity of social and literary criticism.

Long before this, Lionel Johnson had summed up Arnold's achievement by linking the poetry and the man. Johnson was a poet of the 1890s, best known for his verses 'By the Statue of King Charles at Charing-Cross'. Indeed, he had a strong flavour of that raffish decade, introducing Lord Alfred Douglas to Oscar Wilde, drinking far too much, becoming a convert to Catholicism, and dying – according to Ezra Pound in Hugh Selwyn Mauberley *– 'By falling from a high stool in a pub'.*

Arnold's poems are of two kinds: there are the narrative poems, whether dramatic or otherwise; and the lyrical, emotional, or meditative poems. Now, it is observable that Arnold is at his best in poems neither long nor short: in poems equal in length to the average Hebrew psalm, the average Greek ode. No doubt there are exceptions: 'Sohrab and Rustum' among the longer poems, 'Requiescat' among the shorter, are nearly faultless. But, for the most part, it is in such poems as 'Thyrsis', 'A Summer Night', 'Stanzas from the Grande Chartreuse', that we find the true Arnold; not in 'Balder Dead', 'Progress', 'Revolutions'. In other words, Arnold, to use his own phrase, had not 'the architectonics of poetry, the faculty which presides at the evolution of works like the *Agamemnon* or *Lear*'. Nor was he in the literal sense a singer, such as was Heine or Catullus. Rather, his quality was meditative; he accepted, at least in practice, Wordsworth's definition of poetry, that it is 'emotion remembered in tranquillity'. But it may be objected that Arnold is genial, exultant, even rapturous; that he wrote nothing in the least like 'The Excursion'. That is true; but let us consider a little more curiously. Arnold was fond of national distinctions, qualities of race and temperament. Were one to distinguish Arnold's own qualities, the conclusion might be of this kind. From the Greek culture, he took a delight in the beauty of life and of fine imagination; from the Hebrew genius, a sense of reverence and meditation; from the French, a certain grace and lucidity of spirit; from the German, a steady seriousness of mind. By descent he was, in part, a Celt: that gave him a 'natural magic' of emotion and of soul; while from his English origin he took that daring common-sense which enabled him to hold in harmony these various qualities. Trained in those chosen places of beauty and high tradition, Winchester and Oxford, with all the strength of his father's influence at Rugby, he was always attached to the English ideal: to the ideals of Milton and of Burke. A scholar, a man of the world, a government official, his affections were not narrow, not provincial; but they were not cosmopolitan, not unsettled. His heart was at home in the quiet dignity and peace of an English life, among the great books of antiquity, and the great thoughts of 'all time and all existence'. Hence came his limitations: not from prejudice, nor from ignorance, but from a scrupulous precision and delicacy of taste. No one loved France more than he; no one abhorred more than he 'the great goddess Aselgeia'.[4] He reverenced the German seriousness, depth, moderation of life and thought; he disliked and ridiculed pedantry, awkwardness, want of humour and of grace. In all his criticisms, the same balance between excess and deficiency appears: he was a true Aristotelian. And so, when it is said that Arnold was not a poet of profound philosophy, not a thinker of consistency, or not a man whom we can classify at all, the only answer is a *distinguo*. It was Arnold's work to find beauty and truth in life, to apprehend the meaning and moral worth of things, to discriminate the trivial from the grave, and to show how the serene and ardent life is better than the mean and restless. His poetry, then, is not didactic; but meditative, in the classical sense, it is.

NOTES

1 Goethe's poem *Hermann and Dorothea* (1797) is set in the context of the French Revolution, though based upon the expulsion of Protestants by the Archbishop of Salzburg in 1732; *Jocelyn*, a poem by Alphonse de Lamartine (1790–1869), was published in 1836.

2 Sir Francis Legatt Chantrey (1781–1841), wood-carver and sculptor, best known for his statuary.

3 Pierre Corneille's *Cinna* was first produced in Paris in 1639 and Jean Racine's *Athalie* in 1691.

4 Aselgeia – dissoluteness.

4

Clough

Clough presented a simple yet confounding problem to a good many readers. Did he mean what he said? Or, how far did he mean it? There was, of course, little difficulty in the social comedy of *The Bothie of Tober-na-Vuolich*, usually known more conveniently as *The Bothie*, nor his *Amours de Voyage*. They were amusing and perceptive accounts of an Oxford reading-party in the Highlands and romance among the well-bred English in Rome. But for most critics these pieces represented the surface charm of Clough's writing.

In the poetry of intellectual debate, on matters of religion and morality, Clough was Jekyll and Hyde. Indeed, he indulged in what Stevenson's Dr Jekyll would have recognized as intellectual and spiritual 'dualism'. When we read a long poem like 'Dipsychus' or the shorter poem 'Easter Day', for example, Clough alternates voices and moods. In one voice, the propositions of atheism or immorality are freely expressed. Though a second voice may contradict them later, they are stated without reservation:

> Christ is not risen, no –
> He lies and moulders low;
> Christ is not risen!

Then there is the morality of human indifference urged upon Dipsychus by the Spirit in 'How pleasant it is to have money'. Is a man always to deny himself pleasure because there is somewhere a poor man who cannot afford it? If that were the case, says the Spirit, no one could ever be happy for a moment:

> Who's to enjoy at all, pray let us hear?
> You won't; he can't! Oh, no more fuss!
> What's it to him, or he to us?

The rich man who enjoys his pleasure and pays for it spreads his wealth. Is that not better than puritanical abstinence?

Was such rhetoric merely a dramatic device, as when Milton put speeches into the mouths of the fallen angels in *Paradise Lost*? Or did

Clough allow a real possibility of truth, in this opposition to religious and moral orthodoxy? Most critics saw in him an upholder of established values. But some caught the hint of moral ambiguity, the moral uncertainties of the post-romantic age. It was certainly the age of Baudelaire's 'Les Litanies de Satan' in *Fleurs du Mal*, 'O Satan, prends pitié de ma longue misère!' In Clough, as in Baudelaire, the reader is apt to feel at times the rock of moral absolutism turn to shifting sands beneath the feet. Even the sardonic lines of 'The Latest Decalogue' had a defeatist as much as a reproving ring in some ears:

> Thou shalt not kill; but need'st not strive
> Officiously to keep alive:
> Do not adultery commit;
> Advantage rarely comes of it:
> Thou shalt not steal; an empty feat,
> When it's so lucrative to cheat . . .

Parallel with this, Clough remained a poet of chattering frivolity between social butterflies in the five cantos of *Amours de Voyage*, following the fortunes of the Trevellyn family on their Roman visit. Whether or not he allowed an element of truth to the tempting Spirit of 'Dipsychus', there was no doubt that the world of fashionable society exercised a strong attraction for him as a subject. He might pity the poor but he preferred to write about the rich. If he criticized social injustice, he did so by portraying the lives of those who had too much comfort rather than directly concerning himself with those who had too little. When he upheld religious faith, as his more sympathetic critics thought he did, it was by spending a good deal of time luxuriating in doubt to begin with.

More than Arnold, Clough might have left his readers uneasy. And yet, more than Arnold, they were apt to feel he came down on the side of belief and morality. Like Browning in 'Cleon' or 'Bishop Blougram's Apology', he seemed to treat spiritual truths in a manner that was worldly or even flippant. That, at least, provided a link between his dialecticism and the social comedy of *The Bothie* or *Amours de Voyage*. In that respect, like Browning again, he found ample room in his poetry for the World, the Flesh, and the Devil.

Charles Kingsley on *The Bothie* (1848) in *Fraser's Magazine* (1849)

Kingsley's unsigned review appeared in Fraser's *in January 1849. The poem established Clough as an observer of sophisticated, dandified, and rather slangy society. The story of the Oxford reading-party in the Highlands during a summer vacation revolved round the love of Philip Hewson, a young well-bred radical, for Elspie, the daughter of a Highland farmer. The poem, written in a burlesque of the metre and poetic ornament of Homer and Virgil, was subtitled 'A Long-Vacation Pastoral'. Under the supervision of their tutor, 'the grave man nicknamed Adam', the young gentlemen of Oxford read and play and dine.* The Bothie *is in some ways reminiscent of Pope's* Rape of the Lock, *where, as Hazlitt said, 'the little is made great and the great little . . . the triumph of insignificance, the apotheosis of foppery and folly'.*

The ritual of dressing for dinner is treated as an Homeric catalogue, along with a sly undergraduate assessment of the tutor's intellectual strengths and weaknesses:

> Be it recorded in song who was first, who last, in dressing.
> Hope was first, black-tied, white-waistcoated, simple, His Honour;
> For the postman made out he was heir to the earldom of Ilay
> (Being the younger son of the younger brother, the Colonel) . . .
> Hope was first, His Honour, and next to His Honour the Tutor.
> Still more plain the Tutor, the grave man nicknamed Adam,
> White-tied, clerical, silent, with antique square-cut waistcoat
> Formal, unchanged, of black cloth, but with sense and feeling
>   beneath it;
> Skilful in Ethics and Logic, in Pindar[1] and Poets unrivalled;
> *Shady* in Latin, said Lindsay, but *topping* in Plays and Aldrich.[2]

By imposing the easy youthful slang of Victorian Oxford on the stately rhythm of Homer, Clough adopted the air of a languid and laconic portayal of human manners. It was merely an outer shell of the Clough of Easter Day. *But, as Kingsley suggests, it was an agreeable and amusing outer shell.*

The poem sets forth, in playful earnestness, how a party from Oxford with their tutor, went to read in the Highlands for the long vacation; 'how they bathed, read, and roamed, all in the joy of their life and glory of shooting jackets;' and how, there and then, 'the eager, impetuous Hewson,' poet and ultra-ultra-radical, realized his theories of the nothingness of rank, and the dignity of dirty work, by flirting with Highland lassies—casting himself, in a sudden revulsion of feeling, at the delicate feet of 'Lady Maria'—and finally falling in love with 'Elspie Mackaye.' The incidents and arguments which flow out of Hewson's strange sayings and doings, together with his most deep and truly poetical 'love-story', make up the staple of the poem.

And here we must notice, first of all, the author's vivid and versatile faculty for drawing individual character. Adam, the tutor; Hobbes, 'contemplative, corpulent, witty;' Lindsay, 'clever, brilliant, do-nothing;' even the characters of whom little but the names appear— Arthur, Hope, and Airlie, Sir Hector, the old chieftain, David Mackaye, the old army farrier, are each and every one of them living, individual persons—you could swear to them if you met them in the street. Hewson the poet is more a type of a class than an individual— so far right. But the women are as vividly sketched as the men. 'Katie', the open-hearted child of nature, who thinks no shame to commence a fresh innocent flirtation with every fresh acquaintance, and, like a butterfly,—

> . . . Takes pleasure in all, as in beautiful weather,
> Sorry to lose it, but just as we would be to lose fine weather.
> And she is strong to return to herself, and to feel undeserted,
> For she always keeps burning a cheerful fire inside her,

might pass for a type of the Celtic girl, such as you will meet with in every village in Wales and Ireland, as well as the Highlands. And as a contrast, Elspie Mackaye, really a noble ideal of the true Scotchwoman, with all her rich Norse character, her wild Dantesque imagination, her shrewd, 'canny' insight, her deep and strong affec-tions, yet all crushed into order by that calm self-restraint which indicates, not coldness, but intense and victorious energy—we must say, that we know no recent fiction of a female character so genial, so original, and yet so natural.

Mr. Clough has all the advantage of a novel subject, and one, too, which abounds in fantastic scenery and combinations, as it were, ready-made to his hands. On such ground he need only be truthful to be interesting. The strange jumble of society which the Highlands would present in the summer to such a party—marquises and gillies, shooters and tourists—the luxuries and fopperies of modern London amid the wildest scenery and a primitive people—Aristotle over Scotch whisky—embroidered satin waistcoats dancing with bare-legged hizzies—Chartist poets pledging kilted clansmen—Mr. Clough was quite right in determining to treat so odd a subject in a correspondingly odd manner.

Ralph Waldo Emerson on *The Bothie* (1848) in the *Massachusetts Quarterly Review* (1849)

There was some discriminating praise of Clough's poem, privately and publicly, in England. Elizabeth Barrett Browning assured Miss Mitford that the 'more-than-need-be unmusical hexametres' were 'full of power and freshness'. Both she and Robert Browning admired the book. In the Pre-Raphaelite review the Germ, *in 1850, William Michael Rossetti looked back on the early fortunes of* The Bothie *and concluded, 'That public attention should have been so little engaged by this poem is a fact in one respect somewhat remarkable, as contrasting with the notice which the* Ambarvalia *has received.' Clough's second book,* Ambarvalia, *shared with another poet Thomas Burbidge, had appeared in 1849 and seemed to Rossetti a mere exercise in poetic styles by contrast with* The Bothie.

It was a feature of Clough's career that he was often more popular in the United States than in England. When his first book was published there, Ralph Waldo Emerson read The Bothie *and found much to admire in it. A good deal of his review was a recapitulation of the story and the setting of the poem. His critical assessment came at the end of this.*

The story leads naturally into a bold hypothetical discussion of the most serious questions that bubble up at this very hour in London, Paris, and Boston, and, whilst these are met and honestly and even profoundly treated, the dialogue charms us by perfect good breeding and exuberant animal spirits. We shall not say that the rapid and bold execution has the finish and the intimate music we demand in modern poetry; but the subject-matter is so solid, and the figures so real and lifelike, that the poem is justified, and would be good in spite of much ruder execution than we here find. Yet the poem has great literary merits. The author has a true eye for nature, and expresses himself through the justest images. The Homeric iteration has a singular charm, half-comic, half-poetic, in the piece, and there is a wealth of expression, a power of description and of portrait-painting, which excels our best romancers. Even the hexameter, which with all our envy of its beauty in Latin and in Greek, we think not agreeable to the genius of English poetry, is here in place to heighten the humor of college conversation.

An anonymous reviewer on *Ambarvalia* (1849) in the *Guardian* (1849)

Clough's poems in Ambarvalia *showed a different aspect of his writing to* The Bothie. *Where the vacation pastoral had been urbane and comic, these were more earnest and uneasy. 'The Questioning Spirit', 'A Song of Autumn' ('My wind is turned to the bitter north') or 'Qua Cursum Ventus', a meditation on friendship turned to estrangement by absence, were among the poems that attracted the attention of the critics. Such pieces showed Clough in a more sombre mood and the tone of them was set in a minor key. Doubt and pessimism clouded the mood in some cases and yet the manner of them was emotionally detached when set beside the more famous verses of* In Memoriam.

Some critics who first discussed the book regarded its author as a romantic or rather a post-romantic of the kind described by Baudelaire in 1846. The landscape of the mind, and an unsettled mind at that, was the preoccupation of his art. The Rambler *for July 1849 saw Clough's poetry as confirmation that 'in all persons of lively and keen sensibilities, there is an inward life, in which they far more truly* live, *then in the external and visible one'. The reviewer of* Ambarvalia *in the* Guardian *on 28 March 1849 summed up the contrast between this collection of poems and* The Bothie *of the previous year.*

Mr Clough is already known to our Oxford readers as the author of a *Long Vacation Pastoral*, not very intelligible, and hardly to be recommended, beyond the walls of the University. His present work, if less witty and amusing, is far more powerful, even in its fragmentary nature, more profound, more interesting, more rich in 'the thoughts that shake mankind'. Scintillations, as the abrupt little pieces are, they shed a light around, deep and wide, on human nature. Rarely relieved as the book is, by the boldly yet finely traced characters that stand out in such roundness from the *Pastoral*, yet is their loss atoned for by glimpses into those mysterious cells of the heart, which, as they lie deepest, so are most common to mankind at large. Mr. Clough must be content with 'fit audience, though few'. Those readers who are fond of 'poetry made easy',—who like the even tenor of superficial faultiness, the tinsel of glittering diction, and a 'false gallop' of thought—such we warn not to run the risk of bewilderment and a headache over these pages. Besides, the book is even more tantalising than it need be—there are very few headings to enable one to stand at the writer's view-point, and thence gaze around with him; no obvious arrangement, if any; not even marked pauses to prevent the shock of plunging from a Polkish love song into a metaphysical reverie (sometimes both are combined into one piece) with the versatility of a barrel-organ; and, at times, an hieroglyphical abruptness of expression which better suits the *déshabille* of an author's note-book than his appearance in public.

Later in the review, the Guardian's *critic grew uneasy at the extent to which Clough laid bare the doubts and reservations of his own mind. Might there not even be a sense of self-indulgence or selfishness in doing so before an audience? The review also discussed Matthew Arnold's first book,* The Strayed Reveller and Other Poems. *It drew a comparison between the two new poets, having said that* Ambarvalia *'would well represent the two phases of Tennyson, grave and sportive, the inner and outer world'. By comparison with Arnold, 'If Mr Clough is a mountain stream, "A" is a sparkling fountain. "A" is more likely to be popular. He gives the head less work — the eye is not so introverted — the enigma of life is not so sternly grappled with.' But the reviewer first discussed the introspective nature of Clough's poems.*

The disgust at shams—the weariness of unmeaning conven-tionalities—the ardent longing for truth, and sense of duty—generous sympathy with fellow workers in the great cause of truth, whose conscience forces them to a different path from the writer's own—the noble elevation of sentiment over the Fetish worship of money or pleasure into a contemplation of the awful meaning of life—all this is truly grand and good. But through the book there runs a morbid self-consciousness, a critical and sensitive distrust of self, which are the very opposite of action, and direct hindrance to it:—

> Unless above himself he can
> Erect himself, how mean a thing is man!

Always to be mapping out the foundations on too vast a scale, and with an eye too curious and fastidious, is not the way to rear a goodly superstructure. Nor is it for human intellect to set about analysing and providing the ultimate principles—facts they are, and nothing more or less—of the reason or emotions. Weariness and vexation can only ensue. Nor is it for man to reject this or that system because it is not faultless. Better for us, perhaps, that we must put up with imperfection. In this world we must work: if we wait for symmetrical theories, whose beauty is marred by no troublesome incongruities, there is danger of evaporating in sentimentality, or stagnating in indifference:—

> The fruit of dreary hoping,
> Is waking blank despair.

The poems bear far more decided traces of thinking, than of reading—a fault, if any, on the right side. But is not this, insufficiently qualified by the other, apt to destroy the balance of the mind? Above all, of course, we who are firmly convinced that what we see so often alluded to, by thinkers of that class to which Mr. Clough belongs, as *mere* forms—worthy of the greatest hatred if they were so—are in reality the channels of important verities, in some instances effete in appearance from neglect or misuse, must be excused if we warn our readers against the bad philosophy which now-a-days ministers with so much subtilty and success to intellectual pride. Moreover, it may be asked, whether it be not merely a more subtle and elevated form of selfishness, that amiable and genial weakness which lays bare to the inspection of others the melancholy workings of its own breast—troubles not peculiar to the complainer—as if leaning helpless on their support and sympathy? Then, too, the excess of self-distrust is almost equally a want of faith with excess of self-confidence. That self-distrust alone has humility for its parent, which leans, for the support it cannot find in itself, upon something external, worthy of being the prop of the human soul. If it be said, that it is possible for men, without any fault of their own, never to have met with this 'something external', we answer, that indeed it is so, but it is equally possible, and far more usual, for men to reject the true prop, having constituted themselves the judges of its unworthiness. Great, indeed, is the sympathy due both to the voluntary and the involuntary wanderer: but the latter only has any excuse—the sufferings of the latter alone can be contemplated without danger by others. *Qui laborat, orat,*[3] is a beautiful thought concerning one who has never been taught to pray, a pernicious falsehood about one who has rejected the practice. With such a one it will soon be *Qui non orat, nec laborat!*[4] We are not, in these remarks, treating these poems so much as autobiographical revelations, as thoughts thrown before the minds of many readers not unlikely, from the fashion that now prevails among men of intellect and cultivation—especially those who have come under the influence of a popular writer lately deceased, as remarkable for self-reliance as for moral honesty and straight-forwardness—to awaken echoes that may, in some cases, deepen into the knell of faith and religion. Byronian mawkishness is no longer in vogue: the fresh upright morality of the teaching of which we speak would dissipate in a moment such unhealthy exhalations. A mixture of misanthropy and debauchery is no longer the obvious way to be thought interesting: nor, when sensuality links itself with opposition to religion instead of hatred of mankind, is it much more popular. The vice now is to fancy oneself 'one of no common intellect, no common feelings,' and to reject, because men of less fine natures have abused them, the means of happiness with which Nature and Providence have furnished the humble as well as the intellectual of mankind. We are very far from hinting that this is applicable to the causes which have produced the painfully real traces of morbid struggling before us: but considering the probable effect upon some of the readers of these poems,—given to the world, we venture to say, without the slightest thought of influencing any one either way,—and remembering also the number of minds that are hampered by too much self-conscious-ness from fresh impulsive action, we cannot doubt that their indis-criminate circulation will do far more harm than good.

Matthew Arnold on Clough in
Last Words on Translating Homer (1862)

Clough's health deteriorated in early middle age. He went abroad and died in Florence on 13 November 1861 at the age of forty-two. It was just twelve years since his first book, eleven years since his second and last. He had written a good deal of poetry after that and his verse-novel Amours de Voyage *had been serialized in the* Atlantic Monthly *in 1858. When he died, there was much that was still unpublished or, at least, unpublished in volume form.*

Matthew Arnold was Professor of Poetry at Oxford at the time of Clough's death. His lecture 'Last Words on Translating Homer' contained the first and most enduring eulogy. 'That of which I think in him oftenest', Arnold wrote, 'is the Homeric simplicity of his literary life.'

And how, then, can I help being reminded what a student of this sort we have just lost in Mr. Clough, whose name I have already mentioned in these lectures? He, too, was busy with Homer; but it is not on that account that I now speak of him. Nor do I speak of him in order to call attention to his qualities and powers in general, admirable as these were. I mention him because, in so eminent a degree, he possessed these two invaluable literary qualities,—a true sense for his object of study, and a single-hearted care for it. He had both; but he had the second even more eminently than the first. He greatly developed the first through means of the second. In the study of art, poetry, or philosophy, he had the most undivided and disinterested love for his object in itself, the greatest aversion to mixing up with it anything accidental or personal. His interest was in literature itself; and it was this which gave so rare a stamp to his character, which kept him so free from all taint of littleness. In the saturnalia of ignoble personal passions, of which the struggle for literary success, in old and crowded communities, offers so sad a spectacle, he never mingled. He had not yet traduced his friends, nor flattered his enemies, nor disparaged what he admired, nor praised what he despised. Those who knew him well had the conviction that, even with time, these literary arts would never be his. His poem, of which I spoke before, has some admirable Homeric qualities;—out-of-doors freshness, life, naturalness, buoyant rapidity.

An anonymous critic on *Poems by Arthur Hugh Clough* (1862) in the *Saturday Review* (1862)

In 1862, Clough's posthumously published poems were issued in England and America. F. T. Palgrave contributed a memoir to them, which was largely a summary of Clough's life and interests. Like a good deal of the literary comment in the aftermath of Clough's death, this was naturally eulogistic. But the Saturday Review *offered a more objective assessment of the poems. Those which dealt with 'ancient doubts and truths' in Clough's own mind were expressed, wrote the* reviewer, as well as they could be. But Clough's true strength was not in poems of religious speculation or personal debate. It lay in his gift for writing about the genial society in which he moved.

It has to be said that these vers de société or novels in verse were more welcome to the poetry-reading public of the 1860s than questions as to whether the religion upon which its conduct was founded might be only a myth. The term 'morbid' was apt to be used for such preoccupations. Certainly the Saturday Review summed up a general feeling about Clough's work and it did so directly and fairly.

There is nothing more difficult to convey in words than the exact meaning of the doubts of a philosophical mind of the present day. Perhaps the doubts of all doubters are substantially the same, and the Book of Job has as much philosophy in it as this world is likely ever to come to. But every generation has its own way of putting things; and we might suppose ourselves capable of stating without much trouble what are the chief doubts and conflicts in which we are engaged; but to state them shortly, and to speak of any individual as thinking in a particular way about them, is almost sure to give an opening for ridicule. It is not so much the thought as the vividness with which the thought is held and expressed, and its whole bearing upon the life and other thoughts of the thinker, that attract us. Mr. Clough was extremely impatient of all subterfuges, he was scrupulously anxious not to be led away by half thoughts, he was sincerely desirous not to deceive himself. He shunned anything like half-belief. At the bottom of all reflection, however, he found the image of a wise and just God. This fear of half-belief—this searching out of God, as a being disclosed to him in the recesses of his own heart, but not lightly to be clothed with attributes and credited with schemes and plans of creation—Mr. Clough expressed as well as he could in verse. That which he had to say is perhaps as old as the human race, and is certainly as old as religious philosophy. His verses are full of power, and of happy, unexpected terms; but are obscure, inharmonious, and incomplete. A man cannot be said to have necessarily done much who has put such thoughts into such verses. He may not have done much, but he also may have done much. All depends on the sense of reality which the thinking produces on us, and on the feelings the verse awakens. If we put the substance of the Book of Job into the form of a logical proposition, it does not seem as if we had got hold of much more than a truism. But there are men to whom the truisms of religious philosophy are living realities, and whose life is spent in dwelling on thoughts which ordinary men dismiss after a moment's hasty reflection. That one writer is superficial and another profound on such points, is a fact only to be learnt by experiment. When we read them we feel the difference, but unless we read them we cannot see where the difference lies. We cannot describe what it is that makes the verses of Mr. Clough seem to us to embody, better, perhaps, than those of any other writer of our generation, these ancient doubts and truths in their modern shape; but as we read what he has written, we become conscious of his superiority.

Mr. Clough has also expressed, with far more than ordinary truth and feeling, the emotions which a man of tender heart and full of the sadness of philosophy experiences when he throws himself upon his fellows and basks in the grateful sunshine of friendship. The best, or at least the most intelligible and harmonious of all his short poems, describes the satisfaction with which he welcomes the belief that all honest men, however they are separated in thought and aim, are carried to the same port at last. He compares them to two ships lying side by side at night, and then carried far apart by dawn of day, although they fancied the same breeze was bearing them on. Mr. Clough also saw much of the humour of innocent society, and his *Bothie* is infinitely the best picture ever given of University life. He alone of the many who have undertaken to describe Oxford has done justice to the subject, and has pictured young men as they really exist—full of nonsense, and pedantry, and animal spirits, interested in all manner of discussions, moral and intellectual, working, rowing, bathing, walking and talking, and smoking for ever. This was the form of external life with which Mr. Clough was acquainted, and he managed to describe it as no one else has ever done. That he has done this, and that he has contrived to invest his description with a glow of poetry, and to glorify the life he yet faithfully represents, is quite enough to show that he was not merely a meditative man of reflection, delighting for ever to weave into verse those questionings which vex the meditative mind. It was unfortunate for his permanent reputation that he had little in his life to force the representation of the outer world and of society on him, and that his distrust of his own poetical powers led him to substitute for poetical effect that absorption in the slavery of exhausting labour which killed him before his time, and at last seemed to him the only worthy end of life, and the only proper result of philosophy.

This volume contains two new pieces of considerable length. One is called *Amours de Voyage*, and embodies what its author was thinking and observing and studying, during his stay at Rome in 1849. It is in the form of letters, supposed to be written by an English traveller to his friend, and by an English young lady to her friend. The pair gradually fall in love, although the gentleman is very long in deciding whether he feels more than the passing tenderness which results from being thrown in the way of a sympathizing and pretty girl. His doubts on this point fill up a large portion of the poem, and he has scarcely ascertained that his feelings are serious when the young lady's family leave Rome, and he has to set off in chase of them. He visits them at Florence, at Milan, and at Como; and the story ends as a story never ended before, in the lover giving his mistress up in sheer weariness and despair, because he cannot find her direction. Of course, the interest of such a story cannot be in the story itself. It lies in the humorous sketches of English society abroad, in the playfulnesses of the young lady in her unbosomings, and in the description of the people, the city, and neighbourhood of Rome. It is not nearly equal to the *Bothie*, but it has many of the same excellences. There are fine passages in it, and many subtle trains of thought, and some spirited satirical sketches.

Henry Fothergill Chorley on
Poems by Arthur Hugh Clough (1862)
in the *Athenaeum* (1862)

Clough's death eight months earlier did not inhibit the reviewer in the July number of the Athenaeum *from dismissing the major poem of the 1862 volumes –* Amours de Voyage – *in forthright terms. It was a mixture of 'gymnastic exercises and namby-pamby sentimentalities'. To some extent, Clough suffered by comparison as an Englishman abroad. Those who disliked his urbane account of the Trevellyns in Rome were apt to think that Lord Byron had done it all far better in* Childe Harold *or* Don Juan. *Worse still, between the time that Clough wrote his poem and the time of its publication in 1862, Italy was the scene of insurrection and liberation, a focus of revolutionary hope for a younger generation than Clough's. Compared with the events of the* Risorgimento, *the adventures of the Trevellyns might seem milk-and-water.*

The book, indeed, is full of coxcombry. 'Amours de Voyage' is a tale, told also in lame hexameters, devoted to the republican days of Rome,—in which, among high thoughts, patriotic sentiments and love-breathings, are interspersed passages outdoing the most prosaic passages which flaw 'Aurora Leigh', or are to be found in *Lucille*[5] and 'The Angel in the House'. Take merely some ten lines from a lady's letter. Hundreds of the same quality could be cited:—

Mary allows she was wrong about Mr. Claude *being selfish*;
He was *most* useful and kind on the terrible thirtieth of April.
Do not write here any more; we are starting directly for Florence:
We should be off tomorrow, if only Papa could get horses;
All have been seized everywhere for the use of this dreadful Mazzini.
P.S.
    Mary has seen thus far.—I am really so angry, Louisa,—
Quite out of patience, my dearest! What can the man be intending?
I am quite tired; and Mary, who might bring him to in a moment,
Lets him go on as he likes, and neither will help nor dismiss him.

Again—

Mr. Claude, you must know, is behaving a little bit better;
He and Papa are great friends; but he really is too *shilly shally,*—
So unlike George! Yet I hope that the matter is going on fairly.
I shall, however, get George, before he goes, to say something.
Dearest Louise, how delightful to bring young people together!

Not being among the initiated, we take leave to characterize the above as poor stuff—doubly impertinent as put forth by one purported to be sincere in his life—which should imply sincerity in art. Any man whose song is of manly sports and wholesome ambitions, who is sick of conventionalisms, should find better use for his powers than committing to paper the boarding-school nonsense which passes in reams through the post-office every day.

William Allingham on 'Arthur Hugh Clough,
1819–1861' in
Fraser's Magazine (1866)

On the publication of the Letters and Remains of Arthur Hugh Clough *in 1865 the book was discussed by the editor of* Fraser's

Magazine, *William Allingham, a friend and correspondent of Dante Gabriel Rossetti. He discussed a point that was central to future interpretations of Clough. In his interior debates, Clough used two voices, as in 'Easter Day' or the long poem 'Dipsychus', where one of the two voices is that of a Mephistophelean presence. Such refrains as 'How pleasant it is to have money' or ' "There is no God", the wicked saith' are what Allingham calls 'a kind of bitter humour, a sarcastic philosophy'. He finds it in some of the songs given to the subversive voice of 'Dipsychus':*

> The world is very odd we see,
>   We do not comprehend it;
> But in one fact we all agree,
>   God won't, and we can't mend it.
>
> Being common sense, it can't be sin,
>   To take it as I find it;
> The pleasure to take pleasure in;
>   The pain, try not to mind it.

The more pious critics of Clough's poetry were apt to say that he merely invented this voice as a foil to his virtuous self. Allingham wonders if it was not, more truly, Clough's alter ego: 'On one side of his mind, at least, Clough had a good deal of sympathy with the way of looking at life which we find in such poets as Horace, Goethe, Byron, Béranger.' [6] *In that case, he was far more precariously balanced upon Browning's 'dangerous edge of things' than his admirers cared to suggest. The moral dualism of Clough's poetic debate is the theme of much of Allingham's discussion.*

Many of the views of life and of art are found in his letters from Rome, which were afterwards worked into his second long hexameter poem, entitled *Amours de Voyage*, first published in America. Like the *Bothie*, incondite in metrical form, and frequently ultra-prosaic, the *Amours de Voyage* also is filled with fine and valuable observations made at first-hand, expressed usually with great precision and point, and often with singular beauty. *Ambarvalia*, a volume of short poems, half by Clough ('the casualties of at least ten years') and half by his old school friend Mr. Burbidge, appeared shortly after the *Bothie*. In 1850, during a visit to Venice, Clough began a longish poem, somewhat of the *Faust* kind, called *Dipsychus*, which 'shows the mark of Venice in all its framework and its local colouring.' This was Clough's method. His mind full of the scenery and impressions of some notable locality—the Scotch Highlands, or Rome, or Venice— he made therefrom a mould, as it were, and poured into it the reflections, guesses, theories, and beliefs that were occupying him, or had occupied him. There is much of the sarcastic in the Venice poem, put chiefly into the mouth of a 'Spirit,' who is, in fact, our friend Mephistopheles, and who drives the well-intending but puzzled Dipsychus to exclaim—

> . . . if indeed it be in vain
> To expect to find in this more modern time
> That which the old-world styled, in old-world phrase,
> Walking with God! It seems His newer will
> We should not think at all of Him, but turn,
> And of the world that He has given us make
> What best we can.

The *Amours de Voyage* (first published in America) was all but unknown in England during the author's lifetime, and is still much less widely known than the *Bothie*. This poem (to which one of the mottoes is '*Il doutait de tout, même de l'amour.*' [7] *French Novel.*) recounts the slight adventures of one Claude, a young Englishman of our time, one of the—

> Feeble and restless youths born to inglorious days.

Sick of London, he makes a tour to Italy and Switzerland. He is disappointed or dissatisfied, or at best unsatisfied, with almost everything and every one he sees,—not ignobly, but with the discontent of a subtle, inquiring, and aspiring soul, which is least of all content with *itself*. At Rome he meets three Miss Trevellyns, and likes them, especially Mary, not forgetting, however, to remind himself—

> Well, I know there are thousands as pretty and hundreds as pleasant,
> Girls by the dozen as good, and girls in abundance with polish
> Higher and manners more perfect than Susan or Mary Trevellyn.
> Well, I know, after all, it is merely juxtaposition,—
> Juxtaposition, in short; and what is juxtaposition?

Claude's attitude throughout is that of a questioner. He is, perhaps, the best type yet given us in literature of the scepticism of modern England. He is high-minded, pure, benevolent, intellectual; but he questions of religion, of morals, of love, of men and women, of history and art, and above all of himself. He is not an ingenious quibbler, he has no touch of affectation; to question and doubt, to consider and reconsider, is as natural to him as thinking or breathing. Of Rome he asks—

> It is illusion? or does there a spirit from perfecter ages,
> Here, even yet, amidst loss, change and corruption, abide? &c.

When the French besiege the city, he thinks—

> Am I prepared to lay down my life for the British female?
> Really, who knows, &c.

He writes to his friend Eustace—

> I am in love you say; I do not think so exactly.

As Georgina Trevellyn remarks, 'he really is too shilly-shally.' Does he care very much for Mary Trevellyn? Does she care very much for him? He cannot decide, and in his indecision allows her and her party to travel northwards without him. Then he pursues, but, by a series of misadventures, fails to find them, and gives up the pursuit, saying by and by—

> After all, do I know that I really cared so about her?
> Do whatever I will, I cannot call up her image;

> After all, perhaps there was something factitious about it;
> I have had pain, it is true: I have wept, and so have the actors.

Meanwhile Mary Trevellyn, who has been anxiously looking for Claude, submits on her part, 'although in a different manner,' to the closing of their acquaintance. In a letter of Clough's of June 1858, he says:

> I have had, mirabile dictu, a letter from Emerson, who reprimanded me strongly for the termination of the *Amours de Voyage*, in which he may be right, and I may be wrong; and all my defence can only be, that I always meant it to be so, and begun it with the full intention of its ending so; but very likely I was wrong all the same.

Love, and Self-questioning, singly or in combination, form the staple of the minor poems, whereof the following may be named as very characteristic:—'Duty,' 'When panting sighs the bosom fill,' 'O tell me, friends,' 'The questioning Spirit,' 'O thou whose image.' Several short pieces printed in the volume of poems reappear embodied in the long composition, which remains a fragment, given in the volume of *Letters and Remains* and entitled *Dipsychus*, that is, the two-souled or two-minded, a man who cannot come to an agreement with himself, 'This way and that dividing the swift mind.' Some of the pieces in question assume a different meaning as part of the long composition. For example, the lines given in *Poems*, page 61, 'Submit, submit!' and which there seem to belong to the poet's own way of thinking, are in *Dipsychus* put into the mouth of the devil; though, again, as the author says in his Epilogue, 'perhaps he wasn't a devil at all. That's the beauty of the poem; nobody can say!'

John Addington Symonds on 'Arthur Hugh Clough' in the *Fortnightly Review* (1868)

John Addington Symonds, poet, critic, and historian of the Italian Renaissance, was one of those commentators who saw in Clough's poem 'Easter Day' a progress from doubt to faith of a kind not dissimilar to Tennyson's poetic pilgrimage through In Memoriam. *Symonds quotes with care from the poem subsequently, insisting that it is 'liable to be misunderstood in its incomplete form'. The reader who was so shocked that he got no further than the declaration that 'Christ is not risen' might indeed have misconstrued it.*

Nothing is more true of Clough's mind than that it worked by thesis and antithesis, not reaching a clear synthesis, but pushing its convictions, as it were, to the verge of a conclusion. The poems, for instance, which begin, 'Old things need not be therefore true,' 'What we, when face to face we see,' and 'Say not, the struggle nought availeth,' are in their tone almost timid and retrogressive when compared with 'Easter Day;' and yet we feel that none of them contain the *dernier mot*. Clough could take the world's or the devil's point of view with wonderful force and vigour. This is clear throughout *Dipsychus*; but it also appears in a published poem, entitled, 'The Latest Decalogue.' To imagine that when he did so he was expressing his *own* view would be to mistake the artist's nature altogether. Yet some people are so dull as to do this. They are shocked at any one venturing to state a base or wicked opinion, even though his object be to call attention to the contrary, and, by revealing

ugliness, to lead the eye in silence to the contemplation of beauty.
In Clough's works there are many stumbling-blocks for such
ugliness, to lead the eye in silence to the contemplation of beauty.
readers—none greater than 'Easter Day,' a poem about which it is
hard to speak, whether we regard its depth of meaning or its high
literary excellence. Of the general scope of this poem it is impossible
to give a better account than that which is prefixed to it in the volume
of *Letters and Remains*. There it is styled

> a semi-dramatic expression of the contrast he (Clough) felt
> between the complete practical irreligion and wickedness of the life
> he saw going on, and the outward forms and ceremonies of religion
> displaying themselves at every turn. How can we believe, it seems
> to say, that 'Christ is risen' in such a world at this? How, if it was
> so, could such sin and such misery continue until now? Yet if we
> must give up this faith, what sadness and what bitterness of
> disappointment remain for all believers who thus lose all that is
> most dear to them! And he abandons himself to this feeling of grief
> and hopelessness, only still vaguely clinging to the belief that in
> earth itself there may be, if nowhere else, a new refuge and a new
> answer to this sad riddle. The mood of mind which he depicts in
> such terrible colours is not to be regarded as his own habitual
> belief. The poem is in no sense a statement of facts or opinions, but
> a strong expression of feeling—above all, the feeling of the
> greatness of the evil which is in the world.

More, however, remains to be said. For though 'Easter Day' 'is not to
be regarded as his own habitual belief,' we cannot but consider it to be
the expression of a mind steeped in the disintegrating solvents of
nineteenth-century criticism. The author has clearly absorbed everything that German commentators have to say upon the subject of the
resurrection—nay, more, has, at least one time of his life, most keenly
felt the cogency of their destructive arguments, and in a mood of
bitterness provoked by human degradation has given the form of fiery
language to the shapeless and uncertain doubts which crowd the
minds of a beliefless generation. 'Easter Day' is unique in the history
of literature. It is a poem fully worthy of that name, in which a train
of close and difficult reasoning is expressed in concise words—such
words as might have been used by a commentator on the Gospels, yet
so subtly manipulated by the poet, with such a rhythm, such
compactness, such vitality of emotion, as to attain the dignity of art by
mere simplicity and power.

Arthur T. Lyttelton on 'The poetry of doubt' in the *Church Quarterly Review* (1878)

Comparisons between the poetry of Arnold and Clough were numerous. In April 1878, when Arnold's poetic career had been over for a decade and Clough had been dead for seventeen years, Arthur T. Lyttelton, Bishop of Southampton, cast his net still wider. He acknowledged Tennyson and Browning as 'definitely Christian' while Swinburne's 'irreligion' was no less certain. As poets, Arnold and Clough offered a more subtle and a more intriguing contrast.

The contrast between Clough and Mr. Arnold can be carried further than the broad differences as to truth and duty. In Mr. Arnold's view of human relations we find the inevitable hopelessness which we believe to be the result of the self-centred attitude of his mind:

> . . . we leave behind—
> As, chartered by some unknown Powers,
> We stem across the sea by night—
> The joys which were not for our use designed,
> The friends to whom we had no natural right,
> The homes that were not destined to be ours.

Clough, too, imagines separation of friends; he also represents life as a voyage; but what a difference in the tone! What a buoyant motion in the very measure, as of a great ship leaping forward before a strong wind!—

> But, O blithe breeze! and O great seas,
>   Though ne'er, that earliest parting past,
> On your wide plain they join again,
>   Together lead them home at last.
>
> One port, methought, alike they sought,
>   One purpose hold where'er they fare,—
> O bounding breeze, O rushing seas!
>   At last, at last unite them there!

His thoughts instinctively turn, after he has felt the parting, to the final goal; the tone is that of joyful hope, while Mr. Arnold ends with calm sadness, looking at the present separation and loss, and at nothing beyond.

But perhaps the strongest contrast—and with this we will conclude—is to be found in their respective treatment of love. Mr. Arnold's we have seen; we have seen him resisting it, reluctantly giving way to the fascination, and wrenching his soul back to its loneliness once more. To Clough it is far more of an interest than it is to his fellow-poet. Many of his poems are occupied with the discussion of love in various aspects; and though this subject cannot escape from his subtle mind without undergoing, like all others, a process of refining away, yet generally in the end he reverts to an extremely simple, and not conventional, but natural position, and at times raises the mingled selfishness and self-renunciation of love into a higher sphere by means of a lofty conception of duty, in the performance of which united lives are of more avail than solitary:

> Yet in the eye of life's all-seeing sun
> We shall behold a something we have done,
> Shall of the work together we have wrought,
> Beyond our aspiration and our thought,
> Some not unworthy issue yet receive;
> For love is fellow-service, I believe.

Lytton Strachey on Dr Arnold in *Eminent Victorians* (1918)

Foremost among debunkers of Victorianism in the early twentieth century was Lytton Strachey in Eminent Victorians *(1918). His essay on Dr. Arnold of Rugby contains a gleeful shaft aimed at Clough, a figure of earnest and somewhat obtuse moralizing in Strachey's view. Clough and his poetry are presented as the perfection of Thomas Arnold's system, by contrast with most of his Sixth Form who were 'weak and brutal'.*

But there was an exceptional kind of boy, upon whom the high-pitched exhortations of Dr. Arnold produced a very different effect. A minority of susceptible and serious youths fell completely under his sway, responded like wax to the pressure of his influence, and moulded their whole lives with passionate reverence upon the teaching of their adored master. Conspicuous among these was Arthur Clough. Having been sent to Rugby at the age of ten, he quickly entered into every phase of school life, though, we are told, "a weakness in his ankles prevented him from taking a prominent part in the games of the place." At the age of sixteen, he was in the Sixth Form, and not merely a Præpostor, but head of the School House. Never did Dr. Arnold have an apter pupil. This earnest adolescent, with the weak ankles and the solemn face, lived entirely with the highest ends in view. He thought of nothing but moral good, moral evil, moral influence, and moral responsibility. Some of his early letters have been preserved, and they reveal both the intensity with which he felt the importance of his own position, and the strange stress of spirit under which he laboured. "I have been in one continued state of excitement for at least the last three years," he wrote when he was not yet seventeen, "and now comes the time of exhaustion." But he did not allow himself to rest, and a few months later he was writing to a schoolfellow as follows: "I verily believe my whole being is soaked through with the wishing and hoping and striving to do the school good, or rather to keep it up and hinder it from falling in this, I do think, very critical time, so that my cares and affections and conversations, thoughts, words, and deeds look to that involuntarily. I am afraid you will be inclined to think this 'cant' and I am conscious that even one's truest feelings, if very frequently put out in the light, do make a bad and disagreeable appearance; but this, however, is true, and even if I am carrying it too far, I do not think it has made me really forgetful of my personal friends, such as, in particular, Gell and Burbidge and Walrond, and yourself, my dear Simpkinson." Perhaps it was not surprising that a young man brought up in such an atmosphere should have fallen a prey, at Oxford, to the frenzies of religious controversy; that he should have been driven almost out of his wits by the ratiocinations of W. G. Ward; that he should have lost his faith; that he should have spent the rest of his existence lamenting that loss, both in prose and verse; and that he should have eventually succumbed, conscientiously doing up brown paper parcels for Florence Nightingale.

NOTES

1 Pindar, a Greek lyric poet of the sixth century BC.
2 Henry Aldrich (1647–1710), canon of Christ Church, Oxford; designer of Peckwater Quadrangle; author of *Artis Logicae Compendium* (1691).

3 *Qui laborat, orat* – Whoever works, thereby prays.
4 *Qui non orat, nec laborat* – Who does not work, neither does he pray.
5 *Lucille* (1860) by 'Owen Meredith', i.e. Edward Robert Bulwer, 1st Earl of Lytton (1831–91).
6 Pierre Jean de Béranger (1780–1857), popular French lyric poet.
7 '*Il doutait de tout, même de l'amour*' – 'He doubted everything, even love.'

5

Swinburne

Algernon Charles Swinburne belonged to a later generation of Victorians. He was born in 1837, the year of the Queen's accession, a good quarter of a century after Tennyson and Browning. Educated at Eton and Balliol, son of an admiral, he had the patrician credentials of the true revolutionary. Yet few would deny Swinburne's natural gifts. In lyricism, colour and imagery, rhythm and language, he seemed a born poet. Coming of age in the 1860s, he put these gifts at the service of a rebellion that was political, social, moral, and – not least – sexual. He worshipped Mazzini's revolution and the fight for Italian independence. He proclaimed the beauty of female bisexuality in *Mademoiselle de Maupin* and the splendour of the condemned poems in Baudelaire's *Fleurs du Mal*. Yet more loudly, he announced the genius and example of the Marquis de Sade, though without having read much of what Sade wrote. When he read *Justine* it merely made him laugh. The whiff of Bohemia in other poets became a pungent odour in his own life and work. Stories of Swinburne in a brothel run by rosy-cheeked ladies in Circus Road, Regent's Park, or screaming drunk in the respectable Arts Club in Dover Street, his hat tumbling in the gutter as he staggered from a homeward-bound cab, confirmed the impression made by some of his verses.

Such scandal gathered about *Poems and Ballads* before its appearance in 1866 that the publisher, Moxon, withdrew the volume. It was issued instead by the shady figure of John Camden Hotten, who combined a line in English pornography with the pirating of American authors still in copyright.

Poems and Ballads produced outrage among the critics, as it was meant to do. The tales of sexual aberration and crime, the apparently anti-Christian tone of some of the verse, upset even those who disliked the stifling propriety of mid-century moralizing as much as Swinburne did. What was worse, the most innocuous-sounding poetry was booby-trapped with mythology to make any young lady and her mama blush to the roots of their hair if it were understood:

O sweet stray sister, O shifting swallow
The heart's division divideth us.
    Thy heart is light as a leaf of a tree;
But mine goes forth among sea-gulfs hollow
    To the place of the slaying of Itylus,
        The feast of Daulis, the Thracian sea . . .

'Itylus', as those who checked the name discovered, was Ovid's story of
Tereus, King of Thrace, who raped his wife's sister, Philomela, in a
most brutal manner and afterwards cut her tongue out so that she
might not accuse him. But Philomela wove a tapestry of the crime.
Tereus's wife, Procne, was so enraged that she killed the son of her
marriage to Tereus, and had the flesh cooked and served to the
unwitting father. Then she told Tereus what he had just eaten.

Poems and Ballads, together with his other earlier books, made
Swinburne famous, or infamous. Thereafter, his talent decayed.
Among his other collections there were good individual poems. But he
was remembered for the brilliance and the scandal of his youthful
work and, had there been nothing else, he would have deserved such
commemoration. When he died, in 1909, it seemed that a great post-
romantic age beginning in 1824 had run its course. Arnold Bennett, at
the beginning of his own fame as a novelist, stood with the crowds
outside the house in Putney during the last hours of Swinburne's life.
He reported the scene with a great sense of occasion:

A few yards beyond where the autobuses turned was a certain
house with lighted upper windows, and in that house the
greatest lyric versifier that England ever had, and one of the
great poets of the whole world and of all ages, was dying. . . .
The next day all the shops were open and hundreds of fatigued
assistants were pouring out their exhaustless patience on
thousands of urgent and bright women; and flags waved on
high, and the gutters were banked with yellow and white
flowers, and the air was brisk and the roadways were clean. The
very vital spirit of energy seemed to have scattered the breath of
life generously, so that all were intoxicated by it in the gay
sunshine. He was dead then. The waving posters said it.

The order of the following extracts is not quite chronological. They
begin with two later accounts of Swinburne and his poetry in 1866, as
explanatory background to the critical rumpus caused by the appearance of *Poems and Ballads*.

Edmund Gosse on 'Swinburne' in
Portraits and Sketches (1912)

Edmund Gosse became an assistant librarian at the British Museum in 1867. There he first saw the slight figure of Swinburne with his shock of red hair, carried out drunk after a 'fainting-fit' in the reading room, 'a Cupido crucifixus on a chair of anguish'. Gosse wrote the first biography of Swinburne, in 1917, omitting the contents of his own 'Confidential Paper on Swinburne's Moral Irregularities'. Gosse gives us a sense of the thrill of being young in the 1860s, when a new generation sought to overturn the social prejudices of the first Victorians and when young men in Cambridge linked arms and swept down the pavements, chanting Swinburne's most outrageous verses.

Men who to-day have not passed middle age can scarcely form an impression of what the name and fame of Algernon Charles Swinburne meant forty years ago to those who were then young and enthusiastic candidates for apprenticeship in the fine arts. Criticism now looks upon his work—and possibly it is right in so looking—rather as closing than as opening a great poetic era. The conception is of a talent which collects all the detonating elements of a previous illumination, and lets them off, once and for all, in a prodigious culminating explosion, after which darkness ensues. But such a conception of Swinburne, as the floriated termination of the romantic edifice, or, once more to change the image, as one who brought up the rear of a long and straggling army, would have seemed to his adorers of 1869 not merely paradoxical but preposterous. It was not doubted by any of his admirers that here they held an incomparable poet of a new order, "the fairest first-born son of fire," who was to inaugurate a new age of lyric gold.

This conception was shared alike by the few who in those days knew him personally, and by the many who did not. While the present writer was still in that outer class, he well remembers being told that an audience of the elect, to whom Swinburne recited the yet unpublished "Dolores," had been moved to such incredible ecstasy by it that several of them had sunk on their knees, then and there, and adored him as a god. Those were blissful times, when poets and painters, if they were attached to Keats' "little clan," might hope for honours which were private indeed, and strictly limited, but almost divine. The extraordinary reputation of Swinburne in the later sixties was constructed of several elements. It was built up on the legend of his mysterious and unprecedented physical appearance, of the astonishing verbal beauty of his writings, but most of all on his defiance of the intellectual and religious prejudices of his age and generation. He was not merely a poet, but a flag; and not merely a flag, but the Red Flag incarnate. There was an idea abroad, and it was not ill-founded, that in matters of taste the age in England had for some time been stationary, if not stagnant. It was necessary to wake people up; as Victor Hugo had said: "Il faut rudoyer le genre humain,"[1] and in every gesture it was believed that Swinburne set forth to "rudoyer" the Philistines.

Donald Thomas on *'Poems and Ballads'* in *Swinburne: The Poet in his World* (1979)

The following survey of the contents of Poems and Ballads *(1866) may make clear the precise objections of Swinburne's critics. Even before the book appeared, Swinburne's 'good angel', Pauline Trevelyan, wrote to him with the gentle wisdom of an older woman to a young friend about whom she heard the first disturbing reports:*

If it is only for the sake of living down evil reports, do be wise in which of your lyrics you publish. Do let it be a book that can be really loved and read and learned by heart, and become part and parcel of the English language, and be on every one's table without being received under protest by timid people. There are no doubt people who would be glad to be able to say that it is not fit to be read. It is not worth while for the sake of two or three poems to risk the widest circulation of the whole. You have sailed near enough to the wind in all conscience in having painted such a character for a hero as your Chastelard, slave to a passion for a woman he despises. . . . Don't give people a handle against you now. And do mind what you say for the sake of all to whom your fame is dear, and who are looking forward to your career with hope and interest.

But Pauline Trevelyan was never to read Poems and Ballads. *She died of cancer on 13 May 1866, just over two months before the book was published. Had she lived to read it, her misgivings would surely have seemed justified.*

Into *Poems and Ballads* Swinburne put sixty-two poems, which represented his major output in the first thirty years of his life. He had, of course, published *Atalanta* and *Chastelard*, but it was upon his collected individual poems that he was most likely to be judged as the successor of Tennyson and Browning. In the light of the indignant response to the volume, it has to be conceded that about a dozen of the poems dealt with subjects which were unlikely to find favour in the drawing-rooms of the 1860s. Indeed, represented with sufficient vividness they would hardly have been more welcome a century later. 'Phaedra' deals with the incestuous passion of the heroine for her stepson; 'Les Noyades' describes the fate of a man and a women tied in a naked embrace to be drowned for their crimes; 'Anactoria' is Sappho's violent declaration of lesbian passion; 'Hermaphroditus' and 'Fragoletta' celebrate the parallel theme of bisexualism; 'Dolores' becomes the litany of sadism.

> Cold eyelids that hide like a jewel
>> Hard eyes that grow soft for an hour;
> The heavy white limbs, and the cruel
>> Red mouth like a venomous flower;
> When these are gone by with their glories,
>> What shall rest of thee then, what remain,
> O mystic and sombre Dolores,
>> Our Lady of Pain?

Not only reading but reading aloud was a pastime of the mid-Victorian family, making it doubtful whether its members would relish chanting Swinburne's assurances that his goddess was the child of Priapus by Libitina. Nor would such readers be likely to feel Swinburne's enthusiasm for some of his idol's aphrodisiac charms.

> Could you hurt me, sweet lips, though I hurt you?
>> Men touch them, and change in a trice
> The lilies and languors of virtue
>> For the raptures and roses of vice;
> Those lie where thy foot on the floor is,
>> These crown and caress thee and chain,
> O splendid and sterile Dolores,
>> Our Lady of Pain.

Had Swinburne prepared a collection of sixty-two poems of which a dozen were in this vein while the rest consisted of lyric virtuosity coupled with unexceptionable Tennysonian moralizing the matter would have been more straightforward. But even in such poems as 'A Ballad of Life' and 'A Ballad of Death', with their Pre-Raphaelite pictorialism and their almost Spenserean lushness, there were passages detailing a girl's breasts and nipples in a manner calculated to bring a family reading to an abrupt halt.

> Ah! that my tears filled all her woven hair
> And all the hollow bosom of her gown –
> Ah! that my tears ran down
> Even to the place where many kisses were,
> Even where her parted breast-flowers have place,
> Even where they are cloven apart. . .

At the same time, in other poems of the collection, Swinburne showed himself to be the supreme lyric poet to whom no objection could be taken. Readers sheltered by their ignorance of its origins were enchanted by 'Itylus'. It took its place in the *Golden Treasury* of F. T. Palgrave, recommended reading for those innocents who never need be told that it was about a girl who was raped and whose tongue was cut out, and her sister who avenged this by killing her own son and making his father eat him in a stew. Similarly those who did not delve too deeply into a poem like the 'Hymn to Proserpine: After the Proclamation in Rome of the Christian Faith', were able to savour its poetic accomplishment in the terms which seemed most attractive to them.

> Thou hast conquered, O pale Galilean; the world has grown grey from thy breath;
> We have drunken of things Lethean, and fed on the fullness of death.
> Laurel is green for a season, and love is sweet for a day;
> But love grows bitter with treason, and laurel outlives not May.
> Sleep, shall we sleep after all? for the world is not sweet in the end;
> For the old faiths loosen and fall, the new years ruin and rend.
> Fate is a sea without shore, and the soul is a rock that abides;
> But her ears are vexed with the roar and her face with the foam of the tides.
> O lips that the live blood faints in, the leavings of racks and rods!
> O ghastly glories of saints, dead limbs of gibbeted Gods!

Aeschylean or not, Swinburne had shown himself capable of a rhetoric as well as a lyricism which clung in the minds and memories of his readers. There was, as it were, an ineradicable force to the rhythm of such poems as 'The Hymn to Proserpine', as well as a power of language. This, like the elegiac cadences of 'Itylus' with all their plaintive insistence, made him, in the literal sense, the most memorable poet of his generation.

By contrast with the exuberance of language and the intoxication of rhythm which he showed, the idylls of Tennyson in his middle fifties seemed lame and insipid. Swinburne's verse had power and drama, a natural attraction for the young men of his own generation. There was a modernity of subject as well as technique, a style of description in such poems as 'Laus Veneris' which might as easily have belonged to the twentieth century as to the nineteenth. Here, at least, the caricature of Swinburne as a facile lyricist with nothing to say was easily proved false.

> Outside it must be winter among men;
> For at the gold bars of the gates again
> I heard all night and all the hours of it
> The wind's wet wings and fingers drip with rain.
>
> Knights gather, riding sharp for cold; I know
> The ways and woods are strangled with the snow;
> And with short song the maidens spin and sit
> Until Christ's birthnight, lily-like, arow.

In the description of wind and weather, the verses have a terse and contemporary quality which reminds one, say, of:

> The empty winds are creaking and the oak
> Splatters and splatters on the cenotaph.

From such instances it might be hard to decide which of the two was more recent, though one is Swinburne and the other Robert Lowell's 'The Quaker Graveyard in Nantucket'.

John Morley on *Poems and Ballads* (1866) in the *Saturday Review* (1866)

Poems and Ballads *was Swinburne's fourth book. The first three won faint praise, limited notice, and a good deal of dismissive comment.*

His two verse dramas in The Queen Mother and Rosamond *made up the first volume in 1860. 'He has some literary talent, but it is decidedly not of a poetical kind,' the* Spectator *announced on 12 January 1861. 'We do not believe any criticism will help to improve Mr Swinburne.' 'We should have conceived it hardly possible to make the crimes of Catherine de' Medici dull,' added the* Athenaeum *on 4 May. It was not a promising start.*

In 1865 came Atalanta in Calydon, *Swinburne's Greek poetic drama. The* Saturday Review *for 6 May 1865 found 'skill and sympathy' in the play but these were marred by 'serious deficiencies'. His verse drama* Chastelard *also appeared in 1865, based on the love of Chastelard for Mary Queen of Scots and his execution after being discovered in her room. The* Athenaeum *on 23 December acknowledged a few 'detached beauties of expression' in the poetry but its criticism of what was morally objectionable was a foretaste of the reviewers' reactions to* Poems and Ballads *in the following year:*

> Nor is it to be disputed that Mr Swinburne shows at times a keen insight into the subtleties of human motive, but his chief characters are out of the pale of our sympathy; besides being inherently vicious, their language will offend not only those who have reverence, but those who have taste. We decline to show by quotation how often the Divine Nature is sported with in scenes which are essentially voluptuous. The incidents, again, are often so repulsive that we gain a sort of relief by reflecting that they are equally incredible.

Such as it was, Swinburne's reputation had already been judged in these terms by many reviewers and their readers before Poems and Ballads *appeared in the bookshops at the end of July 1866. Almost two decades earlier the objection to Matthew Arnold's classicism was that it appeared too cold and formal. But in Swinburne's case, the legend of antiquity seemed – even to a liberal moralist like John Morley – to be a convenient mask in which the sexual vices or perversions of London's Haymarket, or Mabille and the Closerie des Lilas in Paris, might be displayed to the drawing-room innocence of Highgate or Bayswater. The lesbian or 'sapphic' overtones of 'Anactoria', or 'Faustine', the sado-masochistic extravagance of 'Dolores', the bisexualism of 'Hermaphroditus' were too much for even the most liberal mind. Post-romanticism, despite its sense of youthful rebellion in Swinburne, seemed to have an air of decadence in such poetry as this.*

It is mere waste of time, and shows a curiously mistaken conception of human character, to blame an artist of any kind for working at a certain set of subjects rather than at some other set which the critic may happen to prefer. An artist, at all events an artist of such power and individuality as Mr. Swinburne, works as his character compels him. If the character of his genius drives him pretty exclusively in the direction of libidinous song, we may be very sorry, but it is of no use to advise him and to preach to him. What comes of discoursing to a fiery tropical flower of the pleasant fragrance of the rose or the fruitfulness of the fig-tree? Mr. Swinburne is much too stoutly bent on taking his own course to pay any attention to critical monitions as to the duty of the poet, or any warnings of the worse than barrenness of the field in which he has chosen to labour. He is so firmly and avowedly fixed in an attitude of revolt against the current notions of decency and dignity and social duty that to beg of him to become a little more decent, to fly a little less persistently and gleefully to the animal side of human nature, is simply to beg him to be something different from Mr. Swinburne. It is a kind of protest which his whole position makes it impossible for him to receive with anything but laughter and contempt. A rebel of his calibre is not to be brought to a better mind by solemn little sermons on the loyalty which a man owes to virtue. His warmest prayer to the gods is that they should

> Come down and redeem us from virtue.

His warmest hope for men is that they should change

> The lilies and languors of virtue
> For the raptures and roses of vice.

It is of no use, therefore, to scold Mr. Swinburne for grovelling down among the nameless shameless abominations which inspire him with such frenzied delight. They excite his imagination to its most vigorous efforts, they seem to him the themes most proper for poetic treatment, and they suggest ideas which, in his opinion, it is highly to be wished that English men and women should brood upon and make their own. He finds that these fleshly things are his strong part, so he sticks to them. Is it wonderful that he should? And at all events he deserves credit for the audacious courage with which he has revealed to the world a mind all aflame with the feverish carnality of a schoolboy over the dirtiest passages in Lemprière. It is not every poet who would ask us all to go hear him tuning his lyre in a sty. It is not everybody who would care to let the world know that he found the most delicious food for poetic reflection in the practices of the great

island of the Ægean, in the habits of Messalina,[2] of Faustina,[3] of
Pasiphaë.[4] Yet these make up Mr. Swinburne's version of the dreams
of fair women, and he would scorn to throw any veil over pictures
which kindle, as these do, all the fires of his imagination in their
intensest heat and glow. It is not merely 'the noble, the nude, the
antique' which he strives to reproduce. If he were a rebel against the
fat-headed Philistines and poor-blooded Puritans who insist that all
poetry should be such as may be wisely placed in the hands of girls of
eighteen, and is fit for the use of Sunday schools, he would have all
wise and enlarged readers on his side. But there is an enormous
difference between an attempt to revivify among us the grand old
pagan conceptions of Joy, and an attempt to glorify all the bestial
delights that the subtleness of Greek depravity was able to contrive. It
is a good thing to vindicate passion, and the strong and large and
rightful pleasures of sense, against the narrow and inhuman tyranny
of shrivelled anchorites. It is a very bad and silly thing to try to set up
the pleasures of sense in the seat of the reason they have dethroned.
And no language is too strong to condemn the mixed vileness and
childishness of depicting the spurious passion of a putrescent imagination, the unnamed lusts of sated wantons, as if they were the crown
of character and their enjoyment the great glory of human life. The
only comfort about the present volume is that such a piece as
'Anactoria' will be unintelligible to a great many people, and so will
the fevered folly of 'Hermaphroditus', as well as much else that is
nameless and abominable. Perhaps if Mr. Swinburne can a second and
a third time find a respectable publisher willing to issue a volume of
the same stamp, crammed with pieces which many a professional
vendor of filthy prints might blush to sell if he only knew what they
meant, English readers will gradually acquire a truly delightful
familiarity with these unspeakable foulnesses; and a lover will be able
to present to his mistress a copy of Mr. Swinburne's latest verses with
a happy confidence that she will have no difficulty in seeing the point
of every allusion to Sappho or the pleasing Hermaphroditus, or the
embodiment of anything else that is loathsome and horrible. It will be
very charming to hear a drawing-room discussion on such verses as
these, for example:—

> Stray breaths of Sapphic song that blew
> Through Mitylene
> Shook the fierce quivering blood in you
> By night, Faustine.

> The shameless nameless love that makes

Hell's iron gin
Shut on you like a trap that breaks
The soul, Faustine.

And when your veins were void and dead,
What ghosts unclean
Swarmed round the straitened barren bed
That hid Faustine?

What sterile growths of sexless root
Or epicene?
What flower of kisses without fruit
Of love, Faustine?

We should be sorry to be guilty of anything so offensive to Mr.
Swinburne as we are quite sure an appeal to the morality of all the
wisest and best men would be. The passionate votary of the goddess
whom he hails as 'Daughter of Death and Priapus' has got too high
for this. But it may be presumed that common sense is not too
insulting a standard by which to measure the worth and place of his
new volume. Starting from this sufficiently modest point, we may ask
him whether there is really nothing in women worth singing about
except 'quivering flanks' and 'splendid supple thighs', 'hot sweet
throats' and 'hotter hands than fire', and their blood as 'hot wan wine
of love'? Is purity to be expunged from the catalogue of desirable
qualities? Does a poet show respect to his own genius by gloating, as
Mr. Swinburne does, page after page and poem after poem, upon a
single subject, and that subject kept steadily in a single light? Are we
to believe that having exhausted hot lustfulness, and wearied the
reader with a luscious and nauseating iteration of the same fervid
scenes and fervid ideas, he has got to the end of his tether? Has he
nothing more to say, no further poetic task but to go on again and
again about

The white wealth of thy body made whiter
By the blushes of amorous blows,
And seamed with sharp lips and fierce fingers,
And branded by kisses that bruise.
And to invite new Félises to

Kiss me once hard, as though a flame
Lay on my lips and made them fire.

Mr. Swinburne's most fanatical admirers must long for something
newer than a thousand times repeated talk of

Stinging lips wherein the hot sweet brine
That Love was born of burns and foams like wine.

And

Hands that sting like fire.

And of all those women,

Swift and white,
And subtly warm and half perverse,
And sweet like sharp soft fruit to bite,
And like a snake's love lithe and fierce.

This stinging and biting, all these 'lithe lascivious regrets', all this talk of snakes and fire, of blood and wine and brine, of perfumes and poisons and ashes, grows sickly and oppressive on the senses. Every picture is hot and garish with this excess of flaming violent colour.

A. C. Swinburne in *Notes on Poems and Reviews* (1866)

Perhaps the worst of John Morley's review was its final words: 'Never have such bountifulness of imagination, such mastery of the music of verse, been yoked with such thinness of contemplation and such poverty of genuinely impassioned thought.' Morley was a Liberal – as well as a liberal – who was to be Chief Secretary for Ireland and Lord President of the Council. He wrote with dignity, like an adult reproving a dirty-minded nursery prodigy. Ironically, this future statesman was actually a year younger than Swinburne.

Elsewhere, there were reviewers who lacked Morley's gravitas. Robert Buchanan was to launch a major attack on Swinburne, the Pre-Raphaelites, and the vices of the age in 'The Fleshly School of Modern Poetry' in 1872. Even children's sweets had been corrupted by the likes of Swinburne. According to Buchanan, 'Among the commoner sorts of confectionery, may be seen this year models of the female Leg, the whole definite and elegant article as far as the thigh, with a fringe of paper cut in imitation of the female drawers and embroidered in the female fashion.' Reviewing Swinburne's poems in the Athenaeum *on 4 August 1866, Buchanan described them as having been 'inspired in Holywell Street, composed on the Parade at Brighton, and touched up in the Jardin Mabile [sic]'. Holywell Street was notorious as a centre of the Victorian pornography trade, the Parade at Brighton had a reputation for raffish immorality, while Mabille offered entertainment and vice in equal proportions. More directly, Buchanan characterized Swinburne's writing as 'prurient trash'. He described the poet as being like Gito, the homosexual favourite in the* Satyricon *of* Petronius, *'seated in the tub of Diogenes, conscious of the filth and whining at the stars'. The chorus grew louder. On 20 August, the* Pall Mall Gazette *reviewed the book as 'Swinburne's Folly', while the* Globe *on 29 November accused him of 'poetic Billingsgate of the choicest description'.*

There were some friendly reviews from critics like Henry Morley in the Examiner *on 22 September 1866:*

> In the *Poems and Ballads* there is the same stern blending of pain and wrath with the delights of wantonness. The theme is not one to be sung *virginibus puerisque*, but shall it therefore not be sung? Shall a young poet be praised for the frivolous songs of love and wine that satisfy conventional ideas of decorum, but condemned for fastening upon the inmost life of such themes, painting such innermost delights as they claim to have in them only to show the rottenness within?

The debate in 1866 was little different from that of our own time. Swinburne and his supporters stood for adult freedoms of books and art – as opposed to the notion of 'family' reading or entertainment which must be fit for children. A nation that banned whatever was unsuitable for its children would soon become childish and even babylike in its sensibilities. The protection of the young from the realities of life and art was too high a price to pay.

Yet the contents of Poems and Ballads *marked Swinburne's reputation as indelibly as* Sordello *had done Robert Browning's. It was said that Moxon withdrew the original edition of* Poems and Ballads *because he feared a prosecution for obscenity. J. M. Ludlow, a leader of the Christian Socialist movement, demanded a prosecution by the Attorney-General but without success. As a publisher, the shady John Camden Hotten was more robust than Moxon. He suggested to Swinburne that it might not be a bad thing to write a pamphlet answering the critics. This was done and then published by Hotten in October 1866. Swinburne insists that he had been restrained compared with Byron or Shelley, though he must have recalled that the works of both poets had been successfully prosecuted in the criminal courts on more than one occasion.*

Certain poems of mine, it appears, have been impugned by judges, with or without a name, as indecent or as blasphemous. To me, as I have intimated, their verdict is a matter of infinite indifference: it is of equally small moment to me whether in such eyes as theirs I appear moral or immoral, Christian or pagan. But, remembering that science must not scorn to investigate animalcules and infusoria, I am ready for once to play the anatomist.

With regard to any opinion implied or expressed throughout my book, I desire that one thing should be remembered: the book is dramatic, many-faced, multifarious; and no utterance of enjoyment or despair, belief or unbelief, can properly be assumed as the assertion of its author's personal feeling or faith. Were each poem to be accepted as the deliberate outcome and result of the writer's conviction, not mine alone but most other men's verses would leave nothing behind them but a sense of cloudy chaos and suicidal contradiction. Byron and Shelley, speaking in their own persons, and with what sublime effect we know, openly and insultingly mocked and reviled what the English of their day held most sacred. I have not done this. I do not say that, if I chose, I would not do so to the best of my power; I do say that hitherto I have seen fit to do nothing of the kind.

Swinburne defends several of the individual poems that had been attacked by his critics - 'Dolores', 'Faustine', and 'Hermaphroditus' among them - but he ends with defiance on the central point at issue, quoting four lines of Théophile Gautier which may be translated as:

> Mothers of families I hereby warn
> That I do not write for their girl-children,
> For whom one cuts up bread and butter;
> Mine is a young man's poetry.

It was not the end of the matter. In 1885 the young novelist George Moore was still carrying on the fight against the Philistines and the censors:

We must write as our poems, our histories, our biographies are written, and give up once and for ever asking that most silly of all silly questions, 'Can my daughter of eighteen read this book?' Let us renounce the effort to reconcile those two irreconcilable things - art and young girls.

In that respect, Swinburne may have fired the first shot but the battle had scarcely begun.

I have overlooked the evidence which every day makes clearer, that our time has room only for such as are content to write for children and girls. But this oversight is the sum of my offence.

It would seem indeed as though to publish a book were equivalent to thrusting it with violence into the hands of every mother and nurse in the kingdom as fit and necessary food for female infancy. Happily there is no fear that the supply of milk for babes will fall short of the demand for some time yet. There are moral milkmen enough, in all conscience, crying their ware about the streets and by-ways; fresh or stale, sour or sweet, the requisite fluid runs from a sufficiently copious issue. In due time, perhaps, the critical doctors may prescribe a stronger diet for their hypochondriac patient, the reading world; or that gigantic *malade imaginaire* called the public may rebel against the weekly draught or the daily drug of MM. Purgon and Diafoirus.[5] We, meanwhile, who profess to deal neither in poison nor in pap, may not unwillingly stand aside. Let those read who will, and let those who will abstain from reading. *Caveat emptor.*[6] No one wishes to force men's food down the throats of babes and sucklings. The verses last analysed were assuredly written with no moral or immoral design; but the upshot seems to me moral rather than immoral, if it must needs be one or the other, and if (which I cannot be sure of) I construe aright those somewhat misty and changeable terms. No moral agenda—where is he going?

W. M. Rossetti in *Swinburne's Poems and Ballads: A Criticism* (1866)

Though Swinburne was not in the strict sense a Pre-Raphaelite, there was a natural sympathy between him and those members of the Brotherhood who felt increasingly under attack by representatives of bourgeois philistinism like Robert Buchanan. In the autumn of 1866, after the publication of his self-defence, Swinburne was gratified that William Michael Rossetti came to his assistance with his little book Swinburne's Poems and Ballads: A Criticism.

The advent of a new great poet is sure to cause a commotion of one kind or another; and it would be hard were this otherwise in times like ours, when the advent of even so poor and pretentious a poetaster as a Robert Buchanan stirs storms in teapots. It is therefore no wonder that Mr. Swinburne should have been enthusiastically admired and keenly discussed as soon as he hove well in sight of the poetry-reading public, for he is not only a true but even a great poet; still less wonder, under all the particular circumstances of the case, that, with his last volume, admiration and discussion should have ended in a grand crash of the critical orchestra, and that all voices save those of denunciation and repudiation should have been well-nigh drowned. As with many poets of whom our literature is or might be proud—a Shelley, a Byron, a Landor, a Whitman, a Mrs. Browning—the time had to come to Mr. Swinburne when the literary interest in his writings paled before some other feeling excited by them—when the literary gauge was thrown aside by his examiners, and some other one was applied, not to the present advantage of himself or his book. Be it added that Mr. Swinburne has done his very best, or worst, to hasten this time, and to aggravate the crisis. He has courted critics to be—and still more to profess themselves—indignant and horrified; they have responded to his invitation, have exorcised his book with abundant holy water of morals and religion, the salt of literary disquisition being but sparingly used—and the result is, that the book is withdrawn from publication in England. It is practically certain, however, to have reappeared, with no alteration save that of the London publishing-house, long before these remarks are in print. We shall endeavour to look upon this book, along with Mr. Swinburne's other writings, calmly, to appraise them justly in literary and all other respects, and to assign him his due place among poets. We will at once and unreservedly say, we are satisfied that this place will, in the judgment of posterity, be a lofty one, and that Algernon Swinburne is one of that rare and electest class—the writers whom contemporaries, even the well-affected among them, are likely to praise too little rather than too much.

Thus, strange as it may seem to say so of a book withdrawn from circulation on account of its outrages to decency, and in which 'passionate sensuousness' really is a very leading influence, we believe that that influence is, in fact, one of the *less* genuine constituents of the author's mind: there is even something about it too determinate and prepense, too uneasily iterative—not exceptionally genuine, but near to being actually factitious. It would even ring almost hollow to the ear and the apprehension of the reader, were not the sound transmitted through so intense a medium of artistic perception and harmonic expression. We are certainly far from justifying Mr. Swinburne's course in publishing to a world which was pretty well known not to want them such performances as 'Dolores', 'Fragoletta', and some others—to have done so was both a miscalculation and an *inconvenance*,[7] for which he has had to pay the penalty which might have been foreseen; but we are equally far from thinking that any positive stigma attaches to his name or his genius on this account, or that there is any true sense of right or justice in those critics who, stopping their ears at his unseemlinesses, refuse to hear, distinct and predominant above them, the flood of noble and divine music which these only mar with casual and separable though perverse discords. To sum up this part of our subject, Mr. Swinburne is 'passionately sensuous' in his poems chiefly because the passionate and the sensuous are two ultimate and indestructible elements of poetry; and he over-enforces them in expression chiefly because a mighty intoxication of poetic diction mounts to his head, and pours in an unruly torrent through his lips, and he forgets the often still nobler office of self-mastery and reticence.

The 'Classic or Antique' influence is an entirely genuine one with Mr. Swinburne, and cannot be called other than genuine in the part which it plays in his present volume. His mind and his sympathies receive nurture from the antique past. He is a manifest pagan; neither believing in a Christian revelation, nor entering kindly, though he can enter with truth of artistic perception, into a Christian dispensation, and modes of thought and life. This classic influence subserves to some extent his passionate sensuousness; for he can think without intolerance, and write with amazing candour and beauty, about 'Hermaphroditus' or 'Anactoria'. The poem bearing the latter name is, indeed, one of the most glorious exhibitions of fervent imagination and poetic execution in his volume. The reader is not bound to like it: if he does not admire it, he has but a purblind perception of what poetic workmanship means. The statue in the Louvre, and the Lesbian loves of Sappho, are not germane to the modern mind: let them by all means remain un-germane! Yet let not the artificer or the student of poetry be a mark for the mere mud of nineteenth-century highroads if some 'elective affinity' prompts him to penetrate somewhat further than parson or pedagogue into moods of mind and aberrations of passion which were vital enough to some of the great of old, however dead and putrescent they may now most legitimately have become. To these subjects a healthy and open mind stands in the relation expressed by the matron to whom naked men were as so many statues. One might almost say, and not be misunderstood by those whose understanding is worth courting, that everything Greek has become to us as a compound of beauty and of thought, a vestige and an evidence of human soul infused as into Parian marble, marble-like in its purity of appeal to us, and which time has privileged us to love with no gross or abject thought, whatever may be the express image and superscription of the monument. Be it confessed at the same time that Mr. Swinburne receives and transmits the impression without availing himself of this privilege so fully as he might, or, with his exquisite sensibility to beauty of subject-matter and perfection of poetic keeping, ought to, have done. 'Anactoria', impure as is its theme, might conceivably be treated with some nearer approach to comparative purity, and certainly without the feline or tigerish dallyings in which 'the lust of the flesh' passes into a positive lust of blood, equally unknown (if we are not mistaken) to Greek passion, and unknowable, unless as a nightmare of the imagination, to normal sensualists. Why lay hands doubly lawless upon what can be claimed as rightful property only by such a son of Belial and cretinism as the producer, predestined to a madhouse and a hardly utterable name, of some

> scrofulous French novel
> On grey paper with blunt type,

and embellished with a 'woful sixteenth print'? In his other classical poems which touch upon somewhat similarly dangerous ground, 'Phaedra' and 'Hermaphroditus', we see no cause for censuring Mr. Swinburne: he imagines and speaks as a poet has a right to do—the only further requirement being the 'fit audience'.

George Saintsbury on 'Mr Swinburne' in *A History of Nineteenth Century Literature* (1896)

Swinburne never again created a storm on the scale of the Poems and Ballads *scandal. Within a few years, a new generation of poets and critics took Sappho and her kind in their stride. 'Venus or virgin, it is all one to me, provided he can make fine poetry out of either,' wrote Alfred Austin in* Temple Bar *in July 1869. A cloud no bigger than a man's hand presaged the advent of 'Art for Art's sake' and a* fin-de-siècle *aestheticism.*

But unfortunately Swinburne never again wrote with the panache or the brilliance of the 1860s. In the volumes that followed – Songs Before Sunrise *(1871) or* Poems and Ballads: Second Series *(1878) – there were good individual poems like 'Ave Atque Vale: In Memory of Charles Baudelaire' or 'The Complaint of the Fair Armouress' in the later volume. He also wrote two novels, the second unfinished, of a strikingly modern and poetic kind* – Love's Cross Currents *and* Lesbia Brandon. *At a more mundane level he published literary criticism and a little mild pornography.*

The truth was, as T. S. Eliot suggested in The Sacred Wood *(1920), that Swinburne's poetry was considerable in bulk but that no one would want more than a selection from it. It is hard to imagine many willing readers for almost a hundred pages of* The Tale of Balen *or* A Century of Roundels. *But the Swinburne of the 1860s seemed like a writer whose pen turned words to gold without effort. Even so, as Eliot sees it, the nature of Swinburne's poetry requires that the selection must be made according to individual taste:*

Of Swinburne we should like to have the *Atalanta* entire, and a volume of selections which should certainly contain *The Leper, Laus Veneris*, and *The Triumph of Time*. It ought to contain many more, but there is perhaps no other single poem which it would be an error to omit.

For most readers, as for Eliot, a selection of what was best in Swinburne's poetry would draw heavily on Atalanta in Calydon *and* Poems and Ballads. *The Grecian choruses of* Atalanta *had a rhythm and energy to match their pagan sexuality:*

> And Pan by noon and Bacchus by night
> Fleeter of foot than the fleet-foot kid,
> Follows with dancing and fills with delight
> The Maenad and the Bassarid;
> And soft as lips that laugh and hide
> The laughing leaves of the trees divide,
> And screen from seeing and leave in sight
> The god pursuing, the maiden hid.

If Swinburne became a popular poet of the 1870s and 1880s, it was largely by virtue of this early work. There was a sureness of technique and a memorability that raised the choruses of Atalanta *high among the poetry of the age:*

Before the beginning of years
   There came to the making of man
Time, with a gift of tears;
   Grief, with a glass that ran;
Pleasure, with pain for leaven;
   Summer, with flowers that fell;
Remembrance fallen from heaven,
   And madness risen from hell.

It was, if nothing else, among the quickest and most sure-footed poetry in the English language.

Because the twentieth century felt even less sympathy towards the more laboured and ambitious poetry of his later years, Swinburne's appeal depended almost wholly on his early poems. In 1926 Harold Nicolson's Swinburne *was a slighter but perceptive successor to his biography of Tennyson. Nicolson suggested the possibility that Swinburne's 'emotional receptivity began to ossify in 1857', when he was twenty years old. Gosse had put the date twenty years later. Thereafter, drink and the devil had done their worst.*

In 1939, Laurence Binyon described Swinburne more generally as a poet whose work could lead to no line of development, perhaps not even within his own writing. 'One could not go on from Swinburne on his own lines; his poetry represents something completed and therefore incapable of growth.' But Binyon also summed up the youthful poet as representative of 'the hothouse air of Romanticism in its last stage, with its thirst for sensation at all costs'. In this, the author of Poems and Ballads *anticipated the writers of the Nineties by quarter of a century. Binyon recalls the best and the worst of 1866:*

Many things contributed to this phase of ferment in the young poet, conscious of extraordinary powers, arrogant and defiant: adoration of beauty for its own sake: an impish desire to shock: enthusiasm for the theories of the Marquis de Sade (addressed in *Dolores* as 'thy prophet, thy preacher, thy poet') and for the antinomianism of Blake: the rejection of the one love of his life. Revolting from the over-sentimental conception of love imposed on the time, he tore through the surface of make-believe to reveal the fury of Lust as a terrible and tremendous force, incarnate through the ages in one 'fatal' woman after another, insatiate and unappeased against a background of sombre grandeur, charged with doom, 'the thunder of the trumpets of the Night'.

Perhaps more than any other Victorian, Swinburne represented to his countrymen the Artist as Bohemian, the divine demand of poetry made tolerable by drink and the brothel. Where else, after all, was a poet's consolation in the tedious intervals between his moods of inspired lyricism? George Saintsbury was a young man of nineteen when Swinburne published Poems and Ballads *and an old man when W. H. Auden published his first poetry. His life spanned a considerable range of literary history and change, from the age of Dickens to that of Orwell. Taking all that he saw and read, he placed Swinburne high among contemporary poets for his rare marriage of spontaneity with technique.*

As a fact, very few people read *The Queen-Mother* volume till their attention was called to it by *Atalanta in Calydon*, which appeared in the winter of 1864-65, and made its mark at once. The magnificent choruses—of which the best known, "Before the beginning of years," is only, and but by a little, the best—caught the ear and the imagination of all youthful lovers of poetry at once, and have never lost hold with some. The new poet had, as regards Tennyson (who was at the summit of his popularity) and Browning (who was at last approaching it), the advantage, in the former case of substituting a rapid and sweeping melody for the slow music of the author of the *Lotos Eaters*, in the latter of being perfectly melodious. He lost no time. *Atalanta*, at first published in a rather luxurious form (which has become rare and very costly), was quickly reprinted, and almost as quickly, in 1866, followed, first by *Chastelard*, a play on the unlucky lover of Queen Mary, and then, in the autumn of the year, by *Poems and Ballads*, a volume of miscellaneous and chiefly lyrical poetry. The merits of *Chastelard* were a little too soon thrown into the shade by the success (both of scandal and otherwise) of *Poems and Ballads*, but they are very great. The blank verse has far more fire and life than that of *Atalanta*, and the subject discouraged instead of encouraging that *stichomythia*[8] which is so effective in Greek and so irritating in English. The beauty of the French verses, "Le Navire" and "Après tant de jours" (which no poet even of that great time of French poetry need have disavowed), was surpassed by the English song, "Between the sunset and the sea," a perfectly wonderful thing, as fresh now as the day it was written—the echoes of its phrase positively quivering with passion, and shaking cascades of poetic colour and light and sound from every stanza.

180

More probably by coincidence than for any logically assignable reason, Mr. Swinburne now fell in with one of those squalls of sudden prudery which have diversified the moral history of a country at other times quite content to bear Restoration comedy for thirty years without a protest, to give almost the fullest reasonable freedom to novelists in the eighteenth century, and not to refuse freedom a good deal more than reasonable, since the very time of which we are speaking, to certain novelists and dramatists of the indecent. Already Mrs. Grundy had been made uneasy by *Chastelard*; she was horrified by *Poems and Ballads*. Its first publisher threw up the charge, which was transferred to another. It was attacked, defended, sought after by some and eschewed by others for its supposed delinquencies, cherished by the wise for its real merits. These merits (which were not unchequered) finally posed Mr. Swinburne as the Third Poet of the later English nineteenth century. It could hardly, in face of this his fourth volume, and of the fact that he was now in his thirtieth year, be denied that he had certain poetic faults, which were perhaps likely to increase—the chief of them all being a tendency to excessive *wordiness*, not unmusical, not even tedious, but failing to carry the poem or the reader any farther—that he was too fond of certain epithets and images, that he was violent and excessive in some departments of thought and expression.

But for the understanding lover of poetry the defects were as nothing to the merits, shown as before especially in the department of lyric. Many poets have been successful in this or that metrical form, unsuccessful in others; to Mr. Swinburne no lyrical measure seemed to offer the slightest difficulties. He could "flood with eddying song" alike elaborate canzonic structures, stately stanzas like that of "The Triumph of Time"; the difficult quatrain, as in "Laus Veneris"; ballad measure; refrain-pieces; light, trilling movements, like "A Match"; the Alexandrine split into eights and fours, like "Faustine." It would be difficult to find any corresponding masterpiece to the triple triumph in sequence of "Dolores," with its peculiar rocking rhythm altered from Praed, of the dreamy languor of "The Garden of Proserpine," and of the magnificent sweeping anapæsts, arranged in a sort of lengthened analogue to the elegiac couplet, of *Hesperia*. Nor could any one say that this was mere metre; poetic imagery, poetic colour, fancy, light, sound were everywhere.

After this remarkable book Mr. Swinburne was, we have said, classed and judged by good wits; but he continued for many years to repeat and vary his diploma-pieces, and among the many books he has issued (*A Song of Italy*, 1867; *Songs before Sunrise*, 1871;

Bothwell, 1874; *Erechtheus*, 1875; *Songs of Two Nations*, 1876; *Poems and Ballads* (second series), 1878; *Songs of the Springtides*, 1880; *Mary Stuart*, 1881; *Tristram of Lyonesse*, 1882; *A Century of Roundels*, 1883; *A Midsummer Holiday*, 1884; *Locrine*, 1887; *Poems and Ballads* (third series), 1889; *The Sisters*, 1892; *Astrophel and Other Poems*, 1894; *A Tale of Balen*, 1896; *Rosamond*, 1900) not one has failed to contain something, hardly one has not contained many things, to show his power. Probably the best of all these is the second series of *Poems and Ballads*. The contents of this are unusually varied, and there is perhaps no single volume—not even the original of the same name—which exhibits the author at a more constantly sustained level of power.

The earlier *Songs before Sunrise*, a little violent in sentiment and uneven in execution, had contained a magnificent overturepiece or prologue. *Erechtheus* has been regarded by some as the best attempt at that (it must be admitted rather artificial) kind of "Greek play in English," in which *Atalanta* is something of a *tour de force*, and Mr. Arnold's *Merope* an estimable failure. The extreme beauty of parts of *Bothwell* was somewhat obscured by its inordinate length; and the same fault was found by some, with less justice, in *Mary Stuart* and *Tristram of Lyonesse*, the latter a poem of extraordinary charm. Of the later books it is difficult to specify parts. *The Sisters*, not generally popular, has great distinctness of flavour, and exhibits well the Northumbrian fidelities which have so advantageously blended with Mr. Swinburne's Southern studies and affections. *A Tale of Balen*, in the same way, mirrors, with an engaging idiosyncrasy and remarkable power of phrase, the poet's own impression of that marvellous Legend of Arthur, which seems to have the power at once of inspiring most true poets, and of inspiring them all differently.

NOTES

1 *'Il faut rudoyer le genre humain'* – 'One must bully the human race.'
2 Messalina was the wife of the Emperor Claudius who ruled from AD 41–54. She acquired a reputation for sexual immorality and was at length either executed or ordered to commit suicide upon Claudius's orders.
3 Faustina was the wife of the Emperor Marcus Aurelius who ruled from AD 161–80. She bore him thirteen children. Though she was later said to have had a scandalous sexual life, there is little evidence of this. One of Swinburne's friends, the painter Frederick Sandys, offered a simpler account of the poem's origins in 1862. Swinburne and several friends had a

bet as to who could produce the most rhymes for the name 'Faustine'. With his usual facility, Swinburne wrote the entire poem in a railway carriage between Waterloo and Hampton Court to win the bet.

4   Pasiphaë, daughter of the Sun, married Minos, King of Crete. When Minos broke his promise to Poseidon to sacrifice a white bull to the god, Poseidon punished him by causing Pasiphaë to fall in love with the animal. She gave birth to the Minotaur, a monster that was half-man and half-bull, which was kept at the centre of the Labyrinth.

5   Purgon and Diafoirus are characters in Molière's play, *Le Malade Imaginaire* (1673).

6   *Caveat emptor* – Let the buyer beware.

7   *inconvenance* – impropriety.

8   *stichomythia* – poetry composed to be spoken.

6

Later critical texts

GENERAL

The columns of the *New Cambridge Bibliography of English Literature* (1969), the annual volumes of the MHRA's *The Year's Work in English Studies*, and the *Philological Quarterly's* list in *An Annual Bibliography of English Language and Literature* remain the most comprehensive guide to articles and reviews, as well as to the greatly increased number of books on poetry of the Victorian period. What follows is no more than an indication of editions, biographies, and critical texts that may be more immediately useful. Some of these are very recent, others have been available for half a century or more without losing any of their importance.

Apart from background reading in the general histories from Oxford or Cambridge, the *Pelican Guide to English Literature: From Dickens to Hardy*, edited by Boris Ford, revised edition (Harmondsworth: Penguin Books, 1982), offers useful chapters on social and cultural background but is necessarily brief on individual poets. As a compendium of information on Victorian poetry, Oliver Elton's *Survey of English Literature 1830–1880* (London: Methuen, 1920) remains useful.

One of the most fruitful interpretations of the age as post-romantic is to be found in Mario Praz, *The Romantic Agony* (Oxford University Press, 1933/Fontana paperback, 1960). Tracing romanticism from Sade and Byron, seeing it in a European context, Praz offers chapters on 'Romantic: an approximate term', 'The beauty of the Medusa', 'The metamorphoses of Satan', 'The shadow of the "Divine Marquis"', 'La Belle Dame Sans Merci', and 'Byzantium'. He concludes with an appendix on Swinburne. The emphasis in English literature falls rather too heavily on Swinburne but Praz is one of the most imaginative and learned writers on the literary undertones of the period.

An unflattering interpretation of the romantic legacy is made by Bertrand Russell in Chapters 18 and 19 of his *History of Western*

Philosophy (London: George Allen & Unwin, 1946 and frequent reprints). In thirty pages, drawing many illustrations from poetry and fiction, Russell contends that romanticism and the example of Rousseau led to the tyrannies of the twentieth century in Communist Russia and Fascist Germany, the Fascist link being the stronger. Romantic individualism was to prove incompatible with social democracy. Of books that have examined nineteenth-century literature for its philosophical content, John Holloway, *Victorian Sage: Studies in Argument* (London: Macmillan, 1953) analyses a number of writers as contributors to the intellectual debate.

Among more specific accounts of the romantic tradition in poetry is Frank Kermode, *The Romantic Image* (London: Routledge & Kegan Paul, 1957). The later development of romanticism is examined in the light of Wyndham Lewis's phrase that the image is the 'primary pigment' of poetry. The discussion moves towards romanticism and symbolism in the poetry of Yeats and Arthur Symons.

The Major Victorian Poets, edited by Isobel Armstrong (London: Routledge & Kegan Paul, 1969) contains four essays each on Tennyson and Browning, as well as two each on Arnold and Clough. Clough is excellently served by the contributions from Barbara Hardy and John Goode, while the less obvious aspects of the other poets are considered by Michael Mason on Browning's *Sordello*, Bernard Bergonzi on Tennyson's *Princess*, Gabriel Pearson on Matthew Arnold's *Merope*, as well as John Killham on *The Ring and the Book*.

A second distinguished collection of short pieces appears in Geoffrey and Kathleen Tillotson, *Mid-Victorian Studies* (London: Athlone Press, 1966), containing a discussion of *Idylls of the King*, *The Bothie of Tober-na-Vuolich*, and the poetry of Swinburne.

As Mario Praz links the post-romantics to their forebears, so Carol T. Christ in *Victorian and Modern Poetics* (University of Chicago Press, 1984) shows the often unacknowledged debt of modernism in the work of Yeats, Pound, and Eliot to its Victorian predecessors. Though having little otherwise in common with Praz, this argument also suggests that modernism is less a rebellion against romanticism than a continuation of it, as Baudelaire and others had expected it to be.

The poetry discussed in the present selection is also the subject of five volumes in the Routledge 'Critical Heritage' series. These are listed in the *Additional Bibliography* following this chapter.

As a convenient introduction to Victorian poetry other than that discussed in the present volume, the *New Oxford Book of Victorian*

Verse, edited by Christopher Ricks (1987) offers a wide choice for the period as a whole.

TENNYSON

A major advance in Tennyson scholarship is *The Poems of Tennyson*, edited by Christopher Ricks in three volumes (Harlow: Longman, 1987). The Tennyson manuscripts at Trinity College, Cambridge, remained under an embargo respecting publication until 1969. The first two volumes of *The Letters of Alfred Lord Tennyson*, edited by Cecil Y. Lang and Edgar F. Shannon, were published by the Clarendon Press in 1982 and 1987.

Among biographies of Tennyson, Philip Henderson, *Tennyson: Poet and Prophet* (London: Routledge & Kegan Paul, 1978) shows the more human and anecdotal reputation of the poet at shorter length. Robert Bernard Martin, *Tennyson: The Unquiet Heart* (Oxford: Clarendon Press/London: Faber & Faber, 1980) is the major biography of the last half-century. It adds to Nicolson's picture the dark influence of childhood and heredity; the fear of epilepsy and family madness; alcoholism and melancholia in Tennyson's father. The long postponement of the poet's marriage to Emily Sellwood after Hallam's death appears not as grief or loyalty but as a fear of heredity on both sides. Tennyson wrote readily about friendship but his inability to sustain it is suggested. In friendship he was 'a born sprinter rather than a long-distance runner'. A useful complement to these lives is Andrew Wheatcroft, *The Tennyson Album: A Biography in Original Photographs*, with an introduction by Sir John Betjeman (London: Routledge & Kegan Paul, 1980) which brings intriguingly close the people and places recalled by Tennyson's life and poetry.

The rehabilitation of Tennyson's poetry is closely linked to the reassessment of his personality. Jerome Hamilton Buckley's *Tennyson: The Growth of a Poet* (Oxford University Press/Harvard University Press, 1960) is more sustained and analytical in its examination of the poems than Harold Nicolson had been. Tennyson is seen primarily through his poetry 'from first to last'. Yet the pattern of combining the poetry and the life is not dissimilar to the one that Nicolson had adopted.

Perhaps the most persuasively argued account of Tennyson's poetry and its background in his life is Christopher Ricks, *Tennyson* (London: Macmillan, 1972). The critique of the poetry in the context of Tennyson's emotional and intellectual development is succinct and incisive in its judgments. Tennyson's writing moves towards an 'unclamorous claim to the central humanity of a great poet'.

A good many books and collections of articles on particular aspects of Tennyson's writing have appeared in the last thirty years. Ralph W. Rader, *Tennyson's Maud: The Biographical Genesis* (Cambridge University Press/University of California Press, 1963) is an illustration of the creative process. In the Princeton 'Essays in Literature' series, Timothy Peltason, *Reading 'In Memoriam'* (Princeton University Press, 1985) follows the poem as an emotional or intellectual process whose total relevance is in its progression. Alan Sinfield, *The Language of Tennyson's 'In Memoriam'* (Oxford: Blackwell, 1971) offers a linguistic account of the poem. The emphasis of the discussion is upon Tennyson's use of diction, syntax, imagery, sound, and rhythm, though this is coupled with a perceptive and more general literary evaluation.

F. E. L. Priestley, *Language and Structure in Tennyson's Poetry* (London: André Deutsch, 1973) is a volume in 'The Language Library' series. However, it includes the moral and philosophical dimension of the poetry as well as an account of its structure, metre, and diction. A collection of essays under the general editorship of the poet's great-grandson is to be found in Hallam Tennyson, *Studies in Tennyson* (London: Macmillan/Barnes & Noble, 1981).

BROWNING

Browning's reputation with respect to Tennyson and his contemporaries stands higher now than at any other time, as the most evidently modern poet of his age. A major complete edition of his poetry is in progress, the first volumes having been issued in 1969 as *The Complete Works of Robert Browning* (edited by Roma A. King Jnr, Ohio University Press). A two-volume paperback of the complete poetry appeared in 1981 as Robert Browning, *Poems* (edited by John Pettigrew and Thomas J. Collins, Harmondsworth: Penguin Books). There is also a Penguin English Poets edition of *The Ring and the Book* (edited by R. D. Altick, 1971).

The first two volumes of a comprehensive edition of *The Brownings' Correspondence*, edited by Philip Kelley and Ronald Hudson, were published by the Wedgestone Press in 1984. The correspondence between the Brownings appeared in a new two-volume edition as *The Letters of Robert Browning and Elizabeth Barrett Browning,*

1845-1846 (edited by Elvan Kintner, Oxford University Press/ Harvard University Press, 1969).

There has been a good deal of biographical writing about Browning in the past twenty years. The two-volume biography by Maisie Ward, *Robert Browning and his World* (London: Cassell, 1968-9) is a reminiscent and enthusiastic account by one who was born in the Victorian age and knew many of its most prominent figures. William Irvine and Park Honan, *The Ring, the Book, and the Poet: A Biography of Robert Browning* (London: Cassell, 1975) is a spacious and scholarly life with a good deal of background material. Donald Thomas, *Robert Browning: A Life within Life* (London: Weidenfeld & Nicolson/Viking Press, 1982; Weidenfeld paperback, 1989) is an attempt to penetrate the enigma of Browning's personality through the evidence of his writing, as well as through the estimates of those who knew him. Vivienne Browning, *My Browning Family Album* (Windlesham: Springwood Books, 1979) is a charming and illuminating memoir, illustrating in words and pictures something of the poet's personal and family life.

Fifty years old and still indispensable for the study of Browning's poetry is William Clyde DeVane, *A Browning Handbook* (London: John Murray, 1937). This lists and examines Browning's poetry in chronological order, giving information about the circumstances in which the poems were written and published as well as the judgments that were passed upon them. Its value is undiminished.

Perhaps the *doyen* of Browning critics since DeVane is Philip Drew, author of *The Poetry of Browning: A Critical Introduction* (London: Macmillan, 1970). The book represents a less biographical approach than some of the critical work on Tennyson. It examines the diction, poetic technique, and levels of meaning in Browning's verse. It argues that he represents a rejection of romanticism rather than a development of it, a thesis that did not commend itself to all reviewers when the book appeared.

Philip Drew is also editor of *Robert Browning: A Collection of Critical Essays* (London: Methuen, 1966). This includes major essays on Browning by well-known authors, among them Henry James, Edwin Muir, George Santayana, and Percy Lubbock.

Ian Jack, the editor of *Browning: Poetical Works, 1833-1864* (1970) in the Oxford 'Standard Authors' series, is also the author of *Browning's Major Poetry* (Oxford: Clarendon Press, 1973). His book offers a clear and specific guide to much of Browning's poetry, though not *The Ring and the Book*, informed by pragmatic judgment and a wide range of literary reference.

Isobel Armstrong is the editor of *Robert Browning* (London: Bell, 1974) in the series 'Writers and their Background'. This volume contains essays by Michael Mason on 'Browning and the dramatic monologue', Barbara Melchiori on 'Browning in Italy', Leonee Ormond on 'Browning and painting', Trevor Lloyd on 'Browning and politics', Penelope Gay on 'Browning and music', Roger Sharrock on 'Browning and history', and Isobel Armstrong on 'Browning and Victorian poetry of sexual love'.

Clyde De L. Ryals, *Browning's Later Poetry* (Cornell University Press, 1975) offers a useful account of poetry after *The Ring and the Book*, which has customarily been less noticed. He comments on the cinematic quality of *Fifine at the Fair* and considers Browning's growing preoccupation in his poetry with his public reputation and the manner in which his work was received by the critics.

ARNOLD

The bulk of Matthew Arnold's poetry and prose is most conveniently available in the Oxford 'Standard Authors' series *Matthew Arnold* (edited by Miriam Allott and Robert H. Super, Oxford University Press, 1986). A fuller edition of the poetry will be found in *The Poems of Matthew Arnold* (edited by Kenneth Allott, Longman, 1965) in the Longman 'Annotated English Poets' series.

No study of Matthew Arnold will easily replace the enlightened moral humanism of Lionel Trilling, *Matthew Arnold* (London: George Allen & Unwin/New York: W. W. Norton, 1939; revised edition, 1949). Though a biography of the poet, a picture of his age and class, it remains perceptive and wise in its critical comments, as in citing 'The Scholar-Gipsy' to exemplify 'the almost constant success Arnold has with the theme of controlled self-pity'. Trilling's book goes beyond academic writing – a pleasure to read and a literary accomplishment in its own right.

Lionel Trilling's successor is Park Honan, *Matthew Arnold: A Life* (London: Weidenfeld & Nicolson, 1981). It is a magisterial and very fully documented account of Arnold's career, and is both extensive and informative.

Few studies have quite approached the intellectual or physical dimensions of these two, if only because Arnold's revival has come somewhat later than those of Tennyson and Browning. Among guides to his poetry, the most important of contributions in the past half-century has been that of C. B. Tinker and H. F. Lowry, *The Poetry of*

Matthew Arnold: A Commentary (Oxford University Press, 1940). In a succinct but valuable chapter, Basil Willey, *Nineteenth Century Studies* (London: Chatto & Windus, 1949) suggests that as Arnold in his poetry is the elegist of a dead world, in his prose he assists the birth of a new world. 'Of the other critics and prophets of that generation, which could have written *Sohrab* or *Thyrsis?* of the other poets, which could have written *Culture and Anarchy* or *Literature and Dogma?*' J. D. Jump, *Matthew Arnold* (London: Routledge & Kegan Paul, 1955) sees in the poetry a conflict of romantic aspirations with the tyranny of circumstances and natural law. 'Dover Beach' appears as Arnold's one great poem representing, so far as such a thing is possible, the main movement forward of mind in the previous quarter of a century.

More recently, Sidney Coulling, *Matthew Arnold and his Critics: A Study of Arnold's Controversies* (Ohio University Press, 1974) affords a useful background to both the poems and prose works. William E. Buckler, *On the Poetry of Matthew Arnold: Essays in Critical Reconstruction* (New York University Press, 1982) offers an appreciation of structure and classicism in Arnold's verse. Joseph Carroll, *The Cultural Theory of Matthew Arnold* (University of California Press, 1982) discusses Arnold's concern in his prose with the synthesis of Hellenism and Hebraism, relating this to his poetry as appropriate.

CLOUGH

Clough's revaluation was still longer delayed than Arnold's. The major edition of his poetry, *The Poems of Arthur Hugh Clough*, edited by F. L. Mulhauser, was published in 1974 in its second edition by the Clarendon Press. *The Poems of Arthur Hugh Clough*, edited by A. L. P. Norrington (Oxford University Press, 1968) is a volume in the Oxford 'Standard Authors' series. This, however, omits such poems as 'Mari Magno' and 'Dipsychus Continued'.

The renewal of interest in Clough appeared early in Katharine Chorley, *Arthur Hugh Clough: The Uncommitted Mind* (Oxford: Clarendon Press, 1962). As Anthony Powell once remarked, the drawback of such intellectual controversies as Clough's for a biographer is that they are 'complicated without being eventful'. Lady Chorley compares Clough with Byron as a poet of society, not much to Clough's advantage, and discusses her subject in terms of Jungian psychological theory.

By contrast with his great contemporaries, Clough has attracted less attention. Far the most comprehensive study is Robindra Kumar Biswas, *Arthur Hugh Clough: Towards a Reconsideration* (Oxford University Press, 1972). As this book suggests, it is perhaps surprising that Clough received little notice during the reassessment of Victorian sexuality in the 1960s. He certainly plays no part in such books as Steven Marcus, *The Other Victorians* (London: Weidenfeld & Nicolson, 1966) or Ronald Pearsall, *The Worm in the Bud* (London: Weidenfeld & Nicolson, 1969). Yet Clough's widow was sufficiently disturbed by its impropriety to remove from his published works a poem like 'Natura Naturans' – Clough's thoughts and feelings while sitting next to an unknown beautiful girl in a railway carriage. Even in a poem like 'Dipsychus' there are lines which, if read carefully, would have evangelicals and feminists competing for the privilege of expunging such thoughts from the pages and minds of the susceptible:

> Speak, outraged maiden, in thy wrong
> Did terror bring no secret bliss?
> Were boys' shy lips worth half a song
> Compared to the hot soldier's kiss?

Clough's religious belief and his expressed doubts are the subject of a crisply argued and penetrating chapter, 'Clough: the real doubter' in A. O. J. Cockshut, *The Unbelievers: English Agnostic Thought, 1840–1890* (London: Collins, 1964). He is also one of the poets included in R. L. Brett, *Poems of Faith and Doubt* (London: Arnold, 1965).

SWINBURNE

Swinburne's later reputation was the contrary of Clough's. He had, after all, been a professed and even a shrill unbeliever. Yet Edmund Gosse's *Life of Algernon Charles Swinburne* (London: Macmillan, 1917), even if it could not quench the whiff of scandal surrounding the author of *Poems and Ballads*, had a lightly deodorant effect. The cult of the 'Other Victorians' in the 1960s might ignore Clough, but ample room was found for Swinburne. His life proved more attractive than his poetry. The poetry survived in such selections as *A Choice of Swinburne's Verse* (edited by Robert Nye, London: Faber & Faber, 1973). But his life was celebrated by a splendid six-volume edition of *The Swinburne Letters* (edited by Cecil Y. Lang, Oxford University Press/Yale University Press, 1959–62). With a few of his favoured correspondents like Richard Monckton Milnes, 1st Baron Houghton, Dante Gabriel Rossetti, or the discreet blackmailer, Charles Augustus Howell, Swinburne's screeching vivacity seems almost to take wings from the page.

Some of Swinburne's previously unpublished work has appeared since 1945. The most significant contribution is the appearance of his unfinished novel, *Lesbia Brandon* (edited by Randolph Hughes, London: Falcon Press, 1952). The chapters of the novel in themselves provide a gloss on Swinburne's poetry.

Among his recent biographers, Philip Henderson, *Swinburne: The Portrait of a Poet* (London: Routledge & Kegan Paul, 1974) gives an account of Swinburne's life, which relies at times upon extremely lengthy quotations from the poetry. Donald Thomas, *Swinburne: The Poet in his World* (London: Weidenfeld & Nicolson/Oxford University Press, New York, 1979) is an attempt to set both the poet and his work in the context of his friendships and compulsions, the social and cultural pressures of his time.

Though the greater interest of his life has eclipsed a more general revaluation of his poetry, Swinburne received far more attention than any other English poet in Mario Praz's description of romanticism in *The Romantic Agony*. In 1970 he was also the subject of a volume in the 'Critical Heritage' series and his verse is analysed by Thomas E. Connolly in *Swinburne's Theory of Poetry* (University of New York/ Antioch Press, 1965). Professor Connolly argues for a clear and systematic theory supporting Swinburne's poetry, drawn from republicanism, Art for Arts's sake, traditions of classical literature, Elizabethan and Jacobean drama, and his own psychology and aesthetics.

Swinburne's own work as a critic of others is well represented by his essays in *Swinburne as Critic* (edited by Clark K. Hyder, London: Routledge & Kegan Paul, 1972).

Swinburne remains under a disadvantage which almost all his critics or biographers acknowledge. Perhaps more than any other poet of his time, we sense his unevenness. Better for his reputation had he died of drink at forty, as many people expected. But he lived to write a good deal more. It is unlikely that a modern reader would derive much pleasure from, perhaps, nine-tenths of his output. But the other tenth contains some of the most accomplished and engaging poetry of his century.

Additional bibliography

Altick, Richard D. and Loucks, James F. (1968) *Browning's Roman Murder Story: A Reading of the Ring and the Book*, Chicago: University of Chicago Press.

Armstrong, Isobel (1972) *Victorian Scrutinies: Reviews of Poetry 1830–1870*, London: Athlone Press.

Bradbury, Malcolm and Palmer, David (eds) (1973) *Victorian Poetry*, London: Arnold.

Bush, Douglas (1971) *Matthew Arnold*, London: Macmillan.

Cook, Eleanor (1974) *Browning's Lyrics*, University of Toronto Press.

Culler, A. Dwight (1977) *The Poetry of Tennyson*, Yale University Press.

Dawson, Carl (ed.) (1973) *Matthew Arnold: The Poetry: The Critical Heritage*, London: Routledge & Kegan Paul.

Delaura, David J. (1973) *Matthew Arnold: Twentieth Century Views*, Englewood Cliffs: Prentice-Hall.

Dyson, Hope and Tennyson, Charles (1969) *Dear and Honoured Lady* (the correspondence of Tennyson and Queen Victoria), London: Macmillan.

Fletcher, Ian (1967) *Romantic Mythologies*, London: Routledge & Kegan Paul.

Gridley, Roy E. (1982) *The Brownings and France: A Chronicle with a Commentary*, London: Athlone Press.

Halliday, F. E. (1976) *Robert Browning: His Life and Work*, London: Jupiter.

Hassett, Constance W. (1982) *The Elusive Self in the Poetry of Robert Browning*, Columbus: Ohio University Press.

Joseph, Gerhard (1969) *Tennysonian Love: The Strange Diagonal*, Oxford University Press/Minnesota University Press.

Jump, John D. (ed.) (1967) *Tennyson: The Critical Heritage*, London: Routledge & Kegan Paul.

King, Roma A., Jr (1969) *The Focusing Artifice*, Columbus: Ohio University Press.

Kinkaid, James R. and Kyhn, Albert J. (eds) (1985) *Victorian Literature and Society*, Columbus: Ohio University Press.

Litzinger, Boyd and Smalley, Donald (eds) (1970) *Browning: The Critical Heritage*, London: Routledge & Kegan Paul.

Page, Norman (1983) *Tennyson: Interviews and Recollections*, London: Macmillan.

Peters, Robert L. (1965) *The Crowns of Apollo: A Study in Victorian Criticism and Aesthetics*, Detroit: Wayne State University Press.

Shatto, Susan (1986) *Tennyson's 'Maud': A Definitive Edition*, London: Athlone Press.

Shatto, Susan and Shaw, Marion (eds) (1982) *Tennyson: 'In Memoriam'*, Oxford: Clarendon Press/Oxford University Press.

Shaw, W. David (1978) *Tennyson's Style*, Cornell University Press.

Strange, G. Robert (1967) *Matthew Arnold: The Poet as Humanist*, Oxford University Press/Princeton University Press.

Sullivan, Mary Rose (1969) *Browning's Voices in the Ring and the Book*, Oxford University Press/Toronto University Press.

Swinburne, Algernon Charles (1965) *New Writings by Swinburne*, ed. Cecil Y. Lang, New York: Syracuse University Press.

Swinburne, Algernon Charles (1975) *A Year's Letters*, ed. F. J. Sypher, London: Peter Owen.

Tennyson, Lady Emily (1982) *Lady Tennyson's Journal*, ed. James O. Hoge, University Press of Virginia.

Thorlby, Anthony (1967) *The Romantic Movement*, Harlow: Longman.

Thorpe, Michael (1972) *Clough: The Critical Heritage*, London: Routledge & Kegan Paul.

Timko, Michael (1966) *Innocent Victorian* (Arthur Hugh Clough), Columbus: Ohio University Press.

Tracy, Clarence (ed.) (1968) *Browning's Mind and Art*, Edinburgh: Oliver & Boyd.

Wellek, René (1966) *A History of Modern Criticism, 1750–1950* (Volumes 3 and 4, *The Age of Transition* and *The Later Nineteenth Century*), London: Cape.

Williams, David (1969) *Too Quick Despairer* (a biography of Arthur Hugh Clough), London: Rupert Hart-Davis.